# KING OF AIR FIGHTERS

# KING OF
# AIR FIGHTERS

## THE BIOGRAPHY OF
## MAJOR 'MICK' MANNOCK,
## VC, DSO, MC

### BY
### FT.-LIEUT. IRA JONES

CASEMATE
*Philadelphia & Newbury*
A Greenhill Book

This edition of *King of Airfighters* is published in the
United States of America in 2009 by
CASEMATE
1016 Warrior Road, Drexel Hill, PA 19026

and in the United Kingdom by
CASEMATE
17 Cheap Street, Newbury, RG14 5DD

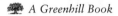 *A Greenhill Book*

ISBN 978-1-932033-99-1

Cataloging in publication data is available
from the Library of Congress and the
British Library.

Publishing History:
*King of Airfighters* was first published by Ivor, Nicolson and Watson in 1934.
It was reissued in facsimile by Greenhill Books / Lionel Leventhal Ltd in 1989.
This new edition has been completely retypeset but the original language
has been left unaltered.

# *Contents*

# List of Illustrations
(Appearing between pages 168 and 169)

TO THE MOTHER OF
MAJOR "MICK" MANNOCK, V.C.
AND ALL WAR PILOTS
WHO DID NOT FAIL IN THEIR DUTY

# *Preface*

This book presents the history of an air fighter who, to quote the citation in the *London Gazette* of the official award of the Victoria Cross, the highest award for valour given to our arms, "was unsurpassed."

His great achievements, his noble selfless character, his manly-boyish spirits, are disclosed for the first time in this, his life-story. His was a spirit in the tradition of our people which we associate in our minds with the qualities required of a Knight of the Round Table. But this romanticised conception of the valorous hero has been so tinged by a false ideal of chivalry, from which we are unable to free our minds, that we always love to think of our heroes in these terms. If a man is brave, we assume he must be a chivalrous Galahad and Lancelot rolled into one. If he is noble, we assume he must be kind; and so on. Mannock reveals the character of the modern hero. Away from the work to which he devoted his great genius, he was all these things. Engaged in air fighting, he expunged all else from his mind, and concentrated to such purpose that he became the most feared, respected, and ruthless air fighter in the British ranks.

He was officially acknowledged by the Air Ministry to be the leading British air fighter of the war, with 73 victories. Many of these he did not officially claim, but they were known to be consistent with his achievements by his comrades and the Air Ministry representative who visited the fighting units in France for record purposes. A microscopic investigation of his achievements unquestion- ably places him on the throne reserved for the King of Air Fighters.

For reasons which will be explained later, the number of victories officially allocated to air fighters of the various nations can never be strictly accurate, in the same way that it is impossible to say whether Captain Albert Ball or Baron Manfred von Richthofen, the British and German aces, were destroyed by gun-fire from the ground or by their enemy's machine guns from the air; but the facts themselves indicate the truth, if they do not actually state it.

Roy Brown's claim to Von Richthofen's death was convincing enough to his comrades in the fight, yet, to many minds, a doubt exists; and that doubt suggests a whole world of possibilities as to what actually took place during three or four minutes of the most breathlessly astonishing episodes of four long years of war between nearly all the civilised peoples of the earth. Similar doubt creeps into many of the statements made after exciting combats by a number of leading air fighters of the war, and whilst it does not always detract from the merit of their astounding achievements, it serves to throw a blazing searchlight on their characters. Of all the great fighters engaged, none exposed more frankly his modesty than Major "Mick" Mannock, V.C., D.S.O. thrice, M.C. twice! None showed more unashamedly the hidden depths of his true character, and none of them comes so closely to a realistic conception of what nobility of mind a character unshaped by birth or education can achieve under the most exacting stress.

To the modern schoolboy, Edward Mannock is the most inspiring figure in the Great War. His achievements may well serve as a beacon to them; a guide along the path of personal endeavour and Duty to their State.

IRA JONES.

ROYAL AERO CLUB,
119 PICCADILLY, LONDON.
*November 1934.*

# Introduction

Professor Werner, writing of the famous German ace, Boelcke, claims that sufficient time has now elapsed for observers to form a dispassionate judgment concerning the history of air fighting. The facts set forth in this book now enable us to see in clear perspective for the first time the place in history of one who is recognised as the greatest of all air fighters—recognised by those best qualified to judge, not only by virtue of their personal association with him during the war, but also as the result of the close examination of all facts and secret documents which have subsequently come to light.

Here he stands, his statue sculpt from the blood-soaked fields of Flanders unveiled at last that his features may remind us, not only of duty done, but of a life sacrificed to the furthering of our prowess in aerial combat.

Here he stands, perhaps the supreme example of a warrior risen from lowly beginnings, faced with the almost insuperable obstacles which militate against one of humble birth, aspiring to place himself upon that topmost rung of heroic achievement—an undertaking which has so often lured men of more exalted station, endowed with equal talents and superior physical attributes. No man grips the imagination with more vigour and virile appeal to the higher senses than does this majestic figure of the Britisher, Edward

Mannock, Major, V.C., D.S.O. and two bars, M.C. and bar.

The course of the war at the date when Mannock entered the conflict had

"witnessed a profligate wastage of some of our finest young manhood ... the silly and bloody game of attrition had already been won by Germany, our diplomacy was a timid and nervous thing ... nothing pleased the Higher Command better than to see us mass our forces for attack in the impregnable West ... such was the net result of the diplomacy and the war direction and strategy pursued by the Allies during nearly two and a half years of a war in which they had started with overwhelming advantages, and through which they had been supported by unexampled efforts and self-sacrifices on the part of the peoples" (David Lloyd George, *War Memoirs*, pp. 103-7).

Sir William Robertson, the famous staff-officer, emphasises the fear that was being felt by the Imperial General Staff, that England might not prove capable of bearing up under the increased strain and effort in every direction which was then becoming inevitable. The time had come when we could no longer let things go on as they had been going as the result of haphazard direction of the war and the inevitable reaction on the spirit of the fighting personnel. The alarm had become general when Mr. Lloyd George seized the reins of power and firmly planted himself in the saddle for a relentlessly concentrated and inspired direction of affairs.

Up to this time we had lived through the war from telegram to telegram, hoping against hope that the various efforts that had already been made would bring us a speedy victory. Few even yet suspected that the war was to drag on for another year and that the crisis still lay ahead of us. None yet suspected that, in spite of the unquestionable advantages held by the Allied Powers, the supreme garland of victory was to be wrested from the tenacious grip of the German hosts on the Western Front only by the valour and endurance of our men.

Fortunately, it was at last realised that the Air Force was destined to play a leading rôle in the conflict. This new arm had entered the war with ridiculous pretensions and absurdly equipped machines; its offensive potentialities had been under-estimated, but it had, through the exertion and personal sacrifices of the men it attracted, become the leading weapon of offence. Brave and resourceful spirits hurtled to their doom, leaving a blazing trail of incredible achievement and heroism which amazed and stupefied the world.

With meteoric speed a tradition of valour had shaped itself from isolated personal examples set by a few choice spirits. On our side gleamed the schoolboy star of Ball, and the fiery example of the heroic Frenchman, Guynemer. On the side of the enemy, the examples of Boelcke and Immelmann kindled the imaginations of the German hosts to the potentiality of this new offensive and highly efficient weapon.

But the builders of this tradition were the first to realise—and it is to their eternal glory that they did so even at the cost of their own lives—in an endeavour to impress the fact on their respective higher commands, the necessity for a closer and more effective co-ordination of their striking powers. History had no precedent to show for the prodigious feats of valour which were performed by these young men in creating the tradition for which they died.

Edward Mannock was the first airman on our side, as Boelcke was the first of the enemy, to realise the supreme importance of applying tactics to formation fighting. Our higher command, divorced from actual experience, was stupefied by the incredible feats of individual valour performed by such brilliant pilots as Ball, Rhys-David, and McCudden, and took some time to realise that a new and audacious air fighter had arisen, whose tactics and methods were to prove such a leading factor in the effectiveness of air fighting. But Edward Mannock, over and above this, exhibited in the performance of his mission a valour that bore little trace of the bounding enthusiasm of the hero of schoolboy fiction, or the ruthless, callous cunning of a hunter and killer who lacks particular object other than that of a desire for fame or trinkets. He was that rare being—not every generation produces one—a man righting for a Cause.

We shall see in the following pages how this character, moved by subconscious impulses, created by his early life and struggles with adversity which remained indelibly stamped on his memory, did not see in the German hosts merely an enemy of his King and Country. Mannock saw that a new and better civilisation, painfully born to life out of the industrial shambles of the nineteenth century, was being threatened by the possibility of a German victory. He saw the whole Liberal-Protestant spirit of Europe menaced by the reactionism of Prussian militarism. Thereafter, he developed a ferocity and temper unsurpassed by any air fighter in sheer intensity and the deadliness of his hatred for the German.

Thus was transformed a man of warm, generous, full-hearted nature into a highly skilled agent of destruction, bitterly and relentlessly determined to achieve victory.

"TO FIGHT IS NOT ENOUGH ... YOU MUST KILL,"
was his final instruction to his fighting comrades.

It is the object of these pages to prove how a man, thus
handicapped by humble birth, lack of education, and
physical disability, but inspired by high ideals, performed the
imperishable deeds which earned for himself the glorious
title of KING OF AIR FIGHTERS.

# I

*Early Life—Part I*

Corporal Edward Mannock, *alias* Corringhame, of the 2nd Dragoons (Royal Scots Greys), was the son of a Fleet Street editor. He enlisted, for an unknown reason, under the assumed name of Corringhame, which was his mother's maiden name. He was a soldier of fine physique. He loved a soldier's life, and volunteered for any scrap the Empire was engaged in.

In 1881 his regiment was stationed in the barracks of Ballincollig, the quaint little Irish suburb of Cork. There he fell in love, and married a sweet, blue-eyed Irish colleen named Julia O'Sullivan.

A year later the newly married couple carried out the first of their many moves during the husband's service career. His regiment was transferred to Glasgow and from there to Edinburgh. At this time the Egyptian trouble fostered by Arabi Pasha was brewing, so out to Egypt Corringhame went, leaving his bride to return to Ballincollig to console herself with her tears. "A soldier's first duty," he told his wife, "is to fight for his King." And on this austere principle he conducted his domestic affairs. He never allowed domestic ties to interfere with what he considered to be his duty. He believed in giving the tax-payer his money's worth.

While in Egypt he served with the Heavy Camel Corps, and took part in the action at Tel-el-Kebir. He returned ten months later wearing the Egyptian Medal and Star, and rejoined his regiment at Edinburgh. During his absence a baby girl had been born—Jess.

In 1886 his regiment moved to the West Cavalry Barracks, Aldershot, and while he was stationed there a son, Patrick, was born. A year later the Corringhame family was at the Preston Cavalry Barracks, Brighton. Here, on May 24th, 1887, was born a son christened Edward, the hero of this book.

From Brighton the regiment moved to Dundalk, Co. Louth, Ireland. During the Curragh Season, which included manœuvres, the father was separated from his family for several months; later he rejoined them when the regiment moved to Newbridge, near Dublin.

At Newbridge, Corporal Corringhame's time expired; he returned with his family to England and settled at Highgate. He had no pension, but as the result of a compulsory regimental money-saving scheme, whereby two-pence a day was deducted from a soldier's pay, he received about £40 on leaving.

He pottered about London for a couple of years, but his heart and soul were still in the King's Service. While on a visit to some relations at Liverpool he suddenly decided to join the Army again. He made a clean breast of his previous service and gave his proper name. His striking personality and soldierly manner soon overcame any obstacles to his re-enlistment, and he was sworn in, this time as a trooper in the 5th Dragoon Guards, who were then stationed in India. So out to India he went, leaving his family to join him later. He found his regiment at Meerut, under the command of Colonel Robert Baden-Powell (now Lord Baden-Powell, the beloved Chief of every Boy Scout).

Mrs. Mannock and her family of four arrived in India six months later. Edward was then between six and seven years of age, and with the other children he commenced his scanty education at the Army school. The family remained in India for nearly six years, and during the summer season the mother and children went for six months to the Hill Stations, as the temperature on the plains was too trying for them.

During this early period, Edward displayed a quiet, reserved nature, which was his primary characteristic during his schooling days. He was neither jovial nor quarrelsome. He never romped about with the other children. He pondered a great deal; while his little friends played, he would be found sitting and thinking or reading; he read any book he could lay hands on. Here is a characteristic attitude which intrigued his elders : a book on his left knee, his chin resting in his right hand, and his brow puckered deep in concentration. This pensiveness and love of reading mystified his elders. This desire to study met with a sudden check one day when the child, for some unknown reason, found his sight almost completely gone. Happily this state was a temporary one, lasting only for a fortnight, although the normal vision did not return for many months. This defect, however, recurred in a less serious form in later years.

He was always truthful, and would invariably admit any breaches of discipline rather than tell a lie and so possibly avoid punishment. His recreations were cricket and football—his favourite sports. It is interesting to note that during his childhood and youth he was quite unlike his famous contemporary richthofen, for he despised hunting and shooting wild game or birds, although he loved shooting at a target with an air-gun and bow and arrow. Animals and birds he loved as pets, and kept rabbits and pigeons. Later in his schooldays, when at Canterbury, he developed a passion for fishing, and occasionally stayed out all night poaching with the aid of a lamp to attract the fish. He would divide his catch between his family and the local priest, Father Power, of St. Thomas's Church. The fish to the former were in lieu of a smacking, while the latter had to be considered in order to adjust his conscience with the Deity!

He revelled in singing, and of musical instruments the kettle-drum and the Jew's harp were his favourites. Later in life he became passionately fond of the violin. He even took it with him to the war. As a boy he enjoyed good health, although he was not robust; in fact, he was growing into a slim, wiry youth, inclined to be tall—the type of youth who persists in his efforts; the race-horse type, sensitive, ambitious, highly strung, and full of grit. He had good features, jet-black straight hair, blue eyes, and a winsome smile.

Although the 5th Dragoon Guards was not the first unit in India on the roster for active service, as the result of the high standard of efficiency which they had attained in 1898 (Sir George White, the Commander-in-Chief, having declared that it was the best unit of all arms then in the country) the regiment was the first to leave India for the South African War, when a sudden call for reinforcements was received by the Commander-in-Chief.

The elder Mannock (once again a corporal) remained in South Africa until the end of the war, and took part in all the engagements which his famous regiment fought in. His family, now five—two boys and three girls—remained in India. When the war was over, Corporal Mannock's period of service was nearly completed, so he returned to England,

being stationed first at Shorncliffe and later at the Cavalry
Depot, Canterbury, where his family joined him. After a few
months he was demobilised and he made a home in Military
Road. Suddenly, and without apparent reason, he
abandoned his family, and he neither rejoined nor supported
them ever again. (In spite of this miserable and unforgivable
desertion, he was not deterred, nearly twenty years later,
from claiming his son's decorations and medals, and
unashamedly receiving them from the hands of the King at
Buckingham Palace, although his son had made a will in
favour of his other relations.) With the indomitable and
characteristic courage of her race and sex, the gallant
mother, with the support of the scanty earnings of her two
eldest children, succeeded in keeping the home together until
the younger children were old enough to fend for
themselves. The children in return, as circumstances
permitted, did not forget the debt they owed to this virtuous
and brave woman.

Edward, now twelve years of age, went to St. Thomas's
School for a short while, but owing to the circumstances
already referred to, he very soon had to commence earning a
living in order to assist his mother. His brother was already
working as a clerk with the National Telephone Company at
Canterbury. Young Edward had always shown a tendency for
practical jobs, preferably in the open air, and decided to start
as a messenger boy; pen-pushing did not appeal to him. His
first job was therefore with a local family greengrocer, who
paid him the handsome wage of half a crown a week for an
average of ten hours' work a day. The boy found the work too
arduous, the hours too long, and the remuneration too little;
so, after a few months, he decided to change his calling to that
of a barber's assistant. The pay was doubled, the work less

arduous, and the job not so sapping to his strength, although he disliked the thought of being indoors so much. He stuck to it for a while, but eventually decided that the nauseating atmosphere of the shop and alcoholic breaths of many of the regular customers were too much for him. He decided therefore to try some other more congenial occupation.

His brother, Patrick, was doing well as a clerk. He was paid fairly good wages; his hours were not long, and he appeared to be perfectly happy. So Edward decided to try the vocation of a clerk with the same company and in the same office, in the hope of eventually gaining an engineer's job. For a while this job suited him. His experiences as an errand boy and as a barber's assistant had given him a taste of the hardships of life in certain vocations, and he was happy and contented with his lot. But after a year or so office life began to affect his health, and the work lost its appeal. He stuck it for several years, until eventually an outdoor vacancy occurred in the, Wellingborough branch of the company; he applied for it and got it. This work was that of a linesman, assistant to the outdoor engineers: Edward's job was confined chiefly to "climbing telegraph poles," as he tersely described it later in life!

He was delighted with his transfer, but sorry to leave Canterbury because of his many friends. Since his arrival in the cathedral city he had made himself very popular with the youths of his age. He was an enthusiastic member of the St. Gregory's Cricket XI and an ardent recruit of the Church Lads Brigade, despite the fact that he was a Catholic. He became the kettle-drummer in the band, a position which was popular and much sought after.

In order to retain his happy connection with the cathedral city, on retiring from the C.L.B., he joined the

Home Counties (Territorial) R.A.M.C. Company at Canterbury, so that he could meet his friends at least once a year. He was a keen member of this Company and attended every annual camp. His keenness and proficiency were soon recognised and rewarded, and he was promoted to sergeant rank, before he resigned to go abroad a few years later.

He soon settled down to his work and surroundings; both appealed to him. The outdoor life suited him, and his attractive personality soon made for him a host of friends. He lived with Mr. and Mrs. A. E. Eyles, who eventually became his firmest friends. Mr. Eyles writes:

"Paddy (as he was familiarly referred to in Welling-borough) soon after his arrival became a great favourite among a large section of the populace. He was a keen cricketer, and played for the Wesleyan Cricket Club as wicket-keeper, a position where an eagle eye and quick thinking are essential. He joined the Parliamentary Debating Society, and very soon he was the secretary of the local Labour Party. His sympathy for the under-dog was pronounced, and bred, I think, from personal experience. In spite of his strong political creed, members of opposite creeds had great affection for him. His happy disposition, his cheerful countenance, and his obvious sincerity appealed to them. His death came as a great shock to everyone, and the town looked upon it as a personal loss. Today in the Council Chamber there hangs a full-size portrait of him, as a just tribute to his achievements, popularity, and memory.

I shall never forget his infectious laughter; his kindliness to children; his love of animals; his love of music, poetry, and literature; his great sense of humour; his good temper (only on one occasion did I ever see him roused to anger, and this was when a water-bailiff threatened to man-handle him as he refused to desist from fishing in preserved waters. He considered that, as the water came from God, and as God had not bequeathed it to any particular person, he was entitled to fish unmolested); his rapier thrusts in debate; his pungent Socialistic speeches. He was a young man with high ideals, and with a great love for his fellow-mortals. He hated cruelty and poverty. He was that rare type of young man who would fight to the death for a Cause which he believed in. For a Cause (thank God) he eventually died. No death more befitted him, for he was fighting as he so often told me: 'For the liberty of our Empire and the World.'

Air fighting to him was not a sport, as it appears to have been to so many other famous pilots. It was a Duty to be done. And he did it."

These virtues moulded into a character which, at the time of his death, was loved, admired, and honoured by men of unquestionable greatness.

# II

*Early Life—Part II*

Although he was very happy and contented enough at Wellingborough, his ambitious nature saw no immediate prospects of advancement in his present occupation, and so one evening, in January 1914, quite unexpectedly, he informed the Eyles family that he had decided to seek his fortune abroad if he could borrow enough money to make the venture. "I'm going to become a successful engineer, tea planter, or rancher," he said; "I feel it is the duty of every man to try to raise himself to whatever heights his ideals take him, whether they be spiritual or worldly. It only requires determination to try."

Mannock's life-story is one fighting chapter of moving forward and upward, and in the words just spoken we have in a nutshell the creed which elevated this barrack-born lad of humble parentage to a MAN among them. A poor boy who not only dreamt dreams, but converted them into reality.

In February, with the aid of money lent by Mr. Eyles and his brother, he sailed in a tramp steamer, and worked his passage to Turkey, in the hope that he could obtain a suitable and more remunerative appointment with an English telephone company in Constantinople, then employed in Government work. The manager, on hearing his story, was so impressed by his enterprise that he engaged him on the

21

spot as an outdoor engineer. Within six months he had made good and was holding the post of district inspector.

His letters to the Eyles family from Turkey not only illuminate his character, but also throw a sidelight on the conditions which prevailed in that country prior to and during the first few months of the war. They are all written from Stamboul and read:

*March 3rd.*—Letter ends: "My feet, eyes, and heart ache."

*July 7th.*—In a letter thanking his friend for a parcel of clothing he adds:

"The book, too, showed foresight on somebody's part, as I wanted so very much to read that poem.

No cricket here. Rowing, swimming, and telephone work are my chief recreations, with a little horse-riding now and then to keep my hand in. I have not much spare time, though, you would be surprised how the time flies out here—and the money !"

This letter was not completed until three days later, when he continues:

"I was not able to complete this letter, as you will observe. Work again, and no overtime paid for it. We have another busy time before us shortly, as the company is going to open another large exchange in town, which means over-work and sleepless nights for me.

The exchanges already existing are now running normally, and everything in connection with them is beginning to obtain the normal routine appearance.

There are quite a number of small exchanges in the outlying districts to be installed yet, but we are too busy with the underground cables to worry about those yet. The company is, in every case, building its own premises, which proves there is plenty of money in the firm. I am still in the good books of my chief, and likely to get on. Old B. would feel mad if he could understand the difference between my job at home and this one here. No more climbing irons for me! Diagrams and a blue pencil! I have been using my head out here. I will tell you a little story. About two months ago there appeared in the *Electrical Review* an advertisement for an Assistant Engineer, for foreign service with the company which I am serving with, but application had to be made to the Headquarters office in London. This, I concluded, was for this branch of the company. In the same issue there was another advert, for an engineer for the Gold Coast Colony—apply by letter to the Crown Agents in London. I applied for this appointment and got a favourable reply, but was asked for credentials from my present employers, which I thought would be the case. Next move. I approached the chief here, telling him of my intention of leaving, but asking him, on the other hand, if there was any likelihood of promotion for me in this present company. It worked. In fact, he would not give me a reference to go to that country, as he thought the job wasn't worth the risk. He held out good prospects for me here. Scene two. One of the rising young bloods here approached the Chief regarding the advert. in the *Review* and was told it had been decided to cancel same for a little while longer. I am fairly well sure of my ground now.

How I long sometimes to have a night with you and the old piano. Not much opportunity here for a good song and accompanist [*sic*]. I am neglecting the little old fiddle too. Your good lady is studying the piano seriously—excellent, for the benefit of my return? I shall want enough music to last me twelve months on that occasion. I miss her cakes and tarts too, and the ginger beer, and all the other nice things I used to have. Woe is me. I sometimes wish I had never left the old place—for the reason of the people I left behind. There are lots of sweet English girls out here too, but I am keeping them at arm's length by saying I am married. I wear the little old signet ring on the marriage finger (at least I think it is the marriage finger), so the girls are giving me up as a bad job. Stiff upper lip, as becomes a rising engineer."

He ends the letter: "Sincerely and Socialistically yours, MURPHY."

*August 28th.*—England had by now declared war on Germany, and the Germans were doing their utmost to induce Turkey to join them. Mannock writes:

"Things very very serious here. War in the air. Great anti-British feeling displayed by the people. Things at famine prices. The company is not paying wages. Banks closed. Credit stopped. Everyone starving. Cannot grumble, I had a bloater last Monday."

*October 21st.*—Letter to Mrs. Eyles, congratulating her on her birthday, reads:

"You will believe me, I am sure, when I tell you I am grieved beyond measure that I cannot send you anything else but a letter as a mark of esteem and token of regard. Believe me also when I say that it is through no fault of my own that such is the case. Nevertheless, there will be something later, when I come back to England, to mark the passing of this birthday. The fact is that I have no money, we are all in the same position. No money owing to the moratorium out here. Never mind, I will bring you something which will make your eyes open—' when Paddy comes marching home again.'

Nothing of any importance has taken place out here up to date. The country is upside down still, and no indication of it being otherwise for some time to come. Through it all, we are alive, well, and hungry. Business proceeds as usual, although a bit slow. I am still at Stamboul, in charge of the engineering here, and doing as well as can be imagined. I have been seriously thinking of throwing all my prospects overboard, and volunteering for service at the front. What do you advise? How long is the war going to last—Xmas? I wonder if it will be the end of old Murphy? A soldier's lonely grave.

I don't feel in form at all to-night, so you must make allowance for this tame and insipid letter. I feel cramped and fettered somehow, and homesick. I want to be home again. England is the best and most comfortable place after all."

*December 28th.*—Owing to the state of war between Turkey and England, Mannock had been a prisoner of war since November, and in the only letter which reached the Eyles family he commences with:

"Dear Comrades," and writes: "Have just had notice that possibly this note may reach you. I haven't had time to write anything elaborate. My Xmas was spent as merrily as could be expected under the circumstances. I sincerely hope that all is well at home. My thoughts are constantly with you. Ali Hamid Bey (one of my faithful henchmen) sends his respectful good wishes, especially to little Derek, and hopes to see him some time or other. (Of course he has seen the p.c. photo you sent of him.) I hope to get out of this crisis all right. I only wish I could think that you all are just as secure at home, as I am here. I trust this note will reach you safely. Of course you cannot write me in return. I sent a note some little while ago, but you may not have got it. I am well, very well, but uneasy owing to no news being received here. Farewell till we meet again. Sincerest thoughts for you all, PAT."

From this date until he returned to England, he neither received any letters, nor did his friends or relations hear from him. As a consequence his friend Mr. Eyles wrote to the American Embassy in Constantinople on January 11th, 1915, asking for information about his whereabouts and health.

The following reply, dated February 19th, 1915, was received from the Secretary of the Embassy:

"SIR, The Embassy is in receipt of your inquiry of January 11th and in reply takes pleasure in informing you that Mr. Edward Mannock is still in Constantinople and in good health."

On the declaration of war, the Turkish Government took over the control of the company which he was working for, and for a few months he continued working as a prisoner of war, but owing to frequent attempts which he made to escape, he was incarcerated in a concentration camp at Stamboul. While confined in this camp, he broke out of bounds on several occasions in order to obtain food for himself and his comrades, and as a punishment he was given meals of black bread and water for days at a time. This treatment naturally affected his health and made him very bitter, particularly against the Germans, whom he contended were responsible for the war and the deliberate ill-treatment of the English prisoners. Mannock's resentment was hardened by the loss of his livelihood at a time when the gates of Life's ambition were opening wide, and at his helpless inaction. He resembled a restless tiger in a cage as he paced backwards and forwards inside the wire entanglements, scheming of ways and means of getting back to his beloved England so that he could fight in her defence. In spite of his restlessness, his gentle and kindly nature did not give at this stage any indication of the renowned air fighter or still less the merciless slayer of his country's enemies which destiny meant him to become.

In spite of the treatment meted out to him as prisoner, his unfailing cheerfulness was a source of comfort to the other prisoners. Miss Florence Minter, who was also a prisoner, writes:

"I see that his comrades invariably spoke of him as a 'sport.' That he was always, and in the dark days of our internment and during that bad time when we were under arrest coming home, he was always cheerful and helpful, and kept the men 'British' all through; he was our philosopher, friend, and guide."

The guards used to tease him, in an effort to annoy, by claiming that "England was ruined." Mannock replied with fingers outstretched from his nose.

As the result of diplomatic overtures he was included in a batch of exchanged prisoners which left the camp on April 1st, 1915. On two previous occasions he was on the point of leaving Turkey, but on account of some comrades, led by him, singing patriotic songs, his freedom was cancelled. His eventual repatriation was on the grounds of age, apparent bad health, and defective eyesight. The Turks, like most Britishers, thought the war would soon be over, and that an obvious "crock" like Mannock was of no military value. Little did they dream that in releasing him they were unleashing an enemy who, by personal effort and leadership, was destined to become the greatest of all air fighters and responsible for the destruction of the equivalent of several enemy squadrons of aeroplanes.

It is well to reflect at this point on the curious congenital defect of sight affecting Mannock's left eye. Quite a number of leading pilots suffered from this defect, and it is also noticeably traceable in a number of men grown to fame and of outstanding genius in history. It is yet to be proved whether this optical astigmatism concentrates more vision in the sound eye or not; but an examination of the photographs of many great men invariably discloses a contracted left eye. It was quite a noteworthy feat in itself, therefore, for Mannock to have succeeded in "bluffing" the medical testing boards who at that time examined pilots for the Air Force. The test was not only rigorous in the extreme, but could only be encompassed by means of a trick on the part of a candidate suffering from such an infirmity. Both eyes of every candidate were required to register as near perfect as could be reasonably expected from normal healthy youths. It is known that the medical officer in a forgetful moment uncovered the sight-boards for a few brief seconds and in this space of time Mannock's good eye had registered and absorbed the requisite data. This peculiarly miraculous instinct of his, by which he could pick out and memorise an object, was one of the chief powers which helped him to shape his talents as an air fighter and leader.

And so, in the midst of the terrible turmoil of war, when rival civilised nations were gloating over the slaughter, destruction, and terror they were inflicting on one another, and the lives of men, the pawns in the game, were merely terms of thousands or hundreds of thousands, a British doctor through lack of "due and proper care" was cheated by a young Irishman. After all, it may be thought it was only a small matter in those days when doctors prodded men like an expert of flesh is wont to prod cattle today. A mistake, yes, but be it remembered that it was a mistake that gave the Allies its greatest air fighter.

As soon as Mannock landed in England, his first thought was to go and report to his old R.A.M.C. Company, which he eventually found in Ashford, Kent. He was immediately promoted to Sergeant, and at his request he joined the transport section of the 3/2nd Home Counties Field Ambulance Company.

A mess-mate writes of Mannock's connections with this Company, and of his personality, which is obviously beginning to assert itself:

"To all his intimates he was known as 'Jerry.' He was what is vaguely called a 'character'—one of those vivid and colourful personalities that make an impression wherever they are found. His career was extraordinarily varied. He joined the transport section of a field ambulance—the 3/2nd Home Counties, commanded by Major Chittenden.

I was a sergeant in the 3/3rd unit, and we 'lay' next to each other at dear, muddy, rat-haunted Halton Park Camp West in 1915—a winter which changed Lord Rothschild's stately park into a slimy mass of chalky mud, dreary beyond conception.

'Jerry' was a member of a combined sergeants' mess j that had roughly about 100 members. It was he who suggested a weekly debate, and this gradually became transformed into a mock Parliament. He was the 'Hon. Member for Newmarket,' a delicate compliment to his knowledge of horses, and he engaged us in many an active debate on Socialism. Those were jolly and stimulating days.

Alas! how many of the good fellows who made speeches and tinkered with the affairs of the nation are lying in hastily made graves in all parts of the world! And now 'Jerry.' The flashing, original, lovable comrade of those transitory days is gone too.

When the transport personnel of the R.A.M.C. of the Field Ambulance became part of the A.S.C., 'Jerry' decided to make a change."

The "flashing, original, lovable comrade" had been quietly examining his conscience a good deal during his moments of quietude. "We are fighting for the freedom of civilisation," he declared passionately one day to the members of the mock Parliament. "We must fight to the last man! We must kill every enemy." He realised that his bitterness regarding the Germans was outgrowing the gentle, sympathetic outlook which should have been an integral part of his make-up as a non-combatant member of the R.A.M.C. He came to the conclusion that he could not and would not assist a wounded enemy. Therefore, he decided to apply for a transfer to a combatant unit. The combatant duties of the Army Service Corps did not meet with his requirements, so he applied for a commission in the Royal Engineers, and obtained it on April 1st, 1916. "I intend to become a Tunnelling Officer," he wrote, "and blow the [—] up. The higher they go and the more pieces that come down, the happier I shall be." Apparently the germ of hatred had by now firmly implanted itself.

The Adjutant of the R.E. Cadet Depot at Fenny Stratford writes of Cadet Mannock:

"I first met Mannock at the Royal Engineers' Depot at Fenny Stratford.

During a tour of duty at that Depot one of the jobs assigned to me was to examine and report upon Cadets qualifying for Commissions. Mannock came to the Depot as a Cadet, and if I remember rightly was in a Class designated S.6.

I still remember vividly our first meeting. I had a list of the Cadets before me and was interviewing them personally one by one. "I came to Mannock's name and looked up. A tall, hard-bitten-looking fellow stood before me, with more the appearance of a Colonial than an Englishman, blue-grey eyes, a thin clean-shaven face, and a rather grim expression. I recollect that it struck me as being strange that he wore Wellington boots and spurs, carried a riding whip, and wore an inverted spur badge on his arm, as he was down on the list as a Sgt.-Major R.A.M.C. I commented on this, and he explained briefly that he was in the Mounted Transport. I followed this up by asking him whether by any chance he knew a Mr. Frank Mannock, an old friend of mine, as the name was an uncommon one. Much to my surprise he replied that Frank Mannock was his cousin. I was surprised, because there was no family resemblance, and the two men were so dissimilar. Frank Mannock was handsome, polished, debonair, cultured, a brilliant conversationalist, and a man of the world. Sgt.-Major Mannock struck me as being the exact opposite. The circumstances of this relationship, however, led to an intimacy between us which probably would not otherwise have developed.

He remained at this Depot for, I should say, about a couple of months, during which time I met him frequently, both officially and off duty. I thus had an opportunity of getting to know the inside of this remarkable man as well as the outside. It took some time to break down the crust of his reserve and gain his confidence, and I probably should never have done so but for my long and intimate friendship with other members of his family.

It is a strange thing that at this time he was not what one might call a 'mixer.' On the contrary, his aloofness was extraordinary in an environment where a withdrawal into oneself was well-nigh impossible—an environment which precluded privacy of any description. The result was that Mannock appeared to make few, if any, friends amongst his fellow-cadets. Few of these young fellows took life seriously. They were a high-spirited, cheerful, happy-go-lucky crowd, full of beans and vitality, and against this vivid background Mannock seemed morose and gloomy. Although he was a much older man than most of the cadets, that fact did not account for his conspicuous insularity.

After a bit, I began to glimpse his point of view. For one thing he had no time for fools or fooling. He was in deadly earnest about the war. I think he chafed at the tameness and monotony of the Training Centre, with its dull routine and eternal sameness. He felt he was being shunted from the main scene of action and that precious time was being wasted. He wanted to come to grips with realities, and here he was living a life of make-believe and soul-destroying routine. The tedium of training made him restless and ill at ease. He had the feeling that he was being cheated of his share in what to him was a great and glorious adventure. Anything in the nature of frivolity appeared to him like fiddling while Rome burned. He was anxious to get on with his job, and to get overseas. Like many others he feared that the war would be over before he had finished training. He had to do and learn many things that were formal and useless. He was forced to repeat many things he knew already, and stuff his mind with the devastating and indigestible contents of Army textbooks. The fact was he hadn't a textbook mind, nor the rigid military mind that could assimilate drill and routine with avidity. On the other hand, he had an individuality that nothing could crush nor absorb. He was a lone figure, but he kept the flame of his personality burning brightly in a system designed to make the individual part of a machine. He sought no friendships nor favour. He had such tremendous strength of mind that one seldom meets. He thought for himself, and when his mind was made up nothing could move him. He was adamant.

His views on life did not come out of books—they were the outcome of his own thoughts and experiences.

His opinions were not second-hand, but came clean and fresh-minted from a keen and original brain.

He hated shams of every kind. Snobbery made him writhe with contempt. Cant, hypocrisy, and pretence he loathed with the loathing of a man who was as straight as a rifle barrel, and whose character bore all the marks of greatness. He was single-minded, and purposeful. He had something of the mystic about him in his visionary idealism. In a way he belonged to another age—the age of chivalry. His patriotism flamed like a beacon on a hill-top. He symbolised all that is best and finest in the English character, especially in his innate sense of justice and fair-play.

There was nothing jingoistic or boastful about him. He was quiet, reserved, self-sufficient, self-confident, and modest. He loved England and the common folk of England with all the depth and strength of his nature, and had he survived he would have fought with all his might for the good of the country and the betterment of the under-dog.

He was out to win the war as a basis for a greater and better England. For him, 'A country fit for heroes to live in,' would have been no empty phrase. He may have been ambitious, but he gave no sign of it at this stage in his career. He seemed to be extraordinarily devoid of self-interest, in any direction whatsoever. I have no idea what made him think of transferring to the R.F.C., but quite unexpectedly he expressed his intention of doing so.

I was amazed at his sudden decision. It appeared to me to be an utterly foolish thing to do.

For one thing, I thought he was too old—he was over thirty at the time—to adapt himself to the newest arm in warfare, and the strange business of flying, especially as the prevailing opinion was, that only young men were suitable for the job. Still the novelty, the danger and excitement of flying, must have appealed irresistibly to his adventurous spirit, and despite all opposition, and the disadvantage of his age, he stuck grimly to his decision, and eventually realising his ambition—obtained a transfer to the Royal Flying Corps. The next time I saw Mannock was in St. Omer. I ran into him quite unexpectedly in a street at the back of the Town Hall. The first thing I noticed was that he was wearing a single M.C. ribbon—his first decoration. I congratulated him, and he told me, with just a touch of pardonable pride in his voice, that he was being awarded a Bar to his M.C.

He was tremendously enthusiastic about flying, and told me that his transfer to the R.F.C. was the best thing he ever did. We were both pressed for time, and after a short conversation about our respective experiences, the details of which I have forgotten, we bade each other good-bye, promising to look one another up when the opportunity presented itself.

I think his last words were: 'Well, Cheerio, old man, good luck!' I never saw him again.

To say that I feel honoured to have known such a man as Mannock, and to have been partly instrumental in getting him his commission, is but a feeble expression of my feelings. He was a splendid man, and a splendid soldier."

A few months with the Royal Engineers at Bedford convinced him that his individuality was being submerged by an ever-increasing amount of red-tape—which he detested—combined with the cunning negative encouragement which he was receiving at the hands of less militant-minded instructors. HE wanted quickly to get to the war; THEY wanted to keep him as long as they could: it was by pursuing this principle that their position was made more secure, and their prospects of promotion made better. This was during the summer of 1916, when Captain Albert Ball, the great British air fighter, was beginning to blaze his trail, and when the nation was going into ecstasies over his valorous deeds. Mannock absorbed every line that he read about Ball and his air-fighting comrades. His imagination carried him high into the heavens above the squalor and the mud; he seated himself in a tiny single-seater fighter with his machine guns spitting fire and barking angrily as he fought enemy after enemy. Tunnelling faded into insignificance. This was the game for him! No senior officer could curb his activities in this kind of warfare. His initiative and his hatred would have full scope to exact its toll. His valour (which he had every confidence in) would have every opportunity of displaying itself. The vain thought of decoration or glory did not enter the picture.

For hours he used to lie on the ground and watch the machines of the Royal Flying Corps in the air. The roar of the engines was a symphony that called him, the sight of the glistening craft in the blue skies quickened his pulse—and his soul. Every evening he studied the aeronautical magazines then published, and his sleep was disturbed with dreams of flying in the air.

Mannock decided to become an airman. But what about his defective eyesight? "An air pilot," the authorities declared, "must have 100 percent, eyesight." How was he going to overcome this apparently insurmountable obstacle? His war record is a fine example of what a determined man could achieve in the way of overcoming official obstacles in order to be at the front, rubbing shoulders with MEN WHO *WERE* MEN, and helping to kill the enemy regardless of his own life.

He applied to be transferred to the R.F.C., and his Commanding Officer with a smile approved. Then came the medical test for flying, the stiffest test of its kind in the war, as only the perfect were chosen from the host of aspirants. He had every confidence in his ability to pass the physical test, though the Turks had turned a despising eye on him, but eyesight ...

"Are your eyes good?" asked the doctor.

"Of course," was the immediate reply.

That examination must have been a great anxiety, and a great achievement for the young Irishman, for the doctor wrote "Fit for pilot" on the papers of the candidate with the defective left eye!

Perhaps the Turkish authorities must be forgiven for repatriating the one-eyed inoffensive young Irishman. The British doctor need suffer no remorse. He was cleverly deceived, but the deception gave the world the King of Air Fighters, a man whose achievements were to outrival those of Richthofen, or any of his contemporaries.

In August 1916, 2nd Lieut. Mannock obtained his transfer to the Royal Flying Corps (R.F.C.), a Corps which had entered the war without tradition, but one which had already by valorous deeds raised itself to indisputable eminence. Mannock fully realised his luck, and an amusing entry in his diary reads:

"When the Adjutant sent for me today and informed me of my transfer to the R.F.C, I could have kissed him, although he has the most repulsive 'mug' of any man that I have ever met. Yes! I could have kissed it; such was my unbounded delight. Now for the Bosche! I am going to strive to become a scout pilot like Ball. Watch me. I wonder what Fate has in store?"

Destiny linked arms with him for a considerable way along War's dangerous path!

# III

*Learning to Fly, and First Tour of Duty in France With No. 40 Squadron*

The No. 1 School of Military Aeronautics, Reading, was one of a number of training depots to which prospective pilots were posted on joining the R.F.C. Here they were instructed in the theory of flight, engines, rigging, map reading, machine gunnery, bombing, and such other subjects as were of use to a pilot on active service. The course varied in length according to the pupil's ability and the urgency of reinforcements required overseas. Mannock, who was now christened "Mick" and "Micky"—popular R.F. C. sobriquets, which went with him to his grave—was at the School from August 14th to September 29th, and of all the subjects, only theory of flight and machine gunnery appealed to him.

Having successfully completed the course and passed out with honours, he moved on to the flying training school— the embryo pilot's paradise. He was originally posted to Hendon, where he qualified in elementary flying and passed his Aero Club Certificate test on November 28th, being allotted the number 3895. Owing to a congestion of pupils, he was moved to No. 19 Training Squadron at Hounslow on December 5th. On February 1st, 1917, he was appointed Flying Officer (on probation), and was attached to the School of Gunnery at Hythe, and after a couple of weeks there he was posted to No. 10 Reserve Squadron at Joyce

Green for advanced instruction. According to his instructor he quickly showed a natural aptitude for flying, particularly during the early stages:

"There are two distinct types of pilots," Captain Chapman says, "who become the most successful flyers: the man with the natural aptitude for flying, and the other with the bulldog tenacity of purpose that causes him to stick the flying game out, despite crashes of the worst description; the sort of fellow who always comes out of the aerial debris smiling. They are always the keenest pupils, being the first on the aerodrome in the morning and the last to leave at night, and invariably fret about the mess on non-flying days, watching the sky from the windows at frequent intervals for a sign of the rain clearing up. I confess that I would sooner teach the first type, for he takes to the air like the proverbial duck to water, and gives very little trouble, generally getting off on his first solo with only a few hours' dual instruction. Major Mannock was a fine example of the first type. He came to me at Hendon, in 1916, for instruction, a raw green 'Hun' (as we called the flying pupils under instruction) from Reading. I do not know, but he seemed not to have the slightest conception of an aeroplane. To do him justice, there were a few wires which he did not loosen in climbing into the cockpit, but then the machine, a Henri Farman (or Rumpty as they were commonly known), was at all times hard to get into. He finally managed to get into the pupil's seat, and we took off the ground. Mannock, unlike many pupils, instead of jamming the rudder and seizing the joystick in a Herculean grip, looked over the side of the aeroplane at the earth, which was dropping rapidly away from him, with an expression which betrayed the mildest interest. I liked him immensely from that moment. He made his solo flight with but a few hours' instruction, for he seemed to master the rudiments of flying with his first hour in the air, and from then on threw the machine about as he pleased."

When he passed on to more advanced instruction, he "was good at flying but poor at landing." It is curious to reflect that, with the exception of McCudden, many of the best air fighters in the war were poor pilots in the aerodrome sense of the term. Complete masters of their aircraft in the air, they were often noticeably deficient in ability to land easily; on the German side, Richthofen and Voss were no exceptions to the rule. Mannock was not a "stunt" pilot: and again it must be remembered that during the war "stunt" pilots rarely displayed courage in face of the enemy. A study of the war careers of pre-war "stunt" pilots will confirm this indictment. Of course, to a good pilot, carrying out aerobatics is merely a question of height and practice; whilst to be prepared to die in an aeroplane becomes quite a different story, especially when there is involved a possible tumble to earth in flames or breaking up into small pieces.

Mannock was fortunate that whilst at Joyce Green he was able to benefit from the advice of one who may be regarded as the finest air marksman of the war—Captain James Byford McCudden, who happened to be giving instruction at the aerodrome, as Wing-fighting instructor. In his excellent autobiography *Flying Fury*, McCudden writes of this period:

"I reported to the Wing at Maidstone, and was told to make my headquarters at Joyce Green for the time being. I was allotted a Bristol Scout for my work, but as it was not yet ready, I used a D.H.2, which I 'spun' regularly to the great consternation of the pupils there, who regarded the machine as a super-death-trap, not knowing that in its day it was one of the best machines in the R.F.C.

Joyce Green is a quiet little spot near Dartford, and the aerodrome is considered a good one, although it is beneath the level of the Thames, which flows past the aerodrome, and the ground is a little spongy.

The machines we are using here are principally the D.H.2s, Avros, and Vickers fighters, which were very good for training pilots preparatory to their flying De Havilland 2s and F.E. 8s.

The pupils here during the period of which I write were very good. One I particularly remember, named Mannock.

One day he came to me and said that I was the cause of saving his life. I had only just previously given him instruction what to do if he unfortunately got into a 'spin,' He had just had his first spin and had remembered my advice, which I think at the time was to put all controls central and offer up a very short and quick prayer. Mannock was a typical example of the impetuous young Irishman, and I always thought he was of the type to do or die. ... I did a good deal of instructional work at Joyce Green, and most of the pupils were eager to learn as much as possible. My work consisted mostly of taking them up in a Vickers fighter which was fitted with dual control, and explaining to them what I wished them to do before we left the ground. When we were up I would put down the nose of the machine and twist and turn it about in all manner of ways in order to get the pupils used to the feel of a machine in all the positions which it is necessary for them to put it, so as to be able to do the aerial acrobatics which are only part of the qualifications of the successful air fighter.

After they had felt the way I manipulated the control, I would let them take charge and repeat the evolutions that I had performed previously. If they were quite good, I would go up in a similar machine and fight them and tell them their faults when we landed again. If they were too bad, they received more instruction until they were proficient or were turned down altogether. ... At this time the pilots were receiving good training indeed, and were quite competent to go into their first fight with a good chance of downing an opponent.

At the time I went to France to fly a fighter aeroplane I had not even flown the type which I was to fly over the lines the next morning, let alone not having received any fighting instruction. I must admit that after I had flown for five weeks over the lines as a pilot, when I went on to De Havilland Scouts, I did not even appreciate the necessity of turning at once when an opponent got behind me, and I only just realised that I had to get directly behind him to get a shot at him without having to make allowance for his speed or mine. Which all goes to show at what a speed does the development of aerial fighting take place. ... Apart from the actual training in the air for fighting, the pupils now receive lectures from pilots who had all flown in France and these lectures include the pilots' own experiences coupled with that of the others."

If similar instruction was being carried out in all other training squadrons, it is difficult to accept recent assertions that pilots were being sent to France during this period completely untrained for fighting duties on offensive patrols.

McCudden and Mannock as a result of this meeting became bosom friends. They were no doubt naturally attracted, not only because of "sympathetic heart-beats," but also because they belonged to the same stock, both being Irish, and both born within the Service and educated principally in Army Schools.

Captain Meredith Thomas (now Wing-Commander) was another pupil at Joyce Green, and as he shared a hut with Mannock, the following impressions and anecdotes give a close-up view of him at this time:

"I first met 'Micky' in February 1917," he writes, "when he came along from Hythe to No. 10 Reserve Squadron at Joyce Green to fly D.H.2s and F.E.8s. We shared a room and he told me many interesting stories of his pre-war life; it appeared to have been a hard one. At this time he was a staunch teetotaler and a fairly regular church-goer, although during chats with him he professed to have no particular religion.

One particular incident regarding his flying training I well remember. That was his first solo on a D.H.2, when he was told, as all were told in those days, 'Don't turn below 2,000 feet; if you do, you will spin and kill yourself.'

Micky proved this wrong early one Sunday morning in March, when he accidentally got into a spin at about 1,000 feet over the munition factory—then just across the creek on the edge of the aerodrome—and came out extremely near the ground and the munition factory, and landed successfully in a small field which was too small to fly out from. He was accused of spinning intentionally, and after a rather unpleasant scene in the Mess and later in the C.O.'s office, was threatened with being turned down.

We were great friends at Joyce Green and had many both amusing and serious talks when waiting in the cold on a petrol bin—at one period for a whole three weeks—for a flight, but I cannot recall anything definite beyond our mutual disgust because of the manner in which the staff threatened the pupils, many of whom had seen pretty severe war service before transferring or being seconded to the R.F.C., whilst the Staff had seen very very little, and in some cases, none.

My first impression of Micky was: he was very reserved, inclined to strong temper, but very patient and somewhat difficult to arouse. On short acquaintance he became a very good conversationalist and was fond of discussions or arguments. He was prepared to be generous to everyone in thought and deed, but had strong likes and dislikes. He was inclined to be almost too serious-minded."

Mannock was much older than his comrades, and his "serious-minded" attitude was due to the fact that unlike his younger comrades he was a profound thinker, and the anxiety which he felt inwardly as to the ultimate result of the war at this period caused him alarm, which he apparently showed in his conversations and manner. He remembered the Indian prisoners whom he had seen caged in Constantinople, with their arms folded and standing like statues facing the Dardanelles. He had heard them say in mystic tones, "The English will come"; and the thought haunted him. He feared that after all "the English will come" would prove to be a myth, and that the wretched starving Indians would be left to the mercy of their callous captors. Hatred (which he concealed) was in his breast, and the seriousness with which he carried out his training caused him to be misunderstood by his more light-hearted fellow-pupils.

On completion of his advanced training on a D.H.2, which synchronised with the crunching of several collapsing under-carriages, he embarked for France on the night of March 31st.

A panoramic view of the history of air fighting on the Western Front as applied to the Royal Flying Corps from the beginning of the war to the date of Mannock's entry into the conflict may prove helpful to the reader in order that he may visualise the rapid and frequent changes and revolutions which were effected by changed tactics and methods; the evolution of better types of fighting planes and their necessary equipment, and the reaction occasioned by these swift-moving phases on the respective belligerents. These years demonstrated to the rivals that upon the success of their air fighters depended the fate of all cooperating aircraft, and ultimately decided to a considerable degree the success of the ground forces.

It is interesting to trace the progress of this vital branch of the Service; to see how we started at zero and finished pre-eminently—the admiration of our Allies and the envy of our foes.

In 1912, the Royal Flying Corps was formed, and consisted of two Wings, military and naval. Their functions were for the most part auxiliary, for they were to assist the Army and the Navy. The means by which they were to do this was twofold: first, by obtaining and reporting information—reconnaissance; second, by using their destructive power—bombing. Both Wings on their formation immediately began to experiment with air armaments. The Naval Wing, which in process of time became known as the Royal Naval Air Service, was still largely experimenting at the outbreak of war. The officers chiefly employed in this research, which took place at Eastchurch, the H.Q,. of the Naval Wing, were the gallant and famous Commander Rumney Samson at first, and later, Lieutenant Clark-Hall, a naval Gunnery-Lieutenant, who was appointed in March 1913 for armament duties. They studied the theory of bomb-dropping in all its aspects, together with the possibility of mounting machine guns on aeroplanes. As a result, Lieutenant Clark-Hall, early in 1914, reported as follows:

"Machine-gun aeroplanes are (or will be) required to drive off enemy machines approaching our ports with the intention of obtaining information or attacking with bombs our magazines, oil tanks, or dock-yards. ... I do not think the present state of foreign seaplanes for an attack or scouting over our home ports is such as to make the question extremely urgent, but I would strongly advocate having by the end of 1914 at each of our home ports and important bases at least two aeroplanes mounting machine guns for the sole purpose of beating off or destroying attacking enemy machines."

The Naval Wing foreshadowed also the probability of Zeppelin attacks on our shores, and experiments were carried out with the object of inventing a projectile to destroy them. At first, they experimented with an explosive grapnel suspended from an aeroplane, which on contact with a Zeppelin would explode. However, after many ingenious devices were tested, the only effective weapon appeared to be the Hales grenade, and it was adopted. This decision resulted in the first Zeppelin being destroyed in the air during the war, and Flight-Sub-Lieutenant Warne-ford, the pilot of the victorious aircraft was awarded the Victoria Cross.

The Military Wing, which was later designated the Royal Flying Corps, while recognising that its chief duty was reconnaissance for the Expeditionary Force, was as much alive as its sister branch to the possibility of future combats in the air; consequently, Major Brooke-Popham, who commanded the first Squadron to get to work in this connection—No. 3—despatched a flight, under the command of Captain P. L. W. Herbert, to Hythe, to determine the most suitable kind of machine gun for use in aeroplanes. After a thorough test of most types, the Lewis gun was chosen, with the proviso that it should go through a series of ground tests. These took a long time, and it was not until September 1914 that the first aeroplane fitted with Lewis guns reached the R.F.C. in France.

The Lewis gun eventually became a much-used weapon in the war, both by the air and ground forces. It was used extensively in air warfare, and played an important part in Mannock's fighting. It was of simple design and the mechanism was not complicated or difficult to understand. There were sixty-two parts in the gun proper, exclusive of the accessories, which were not part of the gun. The parts could not be wrongly assembled, and when in place required no adjustment. The gun was air-cooled by an ingenious design, whereby the powder blast at each discharge ultimately caused the sucking of cool air over the barrel of the gun. Incident to the cooling system was the increase of velocity of the bullet. It was found in practice that the gun gave a slightly greater velocity to the bullet than could be obtained from the same length of barrel in a shoulder arm firing the same ammunition. The recoil was negligible. The rate of fire was between 600-800 rounds per minute according to the adjustment. The ammunition was fed to the gun from a rotating drum, which held 99 rounds of 303. The bullet when fired travelled during the first second at over 820 yards per second, and killed at range of 1,000 yards.

In July 1914, several machines which were used later in the war as "fighters" were being designed; and some including the Bristol Scout, Vickers fighter, and F.E.2 were even being experimented with; but the fact remains that the R.F.C. had designed its machines and trained its pilots primarily for reconnaissance, and the result was that it actually entered the war, like the enemy air force, armed only with rifles and revolvers.

It is interesting to trace the cause which led up to the first air combat in which a British aircraft pilot took part. Nos. 2, 3, 4, and 5 Squadrons, the Aircraft Park and Headquarters Staff of the R.F.C, the first organised National Air Force to fly to a war overseas, had arrived in France on August 15th, 1914, with an assortment of aeroplanes— B.E.s, Henri Farmans, Blériots, Avros, and B.E.8s.

On August 19th, operations were commenced from their aerodrome at Maubeuge. Three days later the first German aeroplane was seen by our pilots. It was an AlbatrossBiplane, which passed over the British aerodrome. As soon as it was sighted, Major Longcroft and Lieutenant Dawes on B.E.s, and Lieutenant Strange on his machine which experimentally mounted a Lewis gun, gave chase; but the enemy escaped.

This was the first opportunity and attempt of a Britisher to engage in aerial combat, and it is most interesting to note that, although this was the first enemy seen in the air, yet the first thoughts of our pilots were—to give chase and destroy him. This was the germ which eventually was to grow into the traditional R.F.C. offensive spirit.

The day of victory was not far off, for on August 25th the first fight in the air took place, and on the same day two hostile aircraft were forced to the ground by our pilots. One enemy landed near Le Quesney, where it was captured; the other was forced down by Lieutenants H. D Harvey-Kelly and H. C. Mansfield, and an accompanying machine from No. 2 Squadron. The officers mentioned landed near their victims, who dashed away from their machine and escaped in a wood, though hotly pursued by their victors. While it is somewhat doubtful which of these machines was forced down first, it is undeniable that this engagement was the prelude to air fighting on a scale which was then undreamed of, and which early proved that the successful co-operation of aircraft with ground forces depended upon local air superiority, which could only be attained by aggressive air fighting. The protagonists were slow in grasping this fact, and the progress of equipping the Air Services with efficient fighting machines was almost leisurely for many more months to come.

It is not difficult to imagine what might have happened had one of the combatants foreseen the importance of air fighting and speedily equipped himself with special fighters. The opposition would have been negligible, and consequently the enemy would have been driven from the skies, and the "eyes of his army" would have been destroyed. On the other hand, the victors' aircraft could have patrolled over the enemy lines unmolested, reporting the enemy's movements as well as lowering his *moral* by continuous bombing and machine-gun attacks.

In September, the German High Command issued an order that all enemy aircraft were to be attacked whenever encountered. This was the official signal for the real war in the air to commence; that is, aeroplanes had to fight one another in deadly combat. The immediate effect of such a declaration was that a keen competition began between the opposing air forces in designing, constructing, and arming aeroplanes, with the result that progress was rapid. As an outcome of this order, combats became more frequent; and on September 7th, the Commander-in-Chief in his despatch was able to say: "Five enemy aeroplanes have been shot down as the result of aerial combat." These combats demonstrated to us the necessity for faster and better-armed aircraft for this type of work. The enemy aircraft at this period were usually faster, easier to manœuvre, and certainly better climbers—three characteristics which make one aircraft superior to another in air combat. This was fortunate for the German, for by his superior speed he was able to refuse combat when he wished; while he was also able to attack our slower machines at will. But whatever material advantage they may have had was more than counterbalanced by the superior *moral* of our pilots, whose dashing and determined attacks often nonplussed the machine-like Teuton. On one occasion an unarmed British machine attacked an opponent so resolutely that the German decided to land.

Sir John French, in his despatch of September 14th, awarded unstinted praise to our airmen:

"The tactics," he says, "for dealing with hostile aircraft are to attack them instantly with one or more British machines. This has been so far successful that in five cases German pilots and observers have been shot in the air and their machines brought to the ground. As a consequence the British Flying Corps has succeeded in establishing an individual ascendancy which is as serviceable to us as it is damaging to the enemy. Something in the direction of the mastery of the air has already been gained."

Sir David Henderson, who commanded the Royal Flying Corps in the field, on September 4th, wired home:

"There are no aeroplanes with the R.F.C. really suitable for machine guns. Grenades and bombs are therefore at present more suitable. If suitable aeroplanes are available, machine guns are better undoubtedly. Request you to supply efficient fighting machines as soon as possible."

Some ten months later, No. 11 Squadron, equipped with the Vickers fighter ("Gun-bus"), arrived in France. This saw the first semi-fighter squadron to be attached to the R.F.C. in the field. Its duty was characterised as "Line Patrol, attacking any hostile aircraft over our territory." It was not, however, until February 1916 that the first single-seater Scout Squadron, No. 24, equipped with D.H.2S, a pusher type of fighter, arrived in France. The chief cause of this delay was a question of output. In the meantime, most squadrons were provided with a Bristol Scout for escorting purposes.

During the Aisne Battle, the Germans used observation balloons, and in an attempt to destroy one, Lieutenant G. W. Mapplebeck, No. 4 Squadron, was shot down by an Albatross pilot, and wounded. He was the first British pilot to be wounded in an air combat.

Towards the end of September, machine guns and rifles were mounted on aeroplanes, and Bristol Scouts appeared in small numbers. McCudden, in his book, says:

"Two Shorthorn Farmans arrived for No. 4 Squadron, and these were fitted for machine guns.... Towards the end of September, two Bristol Scouts, fitted with 80-h.p. Gnomes, arrived from England.... These Scouts were far ahead in performance of anything the Germans had in the air at the time, but the trouble was that no one had accurately foreseen developments as regards fitting machine guns so that they could be used with effect from single-seater machines. The Bristol in No. 3 Squadron was fitted with two rifles, one on each side of the fusillade, shooting at an angle of about 45° in order to miss the air screw."

With the development of trench warfare in September, the Cavalry were of no further use for reconnaissance duty, "open flanks" being non-existent. Consequently, both tactical and strategical reconnaissance had to be carried out over the heads of the enemy ground forces. The question of observation for the Artillery also arose; observation balloons were no longer able to cope with the situation, so aircraft were called upon to fulfil this important duty. This trench-war complication encouraged air fighting on an extensive scale; each belligerent had now to fight for his information. "Every enemy must be attacked on sight," was the official instruction of opposing Headquarters.

Fighting in the air was still in the tentative stage when the Old Year died out. No concentrated efforts had yet begun: individual combats were the order of the day, and even these were few and far between. As the majority of aircraft were on reconnaissance duty, they rightly avoided combat; so much depended upon the information which they had obtained at great risks. A few enthusiasts like Lieutenant Louis Strange (later Lieut.-Colonel) and Captain Hawker (later promoted Major, awarded V.C., and killed), however, made a keen study of air armament. As occasion presented itself, our airmen attacked any hostile aircraft over our territory, often with success; while our machines carried out their duties over enemy territory practically unmolested and with few casualties.

There is no doubt that at this period what superiority could be claimed was more in our favour than in the enemy's, for although he had better aircraft, the offensive spirit of our pilots was irresistible.

During 1915, both sides worked feverishly to produce more powerful aeroplanes equipped with better armament and quicker to respond to the pilot's control. The first victory was won for Germany, by a brilliant Dutch designer named Fokker, who was working for the German Government when war was declared, as it was the only Government which encouraged his early efforts. His decision cost hundreds of British lives, and according to him, our Government became so alarmed as to offer him £2,000,000 if he would transfer his genius. The German Secret Service prevented the offer reaching him!

While we were pottering about with rifles fixed at different angles in single-seaters, as described by McCudden, Fokker was inventing the synchronised machine gun firing through the propeller; an invention which revolutionised air fighting, and gave the enemy a superiority which ultimately led to the "Fokker Scare" in 1916. British machines, especially of the B.E. type, were being bowled over like skittles at a fair, and it was only the characteristic doggedness of the British airmen which prevented an aerial debacle, the effect of which would have produced a demoralising effect upon our Expeditionary Force.

Lieutenant Albert Ball, the first British ace, of No. 11 Squadron and later of No. 60 Squadron, led the Flying Corps in their resistance. Like a tiger, he fought any enemy he met, irrespective of numbers, setting a brilliant example to his comrades, which they followed with enthusiasm and confidence.

Fokker's inventive genius is well illustrated in his invention of the synchronised gun (as told by Fokker in his excellent autobiography *The Flying Dutchman*), and the story connected with it is of sufficient interest to be quoted in detail (the reference in para. 1 to air fighting refers to the use of machine guns):

"The first air fighting in the war opened up in 1915. French pilots in the pusher type Farman observation planes (with propeller in the rear) mounted machine guns in the front cockpit. The pilots were able to fire ahead in almost a-half-circle, but of course they could not shoot back through the propeller. Pilots in tractor planes, whose Propeller was in front, were similarly restricted in their firing. They could shoot out each side and up. Such devices were inadequate for any real combat work, and the best minds of all the forces were bent on improving this situation in order to gain ascendancy in the air.

Observation planes quickly became the eyes of the Artillery and the General Staff, and the only hope of clearing them from the sky was by attack from other planes. Infantry men shot at airplanes, particularly when pilots swept low to strafe them with their newly installed machine guns or bombs, but their success depended more on luck than aim. Anti-aircraft fire was only a little more successful. Its chief result was to force observation planes to fly several thousand feet high, but 'Archies' rarely scored a direct hit. If it were possible to develop a speedy airplane, from which a machine gun could shoot easily, the whole problem of supremacy would be more or less solved.

Suddenly a deadly French single-seater appeared in the air. German pilots, watching this plane fly towards them with its propeller spinning like a solid disc in front, confidently flew on, feeling safe from attack. To their astonishment the nose of the ship began spurting a stream of lead. Several of the German planes were downed. No one knew the secret, although spies were instructed to discover, if possible, the trick and the identity of the flyer.

As luck would have it, a faulty motor brought the plane down within the German lines. Pilots landing in enemy territory were instructed to burn their machine; but before this one was fully consumed, it was captured. The airman proved to be the famous Roland Garros, one of France's greatest stunting pilots before the war. Then his secret was out.

Garros had ingeniously attached a machine gun in front of his cockpit so that its bullets shot straight ahead. To prevent the propeller, which was of special shape, being shot to splinters, he had fitted the near side of each blade with a triangular steel wedge to deflect striking bullets. It was a dangerous device for the pilot. Despite the deflecting wedges, the impact of a bullet might break the propeller, and the ricochetting bullets might strike his own plane. Nevertheless, crude though it was, it had worked. Garros had shot down a number of unsuspecting German pilots before he was captured.

The Air Corps had no thought but to imitate Garros' device, and called me to Berlin, where the remnant of his plane had been shipped, to take over the job of adapting it to German use. Until Garros' gun was given to me I had never had a machine gun in my hand. I had only a vague idea how it shot, and of its practical workings I was entirely ignorant. The German Parabellum machine gun was turned over to me about five o'clock of a Tuesday evening. I caught the next train to Schwerin with it under my arm. The following Friday I returned to the Air Corps Headquarters with the actual synchronised machine gun used in all subsequent aerial warfare. For my gun was copied by the Allies immediately after one of the German planes equipped with it had been captured. The invention and development had all been completed in forty-eight hours of day and night work, after I had hit upon the essential idea.

For the purpose I had adapted the Parabellum gun, the first air-cooled infantry gun, shooting continuous bands of 100 bullets. It had just been developed. Taking the gun apart, I first learned how it worked, shooting it until I had thoroughly familiarised myself with its action. Then I put the problem in technical form, so that it could be considered logically.

The technical problem was to shoot between the propeller blades, which passed a given point 2,400 times a minute, because the two-bladed propeller revolved 1,200 times a minute. This meant that the pilot must not pull the trigger or fire the gun as long as one of the blades was directly in front of the muzzle. Once the problem was stated, its solution came to me in a flash.

The obvious thing to do was to make the propeller fire the gun, instead of trying to shoot the bullets through the

Propeller. Inasmuch as the machine gun would shoot only about 600 times a minute, this required some practical working out, but the principle had been found, which was the important thing.

For a temporary device, I attached a small knob to the propeller, which struck a cam as it revolved. This cam was hooked up with a hammer of the machine gun, which automatically loaded itself, of course. Thus as I slowly revolved the propeller, I found that the machine gun shot between the blades.

During the night I found out the basic operation, and began next morning to perfect the device. One blade was enough to strike the cam, because the gun could shoot only 600 times a minute, while the blades passed a given point 2,400 times a minute. To the cam was fastened a simple knee lever, which operated a rod, held back by a spring. In order that the pilot could control the shooting, a piece of the rod which struck the hammer was hinged to hit or miss as the operator desired. That was the entire device.

Further experimenting disclosed that it worked far from perfectly. The gun insisted on shooting more than one shot at a time. It reloaded so fast that two shots were caused when the cam struck but once. Therefore, it had to be adjusted to operate faster. Another day's hard work brought it to a point where it would shoot through the propeller without hitting it.

To check up where the bullets were actually going in relation to the propeller, I fastened a wooden disc to the hub. The bullets passed through the disc within a short distance of each other, well out of line of either blade. The bullet pattern showed how much time there was between the striking of the cam and the actual firing of the bullet.

It gave me an immense feeling of pride to invent something which I knew would have a fundamental effect on strategy in the air, once it was adopted for combat work.

In order to demonstrate it myself, because I felt so elated over conquering the problem, I installed the synchronised gun in a little monoplane we had at Schwerin, lashed the tailskid of the monoplane to my 80 horse-power Peugeot touring car, and set out Thursday night for Berlin, 220 miles away, arriving there Friday morning. At the military field I told everyone I was going to demonstrate the synchronised gun that morning.

No one believed that it would operate successfully because of the short time that I had been working on the problem. Most of the important staff officers were present. They saw that the propeller had none of the steel wedges that Garros had employed, and could not conceive how I expected to miss it. Nevertheless, everyone desired to witness the try out. I was confident that their doubts would soon be changed into complete belief.

In my confidence, I had not figured on the conservative military mind, which not only has to be shown, but then wishes to be shown all over again, after which it desires a little time to think the whole matter over once more.

First I demonstrated the machine gun from the ground, starting the engine and shooting through the propeller towards the rifle butts. Pulling the trigger, I shot three bursts of ten shots each before stopping the engine.

Gravely they examined the propeller, found no flaw in it, but suspected that there was some trick in the fact that I had shot only bursts of ten. They were not sure the gun would shoot a whole band of bullets. They thought I had slipped something over on them. This was absurd, but the easiest way of proving it absurd was to shoot a band of 100 bullets. That was just as simple as shooting bursts of ten.

Satisfied that the gun would operate while the plane was on the ground, the military men doubted that it would be successful if shot from the air.

I decided to teach them a lesson which would make them think twice before being sceptical again. Directing that some old wings be placed on the field, I took the air while they crowded fairly near the wings to watch the bullets strike. From about 900 feet I nosed over, pointed the plane towards the wings and began firing. They had not foreseen that the bullets striking the stone underneath the wings would ricochet in every direction. I had. When they took to their heels, running like mad for the safety of the hangars, I decided they would never forget that the gun shot from the air as well as it shot from the ground. Timidly, they crept out, after I had landed, and viewed the bullet-riddled wings.

Still they were not satisfied, contending that the only certain test of the gun was to shoot an airplane down The suggestion was made that I, a foreigner and a civilian go to the Front, find a French or British flyer, and demonstrate by actually bringing down an enemy plane that my gun was practical.

My protests were useless. The official mind was made up. Without being given a choice, I found myself bundled to the Front, and introduced to the liaison headquarters of General von Heeringen, one of the Army Corps heads near Laon."

Although a civilian, Fokker was dressed up in the uniform of a German pilot (in case he was captured) and *morally* compelled to fly over the lines. He did so for several days before an opportunity of testing his gun occurred.

Eventually he came across a Frenchman in a pusher two-seater at 6,000 feet, who was flying leisurely along. Now was his chance: it was just like shooting a sitting rabbit. He was attacking him from behind and the Frenchman could not fire back, owing to the propeller being behind him. Fokker suddenly decided that it was just cold-blooded murder, and that the job was too distasteful to him as a neutral (he was not an enlisted soldier at this time; later, against his will he was compelled to be):

"Suddenly," he writes, "I decided the whole job could go to hell. It was too much like 'cold meat' to suit me. I had no stomach for the whole business, nor any wish to kill Frenchmen for Germans. Let them do their own killing!"

As a result of this attitude of Fokker, the machine was handed over to a Lieutenant Oswald Boelcke, who thus was given the opportunity to make himself and the aeroplane famous and feared. On his third flight he brought down an opponent; this victory was the signal for much rejoicing in the enemy Air Force. Orders for machines equipped with this gun were immediately issued. Lieutenant Max Immelmann was the next pilot to fly a Fokker, and he did so with great success. Within a month several machines were flying at the Front, eating up "Fokker fodder" as the enemy nicknamed our slow and cumbersome two-seaters. Immelmann was the first real ace of the war, one might almost say before the term was coined by the French to mean a victor in five or more air combats. This term was rightly ignored during the war by the British, as it only applied to fighting successes. All pilots and observers were assumed to be doing their best, and anyone displaying outstanding zeal in the execution of his duty or obtaining results in excess of the official standard was appropriately rewarded.

The enemy's tactics were simple and efficient and based on Immelmann's methods.

"Dropping out of the sun, a Fokker pilot would dive, pull up underneath the enemy plane and simply sew the opposing airman in a shroud of bullets. The courage of the English and French in facing such disheartening odds seemed almost superhuman to me," writes the designer when describing the tactics.

He forgot, however, to add that if the attack was unsuccessful, the enemy would make a steep climbing turn, half rolling on the top, coming down on his opponent again as before. This manœuvre became known as "the Immelmann turn." It was such an efficient manœuvre that pilots of all nationalities often used it in a fight until the end of the war.

And so, with the appearance of the Fokker I, powered by an 80-h.p. Gnome, flying at a speed of 70 m.p.h. at 6,000 feet, with a duration of two hours, the enemy, thanks to the Dutchman, had convincingly won the first round of the air fighter's war, but the loser had fought gamely: he was not knocked out in spite of the disparity in aircraft. The time had, however, definitely arrived which made us realise that fighting in the air was soon to become a business rather than a cheerful sport.

On April 8th, 1916, we captured a Fokker. The gun design was examined and improved upon by an invention of a Rumanian named Constantinesco, who invented a gun gear which did not rely for its working entirely on mechanical gear, but on hydraulic oil pressure, working on the principle of automobile brakes; this gear when perfected was a great success, and is still in use in the Service.

The eventual vanquishers of the Fokker were mainly "pushers," whose main armament was a movable Lewis gun, which could fire forward but not backward, because the engine was installed behind the pilot's seat. The machines which sealed the fate of the enemy and enabled us to dominate the air situation during the opening of the Somme Battle were, however, tractors, the Nieuport Scout and the Sopwith two-seater, known as the 1½-Strutter. The Nieuport Scout was a French design, and driven by a 110-h.p. Le Rhône engine. Its main characteristic was its lightness of control, good visibility, and quick climb—it could reach 10,000 feet in ten and a half minutes. It was armed with a single Lewis gun mounted on the centre section, so that it fired over the propeller at an angle slightly above the horizontal. Painted with silver-coloured "dope," it was known as the "Silver Hawk." Certainly, at the time of its first appearance on our front in March 1916, it had no superior as a fighter. It was on this type of aeroplane that both Ball and Mannock won their early successes; Ball, however, had the advantage of its superior performance over the enemy; Mannock was not so fortunate. The Sopwith 1½-Strutter was a two-seater which had the pilot's seat in front of the observer's, so that the latter could have a larger field of fire with his movable gun, which protected the tail of the machine. The machine had the additional advantage of a fixed Vickers gun firing through the propeller. This was possible as the result of an invention of a mechanical synchronising gear by the same makers as the gun. These two machines in the hands of brave pilots sent the enemy helter-skelter whenever they were met.

It was Tom Sopwith, Harry Hawker, and Fred Sigrist of the famous Sopwith firm; Geoffrey de Havilland, and the designers of the Royal Aircraft Factory, Farnborough, aided by the French Nieuport firm, who now dominated the scene in designing machines for subduing the aggressive Fokker and its accomplices. Their joint efforts, combined with the French Air Force's gallant work at Verdun, which accounted for a large number of enemy machines, enabled our Air Force to command the air over the Somme Battle during the first two months of the engagement.

It was during this battle that we commenced our renowned Offensive Patrol policy. Briefly, the aim was to pin down enemy aircraft over their own aerodromes, particularly fighting aircraft, and so prevent them from molesting our aircraft co-operating with the ground forces. Although this policy was excellent in its conception, it was most difficult to achieve, for two reasons. First, the enemy refused combat, and patrolled at such low heights over his territory that it was often inadvisable for our fighters to attack him because they would lose the tactical advantage of height as well as render themselves liable to heavy casualties from "Archie" and other ground defences. Secondly, the enemy fighters sneaked up at low heights to the front line and carried out spasmodic raids on our cumbersome co-operating aircraft, which, because of the gallantry of the pilots, were usually a few miles on the enemy side. In return, our fighters only attacked the enemy co-operating aircraft at the end of a patrol when the leader had given up all hope of being able to engage any enemy fighters. In this manner much precious time was wasted. The ultimate result was that, after a few fruitless patrols, pilots would become impatient and attack enemy formations without previously working out tactical schemes. This haphazard method of attack often produced heavy casualties.

These Offensive Patrols did succeed in reducing casualties among our co-operating aircraft, but they did not prevent enemy co-operating aircraft from carrying out their duties, in spite of the heavy casualties inflicted on them; however, they were not entirely successful in pinning down the enemy fighters over their aerodrome area, yet what they did accomplish was all-important. They lowered the *moral* of the enemy Air Force and increased that of our own. Our pilots never thought the war had begun until they crossed the front-line trenches; the enemy had to search the sky before he dared take off from his aerodrome. Occasionally our pilots became so weary of the enemy's timidity that they sat over his aerodrome at dangerously low heights waiting for him to come up and fight. A number of pilots actually waited *too* long and ran out of petrol! Had the enemy's *moral* been higher, there is no question that our casualties would have been much heavier, particularly among our co-operating aircraft. Again, there is no knowing what results the enemy's ground forces would have achieved during their desperate attacks on March 21st and April 9th, 1918, if they had pursued a similar offensive policy to ours, or if we, by adopting a defensive policy, had permitted German aircraft to work unmolested over our retreating army, as our machines did over theirs during the early part of the Somme Battle. A hasty and semi-orderly retreat might easily have been converted into a rout by large numbers of aggressive and harassing aircraft, bombing, and machine gunning. Finally, the policy of Offensive Patrols naturally suited the type of Britisher who became a fighting pilot, for he was obviously temperamentally inclined to adventure; and adventure was to be found in plenty and with more spice over aerodromes where the enemy lived and hid. Our pilots realised that the aeroplane was more destructive in attack than in defence. Any other policy would have cramped their style and broken their spirit.

The Germans, alarmed by our Offensive Patrol tactics, and their attendant successes during the Somme Battle, decided to overhaul the organisation, administration, and tactics of their Air Service. This they did with instant success, and the credit must go to General von Hoeppner, an officer of outstanding organising ability; Lieut.-Colonel Thomson, an astute strategist, who was responsible for the formation of the pursuit squadrons (*Fagdstaffeln*), and Captain Oswald Boelcke, a brainy pilot with tremendous personality and judgment of a good air fighter.

The middle of September saw a distinct change in the air war during the Battle of the Somme. The Germans sprung a surprise in equipment and personnel, which is well illustrated by H. A. Jones, the British Official Air Historian, in Vol. II of *The War in the Air*:

"Sunday the 17th of September was a day of somewhat heavy air casualties for the Flying Corps, most of the victims falling to a new fighting squadron which, under Boelcke's brilliant leadership, came out in force for the first time on this day. The single-seater fighter (*Kampfeinsitzer*) squadrons which had been formed in the middle of July could do little to affect the predominance which the Allied Air Force had established. When the enemy air commander, Lieut.-Colonel Thomson, realised how inadequate these squadrons were, he suggested a reorganisation of the fighting units into special pursuit squadrons (*Fagdstaffeln*), equipped with the fastest types of fighters manned by carefully selected officers who had already proved their fighting worth on active service. It was proposed to use these squadrons defensively. It was recognised that the Fokker monoplane was no longer a match for the British fighters and, in August, the Fokker was replaced by the first Halberstadt and the D type Albatross, which had as armament two fixed machine guns firing through the propeller, a new and surprising innovation. As fighters they outclassed every contemporary British aeroplane opposed to them. The enemy left no stone unturned to get the very best from his new fighting units. Not only were the officers carefully selected, but they were given a special course at single-seater fighting schools in Germany, and then passed on to an advanced fighting school at Valenciennes, finishing their training when they joined their fighting squadrons at the Front. The formation of these pursuit squadrons was to have a profound influence on the whole future air war on the Western Front.

Boelcke, after making a reputation at Verdun, had gone off on a visit to the Turkish, Macedonian, and Russian fronts. He was at Kovel in the middle of August visiting his brother, who was flying with a squadron near the town. Another officer at Kovel was Manfred Freiherr von Richthofen. Boelcke, who had been empowered to organise one of the new pursuit squadrons for the Somme, had a free hand in the choice of his officers, and invited Richthofen to join his new unit, an invitation which was readily accepted. The new unit, known as Jagdstaffel 2, was formed on the 30th of August, 1916, at Lagaicourt, where the pilots impatiently awaited the arrival of their new aeroplanes. Meanwhile Boelcke made occasional patrols alone.

On the 16th of September the first batch of new aeroplanes arrived and, on the following morning, Boelcke led five of his pilots in close formation towards the British lines. At the same time as the German fighters were getting into the air, eight B.E.s of No. 12 Squadron, carrying eight 112-lb. and thirty-two 20-lb. bombs, escorted by six F.E. 2b's of No. 2 Squadron, were leaving for a visit to Marcoing station. Boelcke saw them soon after they had crossed the lines, and followed to cut them off. But the British pilots reached Marcoing and, taking deliberate aim, dropped their forty bombs about the station, which was set on fire. Just outside the station an explosion which followed the burst of a bomb sent clouds of smoke high in the air. Almost as they released their bombs the aeroplanes were mixed up in fierce fight. In addition to Boelcke's five, some seven other German fighters appear to have joined in. The F.E.s did all they could to protect the bombing aeroplanes, and in doing so four of them were shot down. In spite of the self-sacrifice of the escorts, two of the bombers also fell victims to their more speedy opponents. The remainder, extricated from further fighting by an offensive patrol of No. 60 Squadron, got safely home. Richthofen, in his book, *The Red Air Fighter*, states that each of the five pilots of his squadron shot down one opponent, and that for all of them, except Boelcke, it was their first victory against the Royal Flying Corps."

This engagement was the prelude to bitter fighting between this *Jagdstaffel* and the Royal Flying Corps, and, as in this fight, almost all the combats took place over the enemy's lines. The German policy continued to be a defensive one in spite of the superior performance of their machines. There appeared to be a timidity of purpose in the direction and the execution of their air strategy and tactics throughout the war, which resulted in the R.F.C. being able to fulfil the varied demands which came from the Army, in spite of inferior equipment at times. Our casualties were, however, heavy, but not unduly, considering the great amount of work that was being carried out over the enemy's territory. Throughout the war our airmen did not once falter in assisting our Army. This proud achievement cannot be claimed for the German airmen.

Oswald Boelcke, by brilliant leadership in the air and on the ground, and his "circus" (as we nicknamed his *Fagdstaffeln*) infused new life into the badly shaken German Air Service, and by the time of his lamented death (one of his pilots collided with him) in October 1916, the air superiority obtained by us on the Somme was being strongly challenged over the lines. As the enemy's equipment, which was superior to ours, increased in numbers, we gradually witnessed the scales of air superiority more temporarily balance in the enemy's favour, and the air prospects for the Battle of Arras in April were not good.

It is not unreasonable to say that the period immediately prior to and at the opening of the opening of the Battle of Arras on April 9th, 1917, represents the darkest chapter in the history of the Royal Flying Corps in France. April 1917 proved to be Richthofen's vintage month; the British were outclassed in everything except leadership and *moral*. "In no other month throughout the war," says the Official Historian, "was the Royal Flying Corps so hard pressed, nor were the casualties so heavy."

In this same month there arrived in France a new and unknown pilot whose qualities of courage and leadership in the air were to enable him to play a leading part in regaining and maintaining our air superiority over the German Air Service.

Second Lieutenant Edward "Mick" Mannock had arrived at No. 40 Squadron (Nieuport Scouts) just in time for the opening of the battle. His baptism of fire was to be fierce and the test of combat severe.

In his stirring and very human diary which he kept for the first few months of his fighting career, we obtain a first-hand glimpse of his powerful character and an insight into his psychological make-up. His powers of self-analysis are revealing and form a sublime contrast to the blustering naïveté of certain aces on both sides who took up the business of air fighting from the day they arrived in the war area with such a precise and clearly defined preference for what Winston Churchill terms terminological inexactitudes, that one is forced to the conclusion that an astonishingly large number of absurd claims were made by fame-seeking pilots which had no more virtue in them than the outpourings of heated and extremely inventive imaginations.

The first thing we note in his diaries is his simple truthfulness and clarity in expressing his likes and dislikes of very simple things such as probably was expressed by every new pilot in France in his letters home. The only note he strikes in his reflective moments is his penetrating awareness of the gravity of the situation and his determination to make good, despite his knowledge of his poor landing abilities. The new fledgling pilot without previous experience of war flying was at a disadvantage, in starting off, not only in accustoming himself to war conditions but in judging ground and air speeds after a fight in the air. It took some time too for a pilot to accustom himself to the unfamiliar and varying landscape beneath him.

Mannock's truthfulness in recording these early events is borne out by the fact that he does not claim a victory until

he has been more than two months with the squadron, and
then only claims that "it went down out of control." His
first victory over a balloon he does not count as important
at all! His expressive frank disbelief of a rumour which is
reported on April 12th about a new pilot bringing down
three Huns and two balloons "first time out" is expressed in
two words: "some lad." By contrast, Mannock's simple
report of his first experience over the lines symbolises his
whole subsequent career. How important this attitude on his
part is, is revealed when the searchlight is turned on the
claims he made for his victories and those put forward by
many of his great contemporaries. Mannock just could not
tell an untruth about himself or enlarge on any matter which
would secure his own advancement. This remarkable trait in
the character of this particular genius is most noteworthy
when we remember the strong temptation to exaggerate
one's achievements, and the comparatively easy way in
which an impudently audacious airman could successfully
conceal his movements from his comrades during a battle
and dash into the picture at the psychological moment. That
this was occasionally practised by certain air fighters is now
well known.

Perhaps the most astonishing claim ever made was that of
a war pilot who is said to have claimed that he had shot
down several aircraft on a particular day when the weather
was, in fact, so drizzling and dismal, and the blanket of
cloud so thick and dark, that subsequent air records show
there were only three or four pilots in the sky over the sector
in question at that particular time, and none of these pilots
was the airman referred to. The claim is all the more
inexplicable when it is realised that the enemy squadron was
found thousands of feet above the clouds. Why fighters

should be flying high in the heavens when the ground was invisible is not understood, particularly as the cloud bank covered the entire Front at that particular time. But of course a discrepancy may have crept in as to date and location.

Again, there is the well-known story of a renowned enemy airman with a decided flair for the spectacular who carried his imaginative flights of fancy to such heights that it affected his brother pilots. On a number of occasions he took new pilots over a section of the line on the Verdun Front, where a French plane lay shattered in a small lake of shell holes. Waggling his wings and making a sudden dive, he would carry out an imaginary attack and fire a few bursts, then point downwards. The new pilots, seeing the enemy plane below them in the lake for the first time, would naturally assume that our "hero" was the victor and corroborate his combat report and claims. The romancing airman altered the position of the derelict enemy with the most studious skill!

There is no questionable doubt whatever that many of our aircraft claimed by enemy airmen were forced to land through engine trouble, lack of petrol, "Archie," machine-gun, or rifle fire from the ground. After the heat of battle, claims were put in that were never challenged on account of the fact that a crash as a result of these mishaps would generally occur some distance from the spot where the attack was begun. By very reason of the fact that our air scouts sought out the enemy many miles behind their own lines, and were continually harassing them on their own aerodromes, there was little chance of obtaining the truth about these occurrences, which were not infrequent. The outstanding fact remains, however, that the British airmen attained a *moral* ascendancy over the enemy which was never less throughout the war despite the dark winter of '16 and early spring of '17. This *moral* ascendancy was in itself a clear definition of the respective fighting spirits of the opposing belligerents. The German airmen, until the formation of the Boelcke "circus," had an instinct not dissimilar from that of beasts of prey in a performance of wild animals in relation to their trainer. They went up each day and did their act, but did not go looking for trouble.

Boelcke organised this consciousness so that they would at least give as good as they got though seldom venturing beyond their own lines to do it. That specific form of enemy venturesomeness was reserved for the high-powered and well-equipped Zeppelin, which could steal over our coastline from some unguarded spot in the darkness, drop its bombs quickly and clear off with miles of sky free from offensive enemy aircraft. The Britisher developed the trainer consciousness in his offensive tactics, bearding the lion in his own den. Through the constant pressure of this offensive spirit upon the enemy's mind, the enemy airmen developed a sense of defence exactly analogous to that of our airmen on home defence who rushed into the air when the alarm was given that Zeppelins were overhead.

This attitude of mind is best described by a story of one of Germany's leading air fighters—in fact, one of the pilots who commanded the Richthofen "circus" after it had lost its famous leader. The story tells of how he is sitting lazing in the sun one day and the "*alarm*" is given that enemy aircraft are approaching. Into the air goes the valiant airman to defend his aerodrome, and after having "driven off "the foe he returns to his lazy nap. How incongruous this all sounds to our own understanding is patent when a brief examination of the specific function of a fighting pilot is made.

What was the function of the airman during the war? It was to obtain information quickly, expeditiously, and with as much accuracy as the conditions allowed. This job was almost confined to the slow, cumbersome two-seater. What, then, was the fighter's duty? His duty was to shoot down these two-seaters. To put out the enemy's eyes, in fact. But each side protected its two-seaters with high-speed fighting scouts. What, then, was the most important task in the air as the war developed? To shoot down the enemy fighting scout so that the two-seaters could carry out their vital duties of reconnaissance and cooperate with the infantry and artillery. A contest between a high-speed scout and a slow, cumbersome two-seater was an unequal combat and, however valiant the occupants, would invariably end in the downfall of the two-seater. It was therefore the gladiatorial affrays between high-speed fighters which became the acknowledged heroic combat. Shooting down a two-seater was regarded as good and essential war-work, but nothing to boast about for a fighting pilot. By carrying the fight deep into enemy territory, the British established the ascendancy of a superior attacker and thus won a renown for offensiveness which puzzled and irritated the enemy to the point of despair. Boelcke at first called it "stupid" and "impudent"; Richthofen called it "foolhardiness" and "recklessness," but in the main the German airmen recognised in this dominating offensive British spirit something of the conceit of valour which left a vague dread in its wake and gave us the dominion of the air. This constant cracking of the whip of offence; this unending defiance of the grim Prussian-disciplined Moloch, produced an inferiority complex which finally hammered the offensive spirit out of the enemy airmen and penned them over their own lines.

When the famous "Backs to the Wall" order rang out over Flanders on that never-to-be-forgotten April morning in '18, when the line at Merville broke and the Allies were forced to retreat before the last supreme effort made by the enemy, our airmen had so mastered the German fighting pilots that the German front-line troops were forced to stumble blindly forward without sufficient information from their aircraft which would enable them to consolidate their gains. Thus, when to the great glory of the Allied arms the moment arrived for Marshal Foch to launch his celebrated counter-attack, the German front line crumbled like old cheese and the enemy hosts were hurled pell-mell backwards, beaten and demoralised.

The arrival of Mannock in France symbolised a further stage in the shaping of that offensive spirit of our air fighters. It was to be his task to transfuse the inspiration of Ball into the squadrons he fought with and led.

The British High Command did not seek to publicise the individual except where the individual created the standard or level which would serve as a general guide for all fighting Pilots. For this reason the High Command of the Air Forces in the field looked disapprovingly on all attempts that were made to single out any particular airman for special praise, and were often unthinkingly blamed for appearing to ignore high feats of valour. Deeds which in the early days of the war merited V.C.s and D.S.O.s later often passed through the Official *Communiqué* as mere recommendations for the M.C., D.F.C., or even curt mentions such as follows: "Enemy aircraft were also accounted for by the following," and then would follow a list of names. Nothing else. Each name probably spelt a combat of high daring and possibly was worthy of an Homeric elegy had it occurred in the earlier days of the war. But now even paper was insufficient to record them on. The pilots themselves grew to this tradition of brevity and quick description which at the end of the war seemed so commonplace. Only the occasional flash of an incredibly outstanding and almost humanly impossible feat of valour, such as Barker's or West's, would light up the official records with the flame of human spirit, to die down again to the everyday records of the "enemy aircraft were also accounted for by the following." This high pitch of efficiency, intensity, and degree of valour permeated the whole force, and Mannock was one of the chief agents of its creation.

The diary begins like the prelude to one of Beethoven's great symphonies. It starts on a low, quiet note devoid of any but topical interest, rising in majestic, even progression to a crescendo of high achievement. A human life lived quickly at its full—unrestrained. As the notes rise, we feel the backwash of his spirit crying out from under the harsh turmoil of the flesh until the mind appears to yield and the body almost breaks, but, like his famous predecessor Ball, and like every other great air fighter, he overcomes himself and masters his nerves and fights himself back to fight. From then on the tone is less hesitant and uncertain, the notes more limpidly full and controlled, giving out less discordances of temper, and finally he grips the situation with a master hand to play the rising wave at full command.

Mannock's introduction to France was not a particularly happy one; it was raining for one thing, and no place can look or be so dismal and unattractive as Boulogne under such climatic conditions. St. Omer was not much better. Its *pavé* streets and grimy-looking houses remind an English man more of an old farmstead than of a town similar to St. Albans. His sleeping accommodation was also unpleasant; a candle and damp sheets obviously completed his discomfort.

1.4.17.—Just a year today I received my commission, and a year to the day earlier I was released from a Turkish prison. Strange how this date recurs. Let's hope that a year hence the war finishes, and I return for a spell to merrie England.

Well! Landed at Boulogne. Saw the M.L.O. and discovered that I was to be away to St. Omer the following day at 3.45 p.m. Rested and fed at the Hôtel Maurice. Quite a nice place as continental hotels go. Wisher, Tyler, and two more strangers (R.F.C.) kept us company. Rotten weather. Rain. I'm not prepossessed with the charm of La Belle France yet.

2.4.17.—Breakfasted on coffee and omelettes. The Eternal Omelette. By the way, they are good. Left at 4.0 p.m. Quite punctual.

Arrived at St. Omer at 8.30 p.m. feeling very fed up and tired. Rotten journey, 2 m.p.h. After portering luggage and practising my execrable French, reported to No. 1 A.D. Orders to put up for the night on our own. Proceeded by tender and devious ways to Hôtel de France. Horrible place—*déjeuner* worse—and filled with subalterns of all sorts, sizes, and descriptions. No room for me—so went to Hôtel de Commerce. Small, cold room. Candles and damp sheets, ugh!

3.4.17.—Rose at 8. The eternal coffee and omelette. Really the hens must be on war work. Tried to find the office again and subsequently managed to do so. Instructions to proceed to aerodrome. Met Lemon, Dunlop, and Kimball on the way. Was catechised and placed in the School—on Bristol Scouts. Censored lots of letters. No flying. Billed at the Y.M.C.A. in St. Omer.

On the same day he wrote the first of many interesting letters to Mr. Eyles:

"ON ACTIVE SERVICE.
*April 3rd, 1917.*

DEAR JIM,

Some trials. Oceans of mud everywhere and raining. Had a very nice crossing from Folkestone and enjoyed myself. Arrived here on the night of the first and stayed at a filthy hotel. Am now comfortably ensconced at a Y.M.C.A. for officers. Haven't done anything in the way of flying yet, but understand I am to fly a new machine, as soon as the weather permits. I have met several of my old chums here, all of whom are less fortunate than I am in the way of prospects. Nothing at all in this town but old men, old women, British officers and men, and motor-lorries, and last but not least— rotten weather. At the present moment there is six inches of snow on the ground and a promise of more to come.

I expect to get away from here during the next fort-night, but my address is :

R.F.C.,
No. I A.D.,
A Repair Section,
B.E.F.

So drop me a line as soon as you can. In any case, any letters addressed as above will eventually reach me wherever I am.

I hope the missus and Derek are in the best of health. What does she think of the 'Wings'?

Yours,<br>PAT."

Before leaving England, he and Eyles had decided on a secret code so that the latter would know his whereabouts. He prepared his friend for any move by requesting him to send some boots. Eyles knew where his squadron had moved to by taking the first letters of the words in the first sentence or two, which collectively spelt a name. For example, the letters of the first two sentences in this letter spell "St. Oomear," which naturally meant St. Omer. The sentences, it will be noticed from time to time, were ingenious and would cause no suspicion to the censor, because they are always topical.

No. 1 A.D., which is short for No. 1 Aircraft Depot, was a fixed supply and repair depot, which maintained a "three months' supply of aeronautical and transport stores, received all new aircraft from England or France, keeping always a reserve in their hangars, manufactured experimental fittings, and overhauled and reconstructed aeroplanes, balloons, transport, and all flying accessories." New pilots were also afforded facilities of flying practice while they remained in the Pilot's Pool, awaiting posting to squadrons.

4.4.17.—Did some flying today. Of course I expected to break something. U/C strut snapped but comparatively a good show. Nasty town. Mainly composed of estaminets, old women, and dirty—very dirty children. The roads and streets remind me of Constantinople in their glistening filth. Went to the cinema in the evening.

5.4.17.—Flying again. Did some stunts and got along well. I rather fancy the Bristol. Got a fresh billet today, No. 11, Lady Ameux and little Jeannette. I attach here with her written thanks on the receipt of a *boîte de chocolat* from me.

"Little Jeannette "was a vivacious blue-eyed blonde of seventeen, who took a great liking to "Mon brave aviateur," as she adoringly addressed Mick. He had a winning way with the fair sex. From this day they became firm friends, and rarely a visit from St. Omer passed that he did not repeat the chocolate gift. When he was eventually killed, little Jeannette was heart-broken and steadfastly refused to accept his death. Her faith in his infallibility was greater than Death itself.

The great days of his career were now fast approaching. He was posted on the 6th to a fighter squadron—No. 40 (Nieuports). His ambition of the moment was realised. Unfortunately for him, at that time the Nieuport was outclassed by the new D.3 (V-strutted) Albatross, which could show it a clean pair of heels whenever it wished—an important adjunct to the defensive armour of a fighting pilot. Mannock, therefore, was to be introduced to the enemy in a good dog-fighting machine, but one which would have to fight its way home once it had engaged in combat, and in one which he could not compel his opponent to fight if the latter did not wish to. In fact, it was not a satisfactory machine for a beginner, and his prospects of long life were not rosy in view of the impending strenuous fighting against the better-equipped Richthofen "circus." However, he did not appear to worry unduly, for he is immediately made happy in his new surroundings, and likes to fly the "silver hawk."

No. 40 Squadron's main duty was offensive patrol and escort to bombing aircraft. It was a squadron with an excellent reputation, having been well served by commanding officers of the calibre of Major Robert Lorraine (the famous actor) and Major Tilney, the C.O. when Mannock joined it. Later it was to be commanded by Major Dallas, a delightful Australian, who, to maintain the Squadron tradition of "always the offensive," flew low over a German aerodrome and dropped a pair of fur-lined flying boots with a note attached which read: "Ground officers— for the use of." Which was an Air Force way of telling the enemy that he had "cold feet." After dropping the boots he flew away, but returned a few minutes later and, as he hoped, found a number of Germans examining the boots, whereupon he proceeded to shoot them up with considerable success.

In the squadron were some pilots whose methods Mannock studied, and whose advice he listened to. They were mostly individualists, though—but good ones: Bond, Keen, Gregory, Blaxland, MacKenzie, Todd, Ellis, De Burgh, Barwell, Mulholland, MacLanachan, Godfrey, McElroy—all great fighters.

There was a vacant chair at dinner on the night of his arrival. Lieutenant Pell, who in the morning had destroyed an enemy, had failed to return from a later offensive patrol. Mannock occupied the seat. He was not superstitious, for he had no fear of death. In fact, his comrades say he treated the matter as a huge joke.

Every battle by now was preceded and accompanied by a tremendous amount of air fighting, in order to afford protection to the Army Co-operation Squadrons which were carrying out bombing raids, reconnaissance, photography, and artillery co-operation duties. The fighting preliminary to the Arras battle was consequently bitter and casualties heavy on both sides. Lieutenant Pell was one of thirty-one officers and seven other ranks who were missing on that day. In order to give the reader a slight idea of one day's R.F.C work in connection with the battle, the following varied particulars of work carried out on the day that Mannock joined his squadron is given:

"Reconnaissance was carried out by all Brigades and 9th Wing, and 700 photographs were taken. Artillery co-operation—123 targets were dealt with by artillery with aeroplane observation, many O.K.s were obtained, and much ammunition exploded. *Hostile Aircraft.*—As a result of the offensive patrols and bombing raids, hostile machines were kept well east of the lines. Thirty-one officers and seven other ranks were missing and two officers Wounded. Some thirty enemy machines were accounted for and fifteen of these were definitely ascertained to have been destroyed. The following summaries taken from the R.F.C. *Communiqués* are typical of the day's combats :

(1) 2nd Lieut. Smart and 2nd Lieut. Hampson, No, 20 Squadron, while on a bombing raid attacked three hostile aircraft. The pilot of one of the hostile machines was shot and the machine broke in the air and fell. The second machine was driven down in a spinning nose dive, while the third, after having been attacked, dived vertically.

(2) A formation of No. 54 Squadron while acting as escort was attacked by a fast hostile scout. The enemy pilot appeared to be very good and manoeuvred with great skill. Finally, however, he was enticed to attack one of our

machines from behind, whereupon Lieut. Stewart dived on the hostile machine and destroyed it.

(3) 2nd Lieut. Vinson and 2nd Lieut. Gwilt, No. 15 Squadron, were taking photographs over Bullecourt when they were attacked by six Albatross scouts. Unfortunately both machine guns fell out of the B.E., and it was forced to land near Lagincourt, as one hostile machine pursued and continued firing at it. The pilot and observer jumped out and got into shell holes. The enemy artillery opened fire on our machine, but just before it was hit by an 8-inch shell, 2nd-Lieut. Vinson managed to obtain the exposed plates of the Hindenburg Line and Bullecourt.

(4) An offensive patrol of Sopwith Scouts of No. 66 Squadron shot the observer in a hostile machine and he was seen to fall from the aeroplane. They drove off three hostile aircraft which were interfering with our artillery machines.

Bombs were dropped on aerodromes, railways, billets, and dumps by all Brigades. Two 112-lb. bombs were dropped on a train on the Menin-Wervicq line from a height of 500 feet. One burst immediately in front of the train and destroyed the permanent way. The train stopped and was attacked with machine-gun fire from the air by an officer of No. 6 Squadron, who was slightly wounded by gun fire from the ground.

Bombing was also undertaken by the 9th Wing. One raid against Valenciennes was made by D.H.4s, of No. 55 Squadron, at a height of 11,500 feet. From this two bombs were observed to fall on the station, two near the engine depot, and the remainder on and around the objective. On the return journey the De Havillands were pursued by hostile fighters, which, however, they were able to out-distance owing to their superior speed."

The Battle of Arras, which was subsidiary and preliminary to the French offensive against le Chemin des Dames, was a limited victory, owing to the failure of the French to achieve their object. We, however, killed a lot of Germans; gained a little ground; lowered the *moral* of the enemy a bit, and that was about all. The war in the air, on the other hand, proved to be more fruitful in casualties to the Germans, but enhanced our *moral* immeasurably, for in spite of our heavy casualties, chiefly among the antiquated two-seater type of aircraft, the exalted *moral* of the pilots never wavered, and at times gave back more than they received. Our pilots showed, as they had done previously during the Fokker scare, that aeroplanes can multiply and change; but it is the man who flies them who determines the final issues of victory and defeat.

The German Albatross and Halberstadt, by avoiding our fighters as much as possible and adopting sporadic attack tactics against our co-operating aircraft, played havoc with our poor old B.E.s, a type which was of pre-war vintage but slightly modified. They had a top speed of about 70 m.p.h. against their opponents' 120 m.p.h. They carried out the main share of the infantry co-operation and artillery observation duties. Sir Douglas Haig (in his despatch of the battle) pays just tribute to the valour and high sense of duty of our airmen. After stating that the strong enemy lines were carried because of the effective artillery preparations, the Commander-in-Chief goes on to say that this success would not have been possible "without the aid of our air service." Then continuing his tribute he says:

"Our activity in the air, therefore, increased with the growing severity of our bombardment. A period of very heavy air fighting ensued, culminating in the days immediately preceding the attack in a struggle of the utmost intensity for local supremacy in the air. Losses on both sides were severe, but the offensive tactics most gallantly persisted in by our fighting aeroplanes secured our artillery aircraft from serious interference, and enabled our guns to carry out their work effectively. At the same time, bombarding aircraft caused great damage and loss to the enemy by a constant succession of raids directed against his dumps, railways, aerodromes, and billets."

6.4.17.—Ordered to proceed to No. 40 Squadron at a place called Aire, Lens and La Bassée sector. Arrived at destination by tender after 1½ hours' run. Cold, wet, but cheerful. Met Capt. McKecknie and old Dunlop. Mess very nice and the C.O. and comrades all that could be desired. Posted to C Flight—Capt. Todd, commander.

Captain Todd relates that Mannock on arrival was reserved to the point of shyness. He showed an impatient desire to get into the air and over the lines. "He seemed like a highly strung pedigree horse at the starting post," he says. "I let him have his head, but at first he was unable to shoot down any Huns, and his efforts were disappointing."

To counter the grouping of enemy pursuit squadrons, the R.F.C. had decided to fly in groups of three or five. The formations, flying in V shape, were led by the Flight-Commander, who was the brains and the spear-head of the attack. It did not take Mannock long to realise that a possible deficiency of brains at the spear-head accounted for most of the fighter casualties, and also for the failure of engaging enemy formations with tactical advantage. He proceeded to study the art with caution and deliberation, for his mature

judgment told him that the war was going to last a long time,
and eventually it was the side which showed greater
determination, perseverance, strategic and tactical skill which
would win. So far as the air-fighting war was concerned, he
was making his plans to do his share, little or great as it might
eventually prove to be. As a consequence, during his first
couple of months, the most trying in an air fighter's career,
although he fought at all times with boldness as occasion
arose, he tempered his boldness with reliable judgment. He
never allowed recklessness and boldness to become mistaken
for one another, and as a result he gained an unwarranted
reputation for having "cold feet." It was due to bad marksmanship that he was producing no results and not for any
other reason. This unpleasant knowledge did not worry
him—he was too big a man—for he knew what he was
about; and he proceeded unashamed along the tedious path
of caution and perseverance. He assiduously practised
formation flying (at which at first he was very bad); he
trained his eyes to spot aircraft in the air, and to distinguish
friend from foe at a distance; he evolved surprise tactics; and
he practised air gunnery on every possible occasion.

7.4.17.—First solo on Nieuport Scout. Lovely "bus."
Tootled around, and went as far as the lines—via Béthune.
Strange sight from above to see the flashes of big guns, and
note the *chevaux de frise* of salient, sap, and trench. Feel
almost at home on the new machine. Rather heavy on the
controls compared to the Bristol.

On the same day he wrote to Eyles, and by code told him
that he was at Aire ("Arrived in real earnest"). He expected
to remain here for some time, as he wrote: "I shall not be
wanting boots for a little while at any rate."

"No. 40 SQUADRON,
ROYAL FLYING CORPS, B.E.F.
*April 7th, 1917.*

DEAR COMS,

Arrived in real earnest. Have found myself comfortably fixed in probably the best squadron in the service. The C.O. is one of the best and all the other fellows are 'top-hole.' I occupy the dinkiest little caboose one could wish for—such a lovely little hut, although I wish I had brought my camp kit along, as it was required. However, I am fixed up now, and quite comfy.

A machine (good 'un, too) of my very own to do what I like with, and it's a glorious state of affairs compared to what one obtains in England.

As regards health, I am feeling fairly well, and as the weather is improving, I anticipate being in the pink of condition soon.

No! I shall not be wanting any boots for a little while at any rate. Thanks for your kind inquiries.

At the last place I was at, I remained for four days, doing a little flying on a very sensitive single-seater—getting primed for the one I am on now.

I am enclosing in this letter a copy of my Will. You might keep it and act accordingly, although I hope I may be able to recover it again some day.

I hope all at home are well—especially Derek. I asked Paddy to write to you. You may be able to let him know things of interest. Well, cheerio—kind people, and write me soon.

Yours,
E.M."

In another letter to his sister Jess, he wrote:

"I'm across. In a very good squadron, good fellows, good C.O., good machines, good work. I hope I'll pull through all right."

That he expected the possibility that he might not "pull through all right" is proved by the enclosure of his Will to Eyles. This Will bequeathed everything to his brother, Patrick, for distribution amongst his family and Mr Eyles, his brother having previously received verbal instructions as to the method of distribution. He felt that his mother would be too distraught on hearing of his death to deal with any legal procedure. His father, whom he despised, was not to benefit by the Will.

8.4.17.—Wrote lots of letters to England. Unfortunate enough to break an axle in landing. Went as far as the lines with the C.O. Nothing doing. Lost the leader after the first half-hour, so proceeded alone. Foggy. Got back safely. Heavy wind turned machine over on landing and damaged upper plane and struts. Returned the bus to St. Omer for repairs. No bus now!

9.4.17.—Poor old Dunlop had a forced landing at Steinbecke. Broke up everything. Broke both legs. Concussion of the brain and strained backbone. Not expected to live. Still unconscious. No flying today for me. Lively on the Sector during last night—something doing.

10.4.17.—Big attack started. Weather awful. Snow and sleet. No flying. Scaramanga forced to land at Choques. Engine.

11.4.17.—Dunlop still unconscious. Had a "rag" in the

mess. Great fun. Boys from No. 10 came and helped. No damage apart from a sore elbow and a dark eye.

To the reader who is not acquainted with the R.F.C spirit, this last entry will appear somewhat callous— "Dunlop still unconscious. Had a 'rag' in the mess. Great fun." Air fighting was generally looked upon as a game by most pilots; just like Rugger. If one of the team in Rugger is seriously hurt, he is carried sympathetically off the field, but the game carries on just the same. This spirit of "Carry on" found its counterpart only to a greater degree in the R.F.C spirit. This aggressively offensive spirit could not tolerate sorrow, for sorrow was liable to lower the *moral*. Though it might hide in the bosom of the R.F.C pilot, it was only permitted to exude in the secret seclusion of his sleeping-quarters. In the mess, it was an unwritten law for pilots to forget their sorrow and assume a cheerfulness which gave the impression to the casual visitor of "living for the day." Thus was *moral* maintained at an unusually high level, and tradition was built. Without such a tradition the strongest of spirit would soon break under the excessive nervous strain of terrifying combats and personal losses. It was the only way and it produced a spirit of devil-may-care which staggered and completely nonplussed the serious-minded Teuton with his inferiority complex.

12.4.17.—Rotten weather. Great doings at Vimy. Bombardment quite audible. My machine arrived today. Went to see Dunlop. Still unconscious and not expected to live. Rotten luck. Met J. L. Browne at Aire this afternoon. Invited me over to Steinbecke to dine any evening. Weather still very bad. Wind high. No Huns venture over our lines. Heard that a new fellow in 32 brought down 3 Huns and 2 balloons in one day. First timeout. "Some" lad!

13.4.17.—Tested machine in the air. Nice. Weather still bad. Ellis (first time over the lines) stumbled across a Hun two-seater behind a cloud, pulled his trigger and managed to kill the pilot. The machine crashed in Hun-land.... Great rejoicing here over the feat. I wonder which was more surprised—the C.O. or Ellis at this piece of luck?

Todd returned today with an armour-piercing bullet thro' his engine, and several holes in the plane. Brings the war nearer!

Same evening I went over the line for the first time. Escorting F.E.s Formation of 6 machines together. Heavily Archied. My feelings very funny. A group burst near me— about 100 feet. I did some stunts quite involuntarily. Lost my leader and deputy-leader, but led the patrol down south. Returned safely after a very exciting time. Saw a few H.A.[1] far away, but could not get near.

The first flight across the enemy's lines was always a very trying one, it was even more tense than receiving the first ball in cricket from a Larwood. Anything might happen, one had to wait and see. Mannock appears to have been fortunate in not being engaged in a fight after having lost his leader, but he demonstrated that he had plenty of confidence in himself, for he assumed the rôle of leader to the remainder of the flight, who like himself had lost their leader after a few erratic manœuvres when being Archied. Anti-aircraft fire had a most demoralising effect on the new pilot, and it required great self-control to ignore it and remain in formation. Few pilots were able to show contempt for the snarling black circling balls of wool with their bark of "Woof! Brupp!" Casualties from "Archie" were rare, but the *moral* effect was tremendous. Now that

[1] H.A. = Hostile Aircraft.

the airman has a parachute, the *moral* effect of the "Archie" should diminish.

14.4.17.—Another O.P. this morning with Brown leading. Kept formation grandly. Brown tried to lose me but failed. Observed fires in Lens. Saw two formations of Hostile Aircraft (H.A.) very far away. They won't wait. Went over again twice. Passed over Lens, Avion, Annay, La Bassée, Vimy, and Arras. Nothing doing at all. Brown forced to land (engine trouble) at Isbergues, fortunately for him we were not over the enemy's lines when it happened. He's O.K.

15.5.17.—Very bad weather. High wind and clouds, Got 3 letters today. First correspondence to be received in France by me. Heavy bombardment from the direction of La Bassée, Advanced again today in the region of Vimy and Avion. Rumour we have lost Lens.

In a letter to Eyles he unconsciously admitted his sub-conscious thoughts on the possibility of his being killed:

"SAME ADDRESS,
*April 16th, 1917.*

DEAR JIM

Answering in return express. What a splendid piece of work that was of the Canadians at Vimy the other week.

In reply to your question—about 20 miles behind and just north.

I'm rather 'swerry' that you look at the matter of the Will in such a light. I feel as if I could punch your head for being snobbish. If Paddy *seems* that way inclined no reason why you should be. Reminds me of an old woman! I am sending the sword along, as you say you would prefer it. I'm glad the kit has been despatched and received O.K. About the tennis-racquet frame. I've still got that with me and I purposely kept it to use out here during the summer! If I don't come back, they will be sent to Mrs. E., and when I do come home on leave I'll bring it along personally.

By the way, the Lieut. Sowrey is not the man of the Zepp. fame.

Had my first taste of 'Archie' last week. I had the wind up, I don't mind admitting. I did stunts on the old machine which I'd never attempt under other circumstances. Still, got away all right, and that was at 14,000 feet.

Well, old son—lots of things I want to say but cannot. Wait till I come home on leave.

Kind regards to those people at 183 who can't find time (or won't) to write.

Love to D.,
Yours, E.

Sent a photo along if to spare."

His thoughts for his mother's comfort were always uppermost in his mind, and he often spoke of the burden which he carried by the thought of being killed and leaving her behind in possible penury. "Will she get a good pension, I wonder?" was a question he often repeated. Unfortunately the pension of a mother—even an aged mother who has sacrificed much to provide the State with a soldier, and a soldier who has won a V.C.—is a small one.

On the 19th he wrote:

DEAR MUM,

I haven't heard from you in reply to my last letter (2nd), so I suppose that it has gone astray. I wrote you from Boulogne, as I hadn't time to send you a line from the other side, before being packed off to France. You will see from the address above that we are prohibited from giving the name of the place at which we are stationed, but I can say that we are in the actual thick of it, and I go across the lines every day (sometimes 3 times) when the weather is not absolutely prohibitive.

The battlefields wear an awful aspect as viewed from above—covered with shell holes and craters, which remind me of photographs of what the earth looked like at the very beginning of things. It's extraordinary how anything can live through such a bombardment. Just like a plum pudding with ten times too many currants and raisins mixed. I fly a machine on my own, and I can tell you it's very lonely being up in the clouds all by one's self, with the anti-aircraft shells coughing and barking all around one, and big guns on the ground flashing and spitting continuously. I've been over the German towns, *but the Huns clear off almost invariably when they spot us coming.*

I hope Norah is getting along all right. Presumably she is still at the same place. Personally I think she ought to get on to aircraft work as soon as possible. Shells and other kindred things will be played out soon. I am writing to Paddy regularly, and hope also that you are hearing from him to your advantage, It is the only way I could arrange to let you have something occasionally.

Now I don't want you to send me anything along, as there is plenty of everything out here—tobacco, food, music, sports (when the weather is bad), but no girls, so don't waste what little cash you have in needless expense. I'm all right here.

There are lots of interesting things I should like to tell you, but the censor forbids, so I'll leave it to your imagination.

In the meantime, keep your 'pecker' up, and get ready for my leave, as I promise calling at the first opportunity

Love,
EDWARD."

There are two sentences in this letter which attract attention. One, regarding the refusal of the enemy to fight; and the other, his flippant remark regarding the fair sex. This is the second occasion on which he has made reference to the difficulty of getting the enemy to fight on anything like equal terms even over his own territory. Although the Nieuport was inferior in performance to Richthofen's Albatross, he and his much-advertised "circus" of picked fighters rarely voluntarily fought machines of their own type. As an example, during April, Richthofen was awarded 21 victories: of these 17 are two-seaters, mostly B.E.s; 1 Spad; 3 Nieuports. One of the Nieuports he reported crashed at Mercatel, on our side of the lines, This claim, his thirty-seventh officially recorded victory, was a figment of his imagination, for the machine which he fought and claimed as a victory belonged to No. 60 Squadron and returned safely to its aerodrome. This interesting fact only goes to prove how unreliable Richthofen's claims actually were. The facts of the mythical victory are as follows: At 5 p.m., on April 7th, a flight of six Nieuports, led by Captain M. B. Knowles, left Le Hameau Aerodrome, near Arras, to carry out an offensive patrol and take some special photographs. Owing to the necessity of taking them at 7,000 feet, the formation was attacked at a tactical disadvantage by Richthofen and some of his "circus" (not over our lines as he states, but over his own). The result of the fight was that three of the Nieuports were shot down in enemy territory by his companions. The victims were Captain Knowles, Lieutenant C. S. Hall, and Lieutenant G. O. Smart. One of the pilots to return safely and unwounded to the aerodrome, although his machine bore traces of good shooting, was Lieutenant H. E. Harvey. His report of the fight in which he was engaged with a red Albatross coincides in every detail with Richthofen's combat report, except that he did not "smoke and burn," neither did his "plane plunge, without catching itself, to the ground near Mercatel" as the Baron stated in his report when claiming an "acknowledgment." I wonder who confirmed this "claim" to make it official?

Mr. Floyd Gibbons, the American biographer of Richthofen, in *The Red Knight of Germany*, gives the name of Lieutenant Smart as the Baron's thirty-seventh victory, and about this I consider there is much doubt. The position of M7d53, which was the map reference of the position where Smart's machine fell in flames, was between 1–2 miles behind the enemy's lines and about the same distance to the north-east of Mercatel, which was in our lines. Mr. Gibbons, in his enthusiasm to find corroboration for some of Richthofen's claims, perhaps missed this point.

Mannock's reference to the fair sex was to amuse his relations, who always used to tease him about getting married. He was very fond of the opposite sex, who were naturally attracted to him, and he placed them on the pedestal which is theirs by right. There was no vileness in his character.

That the initial war excitement and excess of flying caused weariness is noticeable by the neglect of his diary. On the 19th, he experienced an extraordinarily unpleasant adventure to which during this particular period he was rendered liable, as he happened to be flying Nieuports, which were suspected of being defective. Due to badly seasoned wood used by French manufacturers, also to a number of small screws which were inserted in main spars, thus weakening them, planes in Nieuports used occasionally to break during a dive.

Mannock was carrying out diving and firing practice on a ground target when his right bottom plane broke, fell clean away, and fluttered to earth. He righted his wounded bird and guided it slowly to earth near the aerodrome. This fortunate escape is a typical example of the luck of flying, and offers a plausible reason why most airmen, and in particular war pilots, were fatalists. Mannock was not in the slightest way perturbed by this unpleasant adventure. Sergeant Bovett, who was the rigger in charge of Mannock's flight, tells the following story of this incident: "It was Mannock who had his bottom plane come off in the air, while diving vertically at the ground target. By skilful piloting he managed to get the machine down safely, but crashed it in a ploughed field without being hurt. It was a splendid effort. I saw the whole thing happen. When his rigger reached the crash, Mannock scared the life out of him by asking him what he meant by it, but seeing the rigger's face drop to forty below zero, he burst out laughing and cheered him up by showing him the defective strut socket which had broken."

Sergeant Bovett, who now lives in Camberwell, and who

was a pre-war R.F.G. mechanic, writing of Mannock during this period says:

"We mechanics among ourselves called him 'Mick.'…When he first joined us, he was rather despondent at seeing no Huns, and used to wonder how other fellows found them. He would not let the armourer sight his guns, but did them himself, fixing them closer than usual so that he could get right on to 'Jerry' before letting him have it.

"One day he returned from a job and his plane had been set alight by tracers, which he managed to extinguish by diving; calling the armourer over, he demanded more tracers than usual in future. 'I'll give the b—s what for,' he said. *And he did*. He was a man with plenty of nerve. When he became a Flight-Commander, he fixed a pair of silk stockings on his struts for streamers, where he got them from we don't know— more nerve, I suppose! Mannock was a real fighting pilot and a gentleman, and I've seen some from pre-war to the finish."

His next entry reads:

20.4.17.—Too tired or lazy for the last 5 days to keep up the diary. Went over the lines again on the 16th, but nothing exciting except a few "Archie" greetings. 17th, 18th were rotten days and nothing doing in the way of flying. Went to Aire on 17th and 19th to see Dunlop. There's a hope that he'll pull through. Went to St. Omer on the 18th for a break. Met Hooper and several others of the old school.

On the 19th did some gun practice, and in one dive from 2,000 feet my right bottom plane broke and fell clean away. Managed to right the machine after desperate efforts with the "joy-stick" and landed slowly and safely about half a mile away from aerodrome. Such a thing has never happened before where the pilot has not been killed or injured by the fall.

Another "rag" in the mess on the night of the 19th. Boxed with de Burgh. Crocked my knee and arm. Old McKechnie's farewell night, as he's proceeding home tomorrow morning. Great doings. Retired to bed at 2 a.m. and to be called at 5.30. Went to St. Omer by sidecar at 6.0 a.m. to fetch a new machine, feeling like a wet rag. Mouth felt like the bottom of a parrot cage. However, felt better after the drive, and brought the old bus back O.K. in 8 minutes. Some travelling. Had tour letters today, from Bright, Paddy, Jessie, and Cambridge, so I look forward to a busy evening. I hear from Buddy B. that Jim Rawson is somewhere near, in the 58th Div. I must look him up.

Over the lines today on Parry's bus. Engine cut out three times. Wind up. Now I can understand what a tremendous strain to the nervous system flying is. However cool a man might be, there must always be more or less of a tension on the nerves under such trying conditions. When it is considered that seven out of ten forced landings practically "Write offs" and 50 per cent. are cases where the pilot is injured, one can quite understand the strain of the whole business.

"Tip" I've picked up: If forced to land in Hunland, strike well inside the lines. Don't land near the trenches but well back. The trench dwellers are not noted for their chivalry.

This then prevailing "tip" was most harmful, and should have been officially denounced. A new pilot should have had it impressed upon him that it was his duty to attempt always to get back to his own lines, whatever the price of failure. It is quite possible that this unwarranted piece of advice was responsible for many pilots landing in enemy territory when they might have just got back into our lines had they but tried.

I well remember receiving similar advice myself from one of my numerous flying instructors and wondering what kind of a war pilot he had been. A fighting pilot without a soul!

23.4.17.—Went over to Choques to a concert. Very decent show (21st). Nothing of any great interest to relate. We are packing up and breaking camp preparatory to moving to Auchel. Expect to be completely transferred by Wednesday. Escorted Sopwiths yesterday morning on a photography stunt. Ran into Huns, but had to keep escort touch. Later, went across with Capt. Barwell to protect a B.E. doing a bit of spotting in barbed wire defences at Givhelli or Gabrille. Saw two Huns, but were too high to reach. This morning chased a Hun across the line with Brown. No luck. Much too good a start of us.

Haven't been feeling very well during the last few days. Probably the change in the weather. Tremendous bombardment all last night from the direction of Armentières. Something big going on. Couldn't sleep for the row. One continual roar—not a rumble—without a break. Pity the poor devils in the trenches.

Although his next entry was not until May 3rd, there are three letters which adequately fill in the interval. They give a clear insight into his highly strung temperament and to his thoughts and mental reactions, as the result of his experiences. The mental agony and the tension which his nervous system was being submitted to may be guessed from the insinuation in his letters dated the 28th, which portends bad news.

"40TH SQUADRON,
R.F. CORPS, B.E.F.,
24.4.17.

DEAR JESS,

Thanks for yours of the 15th, which is one of the nicest and most reasonable letters I have ever received from 'ole Jess.' The news that you had moved did not surprise me, as I expected something of the sort. I hope it's for the best. Anyhow, I'll help in a practical way as much as I can, and we must hope for the best. We all have crosses to bear, and I may tell you mine is a heavy one, but I don't complain.

Had an experience the other day, but you can't understand what it means unless you possess technical knowledge. One of my wings (of the machine) dropped off in mid-air (about 2,000 feet), but I managed to get the old bus down safely without a scratch. 'Some pilot!'

Talking about parcels. Don't send me anything of the sort. We are much better off from all points of view out here than you are at home. So don't waste money on foolishness. The food is good and plenty. The boys here are A1, and the days are full of excitement. My only trouble is I cannot sleep for 24 hours at a stretch. No licensing restrictions here, so I can get a whisky and soda whenever I like. That alone makes life worth living. In fact, I'm looking forward with dread to my ten days' leave at home.

No more now. I'm due in the air in twenty minutes.

Love to the kiddies,

Yours,

E."

"40TH SQUADRON,
R.F. CORPS,
27.4.17.

DEAR MUM,

Yours of the 22nd inst. received with many thanks, I was

just wondering if everyone in Blighty had forgotten me, or whether I had been reported missing, receiving no letters.

Things are going on well out here. The boys are doing wonderful things, and it made my heart burst almost to see them laughing and marching along the awful French roads, merry and joyful—one wouldn't think that there was a war on a few miles away. The guns are going on all night long—viewed from above, looks awful and wonderful. I've had some aerial scraps and have come out all right, although I had the 'wind up' terribly and my knees were knocking together like a pair of clappers. The Germans shell us every time we go over the lines, even at 18,000 feet, but we have got quite used to that—horrible black burst of shells, which absolutely bark and snarl at you as they pass by.

I don't see that you have much cause to grieve yet, old girl, even though I do go under (which the good God forbid). You should think of the hundreds of thousands of other sons (lots of them *only* sons) already passed over the Divide, leaving behind mothers, wives, children, or sweethearts. Thank goodness I haven't a sweetheart to mourn for me, although I have sometimes wished for a pal of that sort. However, I have lots of chums of the male persuasion, who would miss me—not that I anticipate going under, mind you, but one never knows.

Talking about 'reading the papers,' I think it's just as well you don't read them. They'd put the 'wind up' anyone, with the casualty lists and obituary notices.

Well, I'm on a very ticklish job to-morrow morning early, with another lad, and anything might happen. It should have taken place this morning, but the weather was prohibitive.

Mrs. Eyles, of Wellingborough, is sending you a photograph along shortly, one which I had taken before leaving England. I hope you'll like it. Plenty more to say, but am forbidden, so I'll leave it until my next leave. In the meantime keep your spirits up, and hope for the best. I want for nothing here, except sleep and lasses, both of which I shall get plenty of, when we all come flying home again after the war.

Cheerio, love to Norah,
ED."

"No. 40 SQUADRON,
B.E.F., R.F.C.
28.4.17, *Saturday.*

DEAR JESS,

Just time to dash off a line or two in reply to yours of the 24th. I'm due over the lines in ¾ hour, and have two more letters to answer, you must forgive me for cutting short this letter. Nothing special to report since my last *communiqué*—except of course the usual visits over the lines, scrapping Huns, getting 'wind up' over the shells snapping all round one.

We have moved from the place I was at when I wrote you last, have been here nearly a week and are moving again to-morrow to—

This new move will enable us to get over the lines within 10 minutes of leaving the aerodrome, and crossing at 10,000 feet.

Heard from Birmingham recently and things appear to be going along as well as can be expected. I wish you people wouldn't worry over me so. As far as I can judge, you are upsetting the old lady by your groundless fears. Just strike an optimistic note, and raise the barometer. It's up to you. I'm all right.

Can't linger any longer now, old girl. Love to the kiddies.

From

E.

P.S.—Got lost in France last night—30 miles away from home at 7.45. Got home in the dark. The old machine stuck it well?."

"40TH SQUADRON,
R.F.C.
*April 28th*, 1917, 5.45 *p.m.*

DEAR COMS,

Your double letter received this afternoon. I am due over the line on a dubious job, at 6.30 p.m. So haven't much time, hence this note—sorry! If I am O.K. I shall write you to-morrow more fully.

Thanks for all kindnesses, tolerances, assistances, sympathies, and all the rest of life's roses and buds. A pen is not very eloquent in a job like this.

Tempus fugit.

Yours, E.

P.S.—Do not regard me as a ghost that haunts your home, but as a guest who loves it."

"40TH SQUADRON,
R.F.C, B.E.F.
*April 29th.*

DEAR COMS,

The morning following the night before. In accordance with the statement in my last letter of yesterday's date, I am dropping you a line to let you know unofficially that I am all right, after the venture previously referred to. Had a very nasty time though, of which more anon. I don't like the

R.F.C. one little bit. One is too remarkably similarised to the position of a coco-nut at a fair! Any-how, a miss is as good as a mile. What annoys me is that the poor unfortunate bird cannot retaliate.

We are moving today to fresh fields or pastures new. See next letter.

Entered into a new method of aerial amusement the other evening. A new game is being evolved. It comprises the act of rushing 'all out' (and by 'all out' is meant opening the engine throttle to its fullest power) around houses, chimneys, barracks, tents, hills and valleys, trees and telegraph poles, at a height from the ground of anything less than ten feet. Nothing more exciting could be imagined, and when one considers that the speed of these machines is anything like—miles per hour, just guess what it means. Well, it's 6.45 a.m. (morning, mark you) now, and we're off again at 7.30, so I must cease. I've neglected my diary during the last week, but shall have to pull up some time today *if possible*.

Another stunt on this morning. No more now. Hope Derek is still in the pink.

Yours,
E."

His offensive spirit is brought prominently to light in his next entry, for in the first place he left his formation to go and search on his own for his first victim. He feels that the timid enemy might engage him alone, while he would avoid the formation. In point of fact it was quite wrong for him to leave the formation, although it was generally recognised as permissible at this period; but later, when formation flying was taken more seriously, pilots were not allowed to leave a formation to go hunting for scalps on their own. By keeping with the leader, they were surer of their own safety, while if the leader manœuvred his flight into a sound tactical position, he could drive home the attack with greater success. Mannock, when he became a leader, never allowed any member of his flight to leave his formation for any reason other than engine trouble (and when he returned, he made sure that *engine* trouble had arisen, and not *heart* trouble); if one did leave him, his wrath knew no bounds. "If you do it again, I'll shoot you. It's cowardice. I'll get you all the Huns you want," he was heard to say while reproving a delinquent. One member of his flight did desert him the second time, just as he was about to engage some Huns. Mannock kept his word. He whipped round angrily and fired a burst over the top of the deserter's machine; they were tracer bullets that he fired, and the retreating pilot could see the flame of the phosphorus in the rear of the bullet as well as hear the angry barking of his Flight-Commander's gun. He never left the formation again! Mannock then calmly carried on his attack on the enemy, and another enemy went floating downwards enveloped in flames.

In the second place, his strong offensive spirit (as well as his high sense of duty) is again indicated. We see him this time, with a jammed gun, deliberately remaining with his formation and crossing the enemy's lines, knowing full well that he will be led to as dangerous a position in the air as any in the war—over the home of the Richthofen "circus" On the way to the objective, we can imagine him anxiously struggling with his gun, trying to rectify the jam to the accompaniment of the "Woof! Brupp!" of the "Archie" bursts, but without success. At last he says to himself, as he fondles his revolver, "I'll have a crack at them with this.

Anyway, my presence alone will have a *moral* effect." Surely this incident, hitherto unrevealed, is one of the finest exploits ever recorded of the war in the air, particularly as we know how imaginative and highly strung Mannock was. It is indeed a fitting opening to an illustrious chapter where voluntary combat, fierce courage, steady resolution, high sense of duty, keenness, tactical skill, and selflessness played a prominent part. Fortune rewarded his daring; and be it remembered that although the line of demarcation is very narrow between temerity and daring, daring men are rare. Mannock early proved that he possessed this incomparable virtue.

His own description of his first fight in the air (one-sided as it was) and its psychological effect reveals his innermost self. First, he despised the pusillanimous enemy who did not attack him, particularly as it must have been obvious that he was defenceless. Later, we espy the soft spot in his heart for the two vacant chairs, and his revulsion to war when he realised the futility of it.

3.5.17.—Have rather neglected the diary lately. Lots of work, and always very sleepy. We moved from Aire Auchel on the Wednesday referred to in previous note—nice aerodrome—and moved again from there on the following Sunday. Am here now at Bruay, 10 miles behind the lines, with the guns roaring away continuously and blowing Vitry and Fresney to little bits. Went over this morning and couldn't see the ground for shell bursts.

Poor old Barwell and Brewis are both missing since four days ago. They hadn't been out here a fortnight. Barwell was the lad who came with me to Givrelle on the 23rd. A heart like a lion.

Six of the boys did a great "stunt" yesterday morning.

Unluckily, I was not on that duty. They went over ours and the German lines at 20 feet, all out, strafed 5 balloons and returned safely, with all machines shot to pieces. One of the finest pieces of heroism that could possibly happen in the R.F.C. Congratulated by wire by General Trenchard and we all had a tall night following. I'm disgusted that I wasn't in it.

Last night, we had a night visitor. Aeroplane dropped two bombs on Auchel and one here. No damage done.

Received a very nice letter from Mrs. D. at Cambridge. How good it is to have the regard and esteem of one's friends. I shall try and justify the good opinions of those splendid people.

I left the formation yesterday, over Vitry, in order to try and get a Hun on my own, but no luck. Really, they are rotten cowards—that is, the majority of them.

Two mornings ago, C Flight escorted 4 Sopwiths on a photography stunt to Douai Aerodrome. Capt. Keen, the new commander, leading. We were attacked from above over Douai. I tried my gun before going over the German lines, only to find that it was jammed, so I went over with a revolver only. A Hun on a beautiful yellow and green bus attacked me from behind. I could hear his M.G. cracking away. I wheeled round on him and howled like a dervish (although of course he could not hear me) whereat he made off towards old Parry and attacked him, With me following, for the *moral* effect! Another one (a brown-speckled one) attacked a Sopwith and Keen blew the pilot to pieces and the Hun went spinning down from 12,000 feet to earth. Unfortunately the Sopwith had been hit, and went down too, and there was I, a passenger, absolutely helpless not having a gun, an easy prey to any of them, and they hadn't the grit to close. Eventually they broke away, and then their

"Archie" gunners got on the job and we had a h—1 of a time. At times I wondered if I had a tail-plane or not, they were so near. We came back over the Arras with two vacant chairs at the Sopwith Squadron Mess! What is the good of it all?

A week ago, the Germans posted a notice up in their trenches which read:

"For God's sake give your pilots a rest."

We sent three B.E.s along at once and machine-gunned the trench where the notice was. Such is war.

Old "Rastus" joined us yesterday from Joyce Green.

This entry is full of interest. Barwell was shot down in flames and claimed by Richthofen as his 52nd victory. The Red Knight's combat report reads:

"*April 29th*, 1917.
7.40 *p.m.*

Between Billy-Montigny and Sellaumines, this side of the lines. No details concerning enemy plane; it is burnt.

*Narrative*

Soon after having shot down a B.E. near Roex we were attacked by a strong enemy one-seater squad of Nieuports, Spads, and Triplanes. The plane I had singled out caught fire after a short time, burnt in the air and fell north of Henin-Liétard."

The fledgling in his inferior machine had not a ghost of a chance against the German ace of aces in his new all-red Albatross, fighting over his own territory and aided by his comrades. But having a "heart of a lion" and intoxicated with the R.F.C. Offensive Spirit, the young pilot threw the gauntlet to the great Richthofen himself. This is an excellent example of the spirit of the Royal Flying Corps during this trying period. It never receded, and the pilots of No. 40 Squadron proudly upheld it.

Barwell was the fourth and last squadron casualty to fall in enemy territory during this black month. The squadron had flown over 700 hours in war flying, mostly spent well over the enemy's lines. The official Royal Flying Corps *communiqués*, which were published weekly, recorded nine victories by pilots of the squadron and the destruction of five balloons during April. Many other possible victories were gained, but owing to the fierceness of the battles and the numbers engaged, it was difficult to watch the tumbling aircraft as they left the scene of the conflicts, and so confirmation of any such victories was impossible. Mannock carried out forty hours' flying during the month, which placed him in the eighth place out of twenty-three. In spite of the number of patrols which he had carried out, he had not been able to engage an enemy in combat. This was not his fault, but a grave reflection on the offensive spirit of the enemy.

In a delightful book called *An Airman's Wife*, which is written round the letters of a brilliant fighter who served in No. 40 Squadron during this period—Lieutenant W. A. Bond, D.S.O., M.C. and bar—is revealed an enjoyable story which rings true of the squadron's activities. The most striking part about this book is the fixed impression it leaves of the timidity of the enemy fighters and the number of times "no Huns were seen during patrols." We are constantly coming across such remarks as: "We were across the lines at 7 a.m. but saw nothing"; "I was over the lines for about two hours this morning. We went out at 7 a.m. and saw nothing"; "I was sent up at 6.30, and during an hour and a half we saw one Hun"; "There were no Huns about"; "I really think that the period during which the Huns very seriously were threatening to be top dog in the air is at an end"; "It was quite an inoffensive patrol, for there were no Huns about—and it was a topping morning"; "I spotted three Huns very low down, but each time I dived they got under small banks of cloud and I lost them": "But there was nothing doing, no Huns"; "This morning, just before we got to the lines, there was a big scrap in which our triplanes got two Huns and our two-seater got one, but two of ours are missing. They haven't been seen in the sky today apart from that"; "Yesterday I did two patrols. There was nothing doing on either"; "Towards the end of the patrol, I saw four red Hun scouts below me and dived on the nearest (Richthofen's pilots). I fired twenty rounds at long range; and the whole four turned away"; "I climbed with one other fellow to head-off five Huns who were coming up from the south, and for twenty minutes we manœuvred until finally the Huns went too far over the lines to follow."

Mannock's disgust at not being included in the dangerous and thrilling balloon-straffing raid signifies his desire to injure the enemy in some definite manner. Most pilots who possessed the offensive spirit in a marked degree usually "had a go" at a balloon if they were getting despondent at their lack of success in downing a Hun.

Actually, balloon-straffing was easily the most dangerous of the war airman's duties. Successful air fighters used to consider one balloon to be the equal of three Huns. The extreme danger of this duty lay in the fact that the attacking aircraft had to go low down to shoot up the balloon, which was usually at least about four miles behind the enemy's lines, and well protected by ground defences of anti-aircraft guns, machine guns, "flaming onion" batteries, and aircraft. One bullet in any vital part of the engine was sufficient to cause a forced landing, and the chance of this happening was great, because of the number which were being fired during the attack and the return flight.

A pilot required a detached mentality to enjoy balloon-straffing, and Mannock soon found that his mentality was not detached, but he attacked balloons just the same, when he could not find Huns. He was not, however, a Beauchamp-Proctor or a Willy Coppens.

It is now made clear why he so enthusiastically described in a recent letter the new game of flying at high speed around houses and other buildings. The citation in the official R.F.C. communiqué describing the balloon-strafing expedition reads:

"Balloons. Lieut. K. MacKenzie and 2nd Lieuts. Walder, Lemon, Thompson, Bond and Morgan, No. 40 Squadron, crossed the lines at 50 feet and under in order to attack German balloons. Previous experience has shown the necessity of flying low in order to obtain satisfactory results in these attacks. These pilots had practised low flying, and had learnt how to use trees, houses and the ground in screening them from infantry and machine-gun fire. Artillery co-operated by putting a heavy barrage on the German trenches, leaving the pilots a certain area in which to cross. As a result of the attack, four German balloons were destroyed. One pilot, who went to within a few feet of the balloon, failed in his attack owing to gun trouble."

His next entry reads:

"*May 6th*, 1917 (I think). Sunday, anyway. Nothing very startling to report since last notes. We've fixed up a tennis court here and manage to get a game of a sort. Lovely weather yesterday—tropical—and today as cold as charity. I'm not feeling well as a result of the change. Ellis did a grand 'stunt' yesterday. Went over high past Douai and returned comparatively low—meeting two Huns landing at their drome at Douai. Caused both to crash by engaging them at once. Met another coming home and brought it down with his automatic pistol. I hear today that he has had a bad landing at the advanced landing ground, and has contracted concussion. Not bad though, and is well on towards recovery. Morgan got one down in flames today, and Gregory also managed to do one in before his gun jammed this evening. MacKenzie was forced to land this side by two of the 'red devils,' but got away scatheless. No luck for me, although I was at the same place half an hour beforehand. I made a rotten landing when returning and turned old 1552 upside down. Just got a bump under the wing at the wrong moment and over she went. These buses are very light. Consolation in the fact, however, that the new flight-commander did exactly the same thing an hour afterwards, but if anything, more so. I noticed today that the Huns are bombarding Vimy Ridge. I think we'll hold it though.

Sudden call yesterday afternoon at 3.0 p.m. Huns were interfering with our B.E.s north of La Bassée, 3rd Army wished for assistance to drive them away. Leaped into the ether with hope budding within me, and as Hall's bus was faulty, I shot off alone. Nothing doing. Went as far as south

of Lille and Armentières. Not a hope. Got 'Archied' north of
Lens, but no Hun 'planes to be seen. Circled round the two
'Quirks'[2] for an hour, they wagging their tails with content
went on flapping their ailerons with gusto, happy in a feeling
of doubtful security, in view of the presence of one of the
'Silver Hawks.' I returned at 5 o'clock feeling disgusted and
fed up.

Blaxland went on leave today. 14 days. Asked him to let
Paddy and Jim know where I was exactly, and what work we
were doing.

Heavy shelling going on now in the Arras-Lens Sector.

Brown and de Burgh left for England a few days ago.
Brown showed signs of nerves—poor chap. I hope they both
get soft jobs until the end of the war. MacKenzie will be the
next to break down, I think."

The person principally responsible for the tennis court was
Padre Keymer, who was much beloved and admired as a
chaplain. Bond, in one of his descriptive letters, writes of
"the Old Man" (as the Padre is referred to in the book):

"The Old Man has asked me to write an article for his
magazine. Really, I could do quite an interesting one on 'The
Vicar as his parishioners do NOT see him.' He is a wonder
parson; a raconteur, a sportsman and a tomboy. Just now he
is working, trying hard to level the ground in the middle of
our huts to make a tennis court. On Sunday night I went to
a service. There were about thirty of us in the ante-room of
the —th Squadron Mess. The walls were thickly decorated
with Kirchner and Pinot studies—of what I call the sub-
limely sacred—and cards were strewn on the tables. Before

[2] "Quirks" was a nickname for B.E.s.

the service could start we had to cut off George Robey—in the middle of a doubtful song—on the gramophone.

The Old Man explained he wanted to make it a meeting rather than a service; therefore after prayers and a few hymns, he proposed we should smoke while he gave us an address.

It stimulated thought, he said.

It is worth a good deal to see him on the aerodrome when any big stunt is going forward.

He was down there to watch us start for the balloon strafe. He was fearfully grave and just walked round the machines—hardly saying a word. I don't think he expected any of us to return.

I was the second to get back. The first was the one whose gun had jammed. I lost my engine on landing and stopped on the far side. The Old Man sprinted out, beating the 'ack-emmas' (mechanics) by yards.

'Any luck?' he shouted. He was fearfully excited.

'Yes, it's all right,' I said.

'Oh, damn good!' he exclaimed. 'Damn good ... Absolutely topping!'

The others came in at intervals, and he beat the C.O. and everyone in welcoming them. He ran about from pilot to pilot, saying, 'Damn good! ... How completely splendid!'

The C.O. joined him in a duet of jubilation, and supplemented his 'damn good' by extracts from the new vocabulary."

This was the only type of Padre who fitted into the scheme of things in a Flying mess during a war. The Royal Air Force is lucky to have many of this type still in the service; particularly one.

Padre Keymer (now deceased) and Mannock were sincere and confiding friends, and of the latter the Padre wrote:

"We were very great friends. He used to confide in me. After so many years, he remains a vivid memory, and quite the greatest personality that I met during the war. His nobility of mind, his fiery enthusiasm to win the war, his modesty and his sincerity had to be experienced to be appreciated. His character was built on a spiritual foundation and not on academical training, of which he had had little. He was a self-educated man; and like most men of this type, he combined academical knowledge with bitter experience, which resulted in a strong, sound, forceful character. He read a tremendous amount. His hatred of the German, which increased with the length of the war, was distinctly more of a hatred bred of civilisation and religion than of the primitive instincts of man. I could write a fat-volumed book on this side of him alone. When he was inwardly sad and depressed, as I often knew he was, he never showed it in the mess, where he was usually boisterous and cheerful. Often he had to be thus in order not to give away his inward feelings. He was indeed a great man. He was particularly depressed at first because he could not shoot down any Germans. This worried me a good deal because he was such a trier. When not on patrol he always seemed to be practising shooting at a ground target which was on the aerodrome. I was afraid that one day he might throw caution to the wind and land on a German aerodrome and shoot them up; he was the type of fellow to carry out such a daring stunt, if he made up his mind. I am glad he did not allow his heart to rule his head, as so many other brave lads did, and so throw his life away.

It was by fighting Life, and the enemy, with his head and not his heart that he achieved greatness. It is sad to think that on the one occasion that he unnecessarily reversed the order Fate decided to desert him and Death accepted the challenge. Of one thing I am certain. His soul rests peacefully in the bosom of our Lord, for there was no vileness in his soul and he always put his trust in Him."

While setting off on offensive patrol there were at least ten possible reasons why a pilot knew he might not return; they were:

Being killed.

Being wounded and losing consciousness.

The machine being set on fire.

The machine breaking up as the result of enemy fire.

Losing control due to broken controls.

Engine put out of action by enemy fire.

Engine failure due to technical defects.

Machine forced to land due to gun stoppage and simultaneous attack by numerous enemies.

Shortage of petrol.

Losing his way owing to incorrect compass or bad weather.

Add to this depressing list the attentions of "Archie" and the fact that the pilot had no parachute, and the reader will easily understand the necessity for periodic rest for the airman, and in particular the air fighter. A rest of a fortnight was usually given after two to three months' active-service flying; and the airman was posted to England for a three-months' rest after any period exceeding six months at the Front, depending upon the amount of work he had been doing, and upon his physical robustness. Owing to pilots being allowed to carry on too long after showing signs of nerves, many never again during the war regained their original health, and as a result became useless for further war flying. Such a close study of this aspect of a pilot's health has been carried out since the war that nowadays a pilot evincing the slightest sign of nerves is immediately "spotted," and treated according to his requirements.

De Burgh (now Squadron Leader), who often led Mannock on patrols during his first month in the squadron, writes a "close-up" of him which again emphasises his personality:

"Mannock joined our Squadron (No. 40) in the middle of April 1917. At the time we were equipped with Nieuport Scouts, which were a very welcome change after F.E. 8s.

Much as we liked the old F.E.8, it was at that period hopelessly outclassed by the German aircraft—after all, a patrol ceiling of about 12,000 feet and a maximum speed of 80 m.p.h. (on the A.S.I.) at that height had its disadvantages!

Though the change was welcome, the squadron looked upon tractors with a certain amount of disfavour—at least the 'old hands' did. When the change took place, half the squadron had never flown anything but pushers, and we all found the lack of visibility forward a great drawback at first.

Mannock was one of the, to us, new school who was used to tractors, and had been taught such things as rolls and half rolls—all of which were more or less strange to us. There was no doubt about it that the new pilots coming out to us about this time had been taught far more than we had about handling an aeroplane.

Mannock was posted to A Flight, which had Todd for a Flight-Commander.

The great question of the moment just about this time was—would a Nieuport's wings come off if you dived it too steeply?

Rumour had been going round—and I believe it was founded on fact—that there was a bad batch of Nieuports coming to the R.F.C. whose timber was rotten.

We noticed that Mannock was in the habit of diving his machine more steeply than anyone else, and we were anxious, and said so.

It was here that I first noticed a characteristic of Mannock which he afterwards showed on other occasions. He was only too ready to seek and accept advice, but he always liked to prove a thing for himself as well.

He continued to dive his machine steeply till one day his bottom plane turned in its fastening and came off! He discovered the way the machine would fly best in this condition, looked for the softest spot—a ploughed field—landed there and turned over with no damage to himself. He had found out how far he could go, and afterwards he went that far and no farther.

Shortly after that I remember discussing with him—I was acting Flight-Commander—how far one could then go and look for 'meat' on one's own. In the past that had been quite successful, but I said that I thought that it was no longer 'healthy.'

Some days later the flight got separated in a dog-fight, and on coming back to the aerodrome Mannock was not with us. He landed about a quarter of an hour later and sought me out saying, 'You were quite right!' He had apparently gone off on his own to find some trouble, had flown round the corner of a cloud into six Huns—and found it all right!

Mannock was an extraordinary character, and a very forceful one. Although I knew him for less than a month, and that 13 years ago, his personality is as clear to me now as if we had only parted the other day.

We had two things in common, he and I, so that I came to know him well (though I doubt if any man saw much beneath the surface of him)—we were both Irishmen, and we both dearly loved an argument.

He was the only man in the mess who would talk beneath the surface. Many was the time that we would argue fiercely on some highly controversial subject such as politics, socialism, or religion—he usually won the argument, though heaven knows what his views really were.

As a curious contrast to the warfare of the tongue, Mannock was very keen on boxing, and as I had done good deal, we often used to blow off steam by having a set to in the mess. In fact, it used to be a stock event, if the evening was livening up, for Mannock and me to have a round or two—and he nearly always said, 'Let's hit out,' and we used to have a good slog at one another. I think, on the whole, that I used to get more than I gave, as he had the height of me, and a slightly longer reach; but I had him at footwork.

As far as I know, there were only two things which would rattle him, and he would always 'rise' to them, if drawn: the first was his very bitter hatred of the Germans, and the second was 'Society' women. The former has been amply confirmed by others. The latter caused us all no small amount of amusement—it was only necessary to leave a copy of one of the weekly papers open showing 'The beautiful Lady ... who is organising a charity concert in aid of ... etc.,' for Mannock to go off the deep end for about half an hour ... and he surely had the power of words!

I often wonder how, and where, he would have fitted into a peace-time world.

I gather that in pre-war days he had led a pretty wandering life in the Near East. What he would have made of the post-war chaos, heaven knows, for he was undeniably a dreamer and idealist, though what those dreams were, I doubt if anyone knew.

Had he lived, he would have made a marvellous politician; he had all the Celtic fire to move multitudes. And what a leader of a lost cause!

But I don't think that present-day politics would have seen much of him. He was nothing if not sincere, and nothing if not a clean fighter. And where would such find a place in Party Politics?

It is a personal regret of mine that I only knew Mannock for such a short time, and that when I was the 'old hand' and he the new. I could so obviously learn far more from him than he ever could from me—but I never had that privilege.

There are very few one meets in the course of one's life who can be labelled as outstanding personalities, but he was one of them.

Of all his contemporaries in the squadron—that strange gang who naturally preferred tractors to pushers—Mannock is the only one who remains clear in my mind, and that by his sheer force of personality."

A similar survey of Mannock's character has been obtained by the writer from innumerable comrades. They all emphasise how his personality towers above that of the others whom they met in those never-to-be-forgotten days.

While Blaxland was at home, he wrote to Mannock's mother and gave her a concise account of the squadron's work.

His remark, "Your son is very good indeed at the job," has more than casual interest. The professional jealousy of certain of his comrades, which was not unusual in the Flying Corps, as in other fields of high endeavour, attempted by the usual sinister methods to discount Mannock's unusual keenness, because of his careful methods and temporary lack of success. The decent fellows in the Mess, however, appreciated him at his true value. The others were compelled to follow.

"LONDON,
18.5.1917.

DEAR MRS. MANNOCK,
    Just before I left France to come home on leave, your son asked me just to write you a short account of the work our squadron is doing, and to tell you how he is getting on.
    He is stationed at present at Bruay, which is south-west of Béthune, and about 10 or 11 miles from the lines. The work our squadron does consists chiefly of patrols on the other side of the lines somewhere between La Bassée and Arras. A patrol generally lasts about 1½ hours and we fly at 11 to 18,000 feet, or sometimes lower, it consists of 3 or 6 machines according to circumstances. The whole idea of the patrol is to find Hun machines and to shoot or drive them down, the latter is generally the case as *they very rarely stop to fight unless they are in vastly superior numbers*, except of course their specially good pilots. Your son is very good indeed at the job, and is very much liked in the Mess.
    No more now.

Yours sincerely,
(Sgd.) L. B. BLAXLAND
(*2nd Lieut. R.F.C.*)."

As the pilot of a single-seater fighter during a war is very liable to experience the same mental fear and reaction as Mannock described from time to time, the knowledge that Mannock during his early days became despondent over the thought that he was not equal to his task as a fighting pilot should prove to be an encouragement to the war pilot of the future, for he definitely proved that loss of self-confidence may be overcome by will-power. "The Will," he said later, "can always triumph over Matter during the early stages of a nervous disability, particularly when that disability is only fear."

A single-seater pilot works in peculiar isolation; he has neither the physical nor the *moral* support of the infantryman or the sailor when in action. He is alone in an immense space, where he can neither remain stationary and hide, nor obtain help if he is wounded. If his machine commences to disintegrate or bursts into flames, he cannot get out.[3] If he is feeling unwell, forebodings of disaster may haunt him during the whole of the patrol, and he will expect engine failure or a surprise enemy attack unnecessarily, and strain his nerves accordingly Young pilots will do well to study and to remember Mannock's psychological triumph. Further, they must not lose sight of the fact that no great fighting pilot was devoid of fear; everyone is to a certain degree afraid; everyone, even the bravest, has to a greater or lesser extent to force himself to fight. Whilst in the fight fear is the chief obsession. It is in fact in the power to force oneself to fight bravely in spite of one's fear that true courage lies. A man who is devoid of fear—I doubt if there is such a person—cannot be brave; because bravery consists in overcoming fear; and if he has no fear to overcome, he

[3] This refers to the last war, when there were no parachutes.

cannot be brave. Again, I believe that a very great number of our best fighting pilots did not enjoy the prospects of a fight. They may have enjoyed looking back at it in retrospect; they may have enjoyed the sensation of actually shooting down their opponent; they may have eagerly grasped at the chance of adding another victim to their score, or some at the chance of gaining kudos or decorations. They may even have enjoyed the excitement of the fight itself. But very few actually enjoyed the prospect of a fight. It is claimed that Ball, Caldwell, Rhys-David, Barker, Meintjes, and one or two others did; but they were quite exceptional. Mannock was not one of these; and England's future air defenders must not lose sight of this fact; it should stimulate them in depression and increase their desire to emulate his greatness.

9.5.17.—Lots of exciting news to tell. Went over the lines from north of Arras to 5 miles behind the German trenches at a height of less than 15 feet, attacking Hun balloons. That was on the 7th—a Monday. Six of us—Capt. Nixon (missing), Hall, Scudamore, Redler, Parry, and myself. All except the Captain (only been with us two days—the new Flight-Commander referred to in my last note), returned safely but with machines almost shot to pieces. Hall crashed on home aerodrome, as did Scudamore; Parry crashed just our side of the lines, at the Canadian H.Q. Redler landed at Savy, but returned here later and damaged his machine on landing. I was the only one to return properly to the aerodrome, and made a perfect landing. We all got our objectives. My fuselage had bullet holes in it, one very near my head, and the wings were more or less riddled. *I don't want to go through such an experience again.*

On the 7th also, I went to Omer to fetch a machine. Early

the same morning (before the balloon "strafes") I had a scrap with a Hun—together with Capt. Keen and Rastus. No luck though, although we put the "wind up" him. I was immediately attacked by several "red devils," but managed to shake them off. I got separated from the others, and went scouting on my own. Keen returned and reported that he thought I went down, whereas there was much handshaking upon my reappearance.

The 8th was a dud day and a party was fixed up for Omer by tender. Went along in the afternoon and returned by 6.30, feeling very rejuvenated by the pleasant break.

Today (9) I had a very disagreeable experience. Capt. Keen, Rastus, and myself on second patrol 9–10.30 a.m.

Rastus left us early owing to engine trouble, so we went on without him. We engaged a Hun over Henin-Liétard and chased him over towards Courcelles. I turned east and Keen went west. I was immediately attacked by three Huns. My guns jammed, Keen was almost out of sight— "Aldis" sight[4] oiled up, and the engine failed at the crucial moment. I thought all was up. We were 16,000 feet up at the time. I turned almost vertically on my tail—nose-dived and spun down towards our lines, zigzagging for all I was worth, with the machine guns cracking away behind me like mad. The engine picked up when I was about 3,000 feet over Arras and the Huns for some reason or other had left me. I immediately ran into another Hun (after I had climbed up to 12,000 again), but hadn't the pluck to face him. *I turned away and landed here with my knees shaking and my nerves all torn to bits.* I feel a bit better now, but all my courage seems to have evaporated after that experience this morning.

[4] "'Aldis' sight" was a gun sight which resembled a telescope.

The CO. was very good, and didn't put me on any more line jobs for the rest of the day, except to bring a new machine from Omer. I was taken to Omer this evening for the purpose by Mr. Leslie of 16 Squadron in a B E 8. Returned to Bruay in the new machine by 8 o'clock, feeling a bit better.

I hope I feel O.K. again in the morning, as I am on the 5.45 a.m. O.P.

The official description of the balloon attack as described in the R.F.C. *communiqué* is interesting:

"*Balloons.*—An attack on German balloons was carried out by seven machines of No. 40 Squadron. The pilots crossed the lines at about 20 feet, and as on a previous occasion, artillery put a barrage on the trenches, but on this occasion 12 other aeroplanes crossed the lines at the same time at a considerable height in order to draw the attention of anti-aircraft gunners. As a result of the attack, seven German balloons were destroyed; three caught fire when high up, two burst into flames when near the ground, and two when on the ground.

The names of the pilots who took part in the attack are:

2nd Lieuts. Morgan, Hall, Cudemore, Redler, Mannock, Parry, and Capt. Nixon, who failed to return."

Enemy fighters might be able to avoid combat, but a balloon could not. And it is thus that Mannock registers his first aerial success.

It is a coincidence that his star should begin to shine on the same day as the brilliantly blazing comet of Captain Ball disappeared.

There were three British fighting pilots, and only three, whose achievements and personality lifted them to a just eminence and gained for them a place in the hearts of all their comrades. They were Ball, McCudden, Mannock. Each in his particular way kindled a torch and lighted the unknown pathways of air fighting for the guidance of their comrades. Ball set an example of valour which was rarely equalled: he was the first British pilot to make a business of killing Huns, and he did so at a period when the enemy was angrily challenging our supremacy of the air; McCudden set an example of caution (without being unduly cautious) and cunning in air fighting, and proved the value of accurate marksmanship; Mannock set up a standard of courage and skill in leadership; he initiated a new era in the art of air fighting—the era of seeking for swift decision by manœuvring for position and then attacking with relentless determination.

Albert Ball was still a minor when he was killed. He was born in 1896, in Nottingham, being the son of Mr. (now Sir) Albert Ball, some time Mayor of the city. When war was declared, he was carried along the wave of patriotism which swept the country its width and length. Ball was one of Kitchener's first hundred thousand, although he was only just eighteen at the time. The Great Adventure appealed to his youthful spirit. He joined the Sherwood Foresters, and within a couple of weeks he was promoted to Sergeant in the 2/7th. In October 1914, he obtained a commission and as a Second Lieutenant he transferred to the North-Midland Cyclist Corps and, whilst encamped near Ealing in the summer of 1915, he took private flying lessons at his own expense at Hendon. His enthusiasm for "this new sport" may be gauged from the fact that as he had to be on parade at 6 a.m. he had to get up very early in order to carry out his flying instruction and get back in time to answer the roll-call. As a pupil he gave every indication of becoming a good pilot in the air, but his landings were not good.

In January 1916, he was seconded to the Royal Flying Corps, and within a month he was a member of No. 13 Squadron (B.E.2s). Although his duty was chiefly artillery co-operation, he had gained three victories over aerial opponents within two months. He thus proved early in his career that he was by temperament more suited to be a single-seater fighter pilot than a two-seater pilot, as he then was. This fact was soon recognised by the authorities, and on May 7th he was transferred to No. 11 Squadron to fly the new Nieuport Scout; and by the end of the month he had shot down two enemy machines. It was on this type of machine that he gained most of his forty-odd victories (by "victories" I mean combats which ended in the enemy leaving the battle apparently *hors de combat*).

Later he served in No. 60 Squadron, and during the Battle of the Somme hardly a day passed that he did not shoot down a Hun. Unlike Mannock, he nearly always flew alone, and thought nothing of charging into a formation of a dozen Huns, shooting a couple down and sending the others about their business, to return to his aerodrome with a bullet-ridden machine. The gods appeared to appreciate his temerity, otherwise it is difficult to understand why he lived so long. At the time of his death he was a member of No. 56 Squadron, which, with such fighters as himself, Crowe, Meintjes, Bowman, Rhys-David, Protheroe, Maxwell, Maybery, Leach, and later McCudden, flying S.E.5s, was the finest fighting unit on the Western Front during this period. They hunted the Richthofen "circus" mercilessly, and it was in search of it on a special mission in which the whole squadron took part that Ball lost his life. Major "Billy" Crowe, who now lives in South Kensington, was the last British pilot to see Ball alive, and in view of the mystery which surrounds his death (the Germans proclaiming that he was shot down by Lothar, the brother of Richthofen), and also of his last moments in the air, it is of interest to read Crowe's story:

"I remember Ball's last flight as clearly as if it was yesterday. The afternoon of May 7th, 1917, was a very 'murky' one, and most of the pilots were lazing around. When we were having tea, a message came through from Wing Headquarters instructing a squadron formation to patrol the area of Douai and Cambrai from 6 o'clock until patrol time was up. Three flights led by Ball, Meintjes, and myself left the ground at about 5.45 p.m. with the express purpose of engaging the Richthofen 'circus' if they were in the air. The weather was very bad. Layers of thick banks of clouds hid the sky, and they ranged from 2,000 to 10,000 feet with varying-sized gaps. We crossed the lines south of Arras between the layers of clouds at 4,000 feet, and Ball, who was leading, shortly after led the formation into a large bank of clouds which resulted in the various members of the formation losing contact with one another. I found myself alone when I got into clear space again, but some distance on my right I could see a number of S.E.s flying in a very loose formation. I made for them, but a cloud bank enveloped me on the way and I lost them. From now on until the end of the patrol, which lasted until dusk, I flew about accompanied by Lieut. Lewis (Uncle Caractacus of B.B.C. fame) whom I had found wandering about like myself looking for a mate. We were soon engaged at frequent intervals in short sharp combats with Albatrosses of variegated colours, including red, which was the hall-mark of the members of the Richthofen 'circus.' As it got darker and darker, I decided to return to our lines, and on the way I saw a solitary S.E.5 flying due north a few miles over the lines and firing Very lights.[5] I immediately proceeded in its direction in an endeavour to join it, and on getting close, I saw it was Ball. He did not appear to see me, for he flew straight into a cloud bank in a north-easterly direction. I followed him. When I got out of the cloud again I saw Ball diving after an enemy aeroplane which disappeared into a cloud and which was hotly pursued by Ball. I followed through the same cloud, which was a big one, and when I got through to the opening on the other side I could neither see Ball nor his opponent, and I did not see him again. The height then was 4,000 feet. As I knew that my petrol must be running low, I reluctantly made for our lines unaccompanied, as Lewis and I had lost one another in the clouds. On the way back I met a two-seater going home and had a quick crack at it without any apparent luck. I eventually had to land owing to the darkness at No. 8 (Naval) Squadron, Auchel, at 8.15. When my petrol tank was examined, it was found to be almost dry. The air seemed to be full of Huns on this night as Piccadilly Circus is full of people on Boat-race night. I have never seen so many. And as a result of the fighting, Ball and a young pilot named Chatworth-Musters were killed; while Meintjes and Leach were both severely wounded, but by force of will-power they succeeded in getting back to our lines. We sent half a dozen of the Hun machines also scuttling earthwards—possible

[5] Coloured lights which burned for a considerable time.

victories. Ball may quite easily have continued to engage the enemy too far east and run out of petrol. As he glided to earth—defenceless, possibly—and as he had done a lot of firing during the patrol, he would have been an easy victim to one of Richthofen's pilots. Equally so, he would have been an easy target for 'Archie' or any other ground defence. I do not believe that there is any foundation for the suggestion that Ball was blinded and that he did not know in what direction he was flying."

Did Lothar Richthofen shoot down Ball?

From investigations of all the information available, which is both contradictory and confusing, it appears possible that Lothar was already wounded and in hospital at the time of Ball's death. His brother definitely states in his book, *The Red Air Fighter*, page 132, that his brother was wounded on May 5th. His brother should know. It would appear that the declaration in the German Press that Lothar shot down Ball was for the purpose of propaganda at the Home Front, in order to revive the drooping *moral* of the people. *The Berliner Tageblatt* even announced that he was shot down by Baron von Richthofen and not by Lothar. The Baron was on leave at the time! A telegram sent to one acting on behalf of our prisoners of war on May 29th stated that he was killed in an aerial fight, but that details were unknown at Field Headquarters. It seems curious that of all people those at Field Headquarters did not know that Lothar Richthofen was his conqueror, if such was the case. Again, Lothar's twenty-second victory, which is claimed to have been Ball, was stated to be a triplane and not a biplane which Ball was flying. It was impossible to mistake one machine for the other even during a fight. The theory that he was shot down by anti-aircraft fire is the one which appeals to me most, and I accept this theory not only because it is known that there was some evidence that his machine was hit by anti-aircraft gun fire, but because of an authentic story given in Wing-Commander T. B. Marson's delightful book, *Scarlet and Khaki*, page 150, which rings much truer than any other that I have heard of or read. He is writing of Ball's death, and he goes on to say:

"Subsequently I met, in America, Capt. Hunter, who was wounded and shot down some days previously, and who was in a German hospital during May in the Lens district. The Germans thought Hunter could give information as to gun positions, and he was visited by one of their officers with the object of getting this information. Hunter had a wounded arm, and was in a very weak state. On the 8th of May, the German officer told him Ball had been killed. Hunter refused to credit it. On the following day the German brought Ball's identity disc, and showed it Hunter as proof of his story's truth. At the same time, he stated Ball was brought down by anti-aircraft fire, and that his machine was badly smashed up. Verification of this is afforded by the fact that the Germans themselves originally reported that Capt. Ball, flying a triplane, had been killed on the 7th of May. At that date the S.E.5 was a new machine, and the debris may reasonably at first sight have been mistaken for that of a triplane."

As Marson truly continues:
"Wounded and possibly semi-conscious, it would only be in keeping with Ball's character to refuse to quit the scene of

conflict, and thus to have fallen a victim to his foes on the ground. In the air he was supreme. Greatly as he was mourned, it was a fitting finale to a hero's career."

The story of Ball's death can be filed in the same dossier as that of his great contemporaries, Guynemer, Rhys-David, Manfred Richthofen, Mannock, for each fell within his enemy's lines dead; and the foeman who fired the deadly bullet or missile is as unknown as the grave wherein lie Guynemer, Rhys-David, and Mannock. Likewise, the deaths of Ball and Richthofen only go to show how difficult it is to assess the correct individual victories of pilots on either side.

With the passing of Ball, the time of the individualist, the lone patroller, also rapidly passed. But the spirit with which he had fought remained; and Mannock held high the brilliant torch.

13.5.17.—Sunday, 12.15 p.m. Lovely day again. Brilliant sun, although we had rather sinister clouds and mist at 4.15 a.m. I was on the early morning patrol with Glin and New. Owing to the weather, we decided to leave New behind (a "new" man), so Glin and I started together at 4.45 a.m. Glin got the "wind up" apparently with the weather and returned at 5.0 a.m. I went over the Lens-Arras sector and amused myself with the clouds. Went thr' rain storm over Arras. Quite enjoyable. The old engine was not going very well. Met three triplanes and some F.E. buses on the same route, and threw a loop or two to show there was no ill-feeling. No Huns to be seen—luckily for them—as I felt rather blood-thirsty. Their "Archie" gunners upset my complacency somewhat for a while. Returned at 6.30 a.m. feeling as hungry as a flea on a china doll.

Rastus and Capt. Keen brought down a Hun yesterday

evening. Just my luck that this should happen when I wasn't with them! Rastus and Keen went out this morning at 6 a.m. on O.P. and I'm sorry to say Old Rastus has not yet returned. I hope he's O.K., possibly landed somewhere on this side. Keen lost him in the clouds. Lemon engaged a Hun this morning without keeping j weather eye open above, with the result that another Hun attacked him from above. Lemon forced to land (on this side, luckily) with his petrol tank shot to pieces.

Hun came over here yesterday morning at 10 a.m. Leaped into the ether and gave chase, but he had too much start of me, being about 18,000 feet up. Chivvied him over his own lines.

The next entry records what was a good fighting pilot's greatest dread—that of "suffering from nerves." Due mostly to ignorance of medical science, the word "nerves" was taboo in a good fighting squadron unless the pilot was a war veteran. A highly strung pilot showing early signs of nerves was looked upon as "turning yellow," and he usually had to bear the cross in unsympathetic isolation. For this reason many brave pilots must have been quite wrongly compelled to suffer Hell. It is amazing to think that Mannock was for a short time a victim of this ostracism.

Captain G. L. "Zulu" Lloyd, a famous fighting pilot of Nos. 60 and 40 Squadrons, relates how he found Mannock a much-misunderstood man when he joined No. 40 Squadron as a Flight-Commander in early July.

"He was not actually called 'yellow,' but many secret murmurings of an unsavoury nature reached my ears,' related Lloyd. "I was told that he had been in the Squadron two months, and that he had only shot down one single Hun out of control, and that he showed signs of being over-careful during engagements. He was further accused of being continually in the air practising aerial gunnery as a pretence of keenness. In other words, the innuendo was that he was suffering from 'cold feet.'"

Lloyd, whose experience of good fighters in No. 60 Squadron—Ball, Cockrane-Patrick, Soden, Chidlaw-Roberts, Caldwell, Pope, Young, Law, Selous, Meintjes, "Jack" Scott—liked the look of Mannock, and decided to have a heart-to-heart talk with him. The result was as he suspected. Mannock was only passing through a phase which most highly strung men who faced the enemy in deadly battle experienced, and a good deal of the chatter was due to the often inexplicable green eye of the yellow god. He found that Mannock was fighting to overcome his own inherent fear—the greatest battle in a man's life. If he wins through he knows he is a MAN, and life thereafter is strewn with roses. Mannock had met a stubborn enemy, but he was winning through. Like all great men, he fought the difficult and unsavoury battle almost in secret and alone. He kept the agony of the combat to himself—a big mistake—thus prolonging the struggle; but making the victory more definite when it had been achieved. To Lloyd, he confessed: "Of course, I've been very frightened against my will—nervous reaction. I have now conquered this physical defect, and having conquered myself, I will now conquer the Hun. Air fighting is a science. I have been studying it, and I have not been unduly worried about getting Huns at the expense of being reckless. I want to master the tactics first. The present bald-headed tactics should be replaced by well-thought-out ones. I cannot see any reason why we should not sweep the Hun right out of the sky." And from then onwards, we meet a new Mannock; a pilot who went out hunting for "scalps," with preconceived plans and ruthless determination. And we see how his phenomenal achievements made his detractors gasp with amazement, and how they were only too happy to have him as their leader. It is a strange, but illustrative coincidence that Boelcke, who was easily the most beloved of airmen in his own Air force, also experienced some unpleasantness through being misunderstood during the early part of his career.

Two letters to Eyles read:

> "40TH SQUADRON
> R.F.C.
> *May 12th*, 1917.

DEAR COMS,

Big roll unexpectedly arrived yesterday. Thanks very much for the music. Very well selected, and I thank you accordingly. You may keep the change—if any!

Business out here still very chock-full of excitement. I have an idea that my nerves won't stand very much of it. It's beyond a joke now. Plenty of scrapping and lots of 'Archie,' although I am feeling perfectly fit and well.

Really I haven't much to say under the circumstances. I always feel tired and sleepy, and I can lie down and sleep anywhere or at any time. We have moved again from the place we were last, and this is not such a pleasant spot, and it's nearer the lines.

Well, I'm dog-tired as usual, and I can't think of anything special to say. On another special mission tomorrow morning. 'Not a hope,' as they say in the R.F.C.

Love to D. and everyone else. You can observe I am nearly asleep.

Yours,
E."

"40TH SQUADRON,
R.F.C, B.E.F.
*May 14th*, 1917.

DEAR COMS,

Brother Rastus unexpectedly arrived yesterday. We are at the same place as when I last wrote you.

Lots of interesting and exciting things have happened recently. I think I thanked you for the music in my last letter. We have been in the wars lately out here, although I am feeling perfectly fit—even excellent. My gear is still in good order, but I think I shall want some more boots before long.

We have started tennis, and I could not find it in my heart to return your racquet. Please buy one and debit to my account.

What sort of weather are you getting at home now? The weather out here is glorious, and we are making as much use of it as possible.

One of my chums has just gone home for a fortnight and he promised to write you. I hope he does.

Have you heard from Johnnie lately? I hope he's all right. There has been a terrible strafe on this front for the last fortnight. We see it all going on from the air. What tales to tell after the war, old boy!

Nothing more now owing to the 'blue pencil' man. Tell Mrs. E. I remember the 14th of the month and if no letter arrives for the occasion, it is because I've been unable to write.

Let's have a line when you can.

Yours,
E."

His diary reads:

14.5.17.—Rastus missing. Went out yesterday morning on 2nd patrol, lost the leader in clouds and hasn't been seen or heard of since. I feel awfully miserable about it. My special chum. His loss is felt throughout the squadron. Everyone liked him. Kismet!

Went to Omer yesterday evening to fetch a machine. Forced to stay there for the night owing to the weather. Hôtel de Commerce. Told Marcelle about poor old Rastus. She was terribly upset. I promised to let her know of any fresh news.

Met Lloyd at Omer. He is on S.E.5S a little further south. They've lost four youngsters in five days. All the young ones seem to go first.

Brought the new machine from Omer this morning at 6 a.m. Another big bombing stunt on today at 10.30 a.m. I expect I shall be on it. More nerves.

Old MacKenzie goes away on leave today. 14 days. He is in need of it. If ever a lad is cracked up, Mac is. I wonder if I shall ever get like that! And what my friends will think of me if I do. Old Paddy the "devil-may-care" with nerves. I feel nervous about it already. Heard a rumour yesterday that we get something in the nature of a distinction for our last balloon stunt. We deserve it.

18.5.17.—Good. Still alive. Some people die on the 17th! Had two glorious days of "dud" weather—which means no work for us. This morning it threatens to be fine—worse luck. Had quite a good time during the last three days. Went to Omer on the 16th with Captain Gregory, Captain Keen, Bond, Jake, Thompson, and Redler. Quite an exciting time, although I think I took a little too much champagne. Anyhow, the Padre advised me to go, as he thought it would do me good.

We took a tender yesterday evening to Béthune. Rather an interesting place in view of the shelled town. Met two Captains of the Canadian Infantry who would insist on showing their appreciation of the R.F.C. in the usual practical manner. After a pleasant time we returned home at 10.45 p.m. quite sober.

No news of poor old Rastus yet. Am afraid he's passed over the Border. Another new lad (two, in fact) arrived here—Bassett—an Australian—quite a good fellow, and Godfrey—a Canadian. Both good lads, but Bassett has the dominant personality. I imagine he'll do big things.

The guns are still booming away over towards Arras-Lens. I imagine things are happening.

Haven't had many letters from home lately! When a fellow gets old, he is ruled out of "society "apparently. Where, Oh! where are all my friends?

Fighting pilots did most of their flying at high altitudes, 15,000–20,000 feet, and the after-effects often produced a very noticeable desire to sleep, and sometimes a splitting headache. Mannock, like most other pilots, was subject to the desire of "snoozing" at every available opportunity. When I served with him in No. 74 Squadron he never failed to take advantage of an hour to "snooze" between patrols.

Headaches were attributable partly to want of oxygen at high altitudes, partly to the natural strain of concentration when searching for enemies, and partly to induced ocular fatigue. Some pilots suffered considerably from ear trouble owing to the rapidity with which fighting scouts changed height. With the change of height, the atmospheric pressure changed, causing a congestion of the auditory organs. Pilots found that the act of swallowing, chewing gum, or continual blowing of the nose during rapid change of height, usually relieved them of unpleasant ear trouble.

21.5.17.—One or two "dud" days, during which many hours of snoozing took place. Occasional odd jobs took place also. Nothing of great import. The Huns seem to have been transferred to the Eastern Front. We roam all over Hunland without seeing an Iron Cross, although their "Archie" devils are just as accurate as ever. Had a forced landing yesterday evening. No, on the 19th. Engine cut out over Vitry, but I managed to make Haute Avesnes—west of Arras. The Colonel insisted that I should stay to dinner— which I did. An R.A.M.C. unit—and all anxious to "do" the R.F.C. boys well. Journeyed Mont St. Eloi and arrived there by tender at 10.30 p.m. Drinks and chats. Major very nice. Got a tender to Bruay and arrived home at 12.45 a.m. very tired. Went back to Haute Avesnes the following morning with mechanics and brought machine back by midday. The magneto had broken, causing the failure.

Went out with Thompson this evening in search of "scalps" but nothing doing. Amused ourselves by dodging about the low clouds and frightening the engines out of sundry crawling "Quirks" doing artillery work. Great sport. You come down vertically at approx. 160 miles p.h. on a poor unsuspecting observer and bank away to the right or left when almost cutting off his tail. You can almost hear them gasp. They're always pleased to see us about, though, and they forgive a little "sky-larking" occasionally.

Had a big mail today. Cambridge, Tottenham, and Richmond.

A letter to Eyles gives an interesting sidelight as to what he and his comrades did when it rained:

"40TH SQUADRON,
R.F.C., B.E.F.,
*May 22nd*, '17.

DEAR JIM,

I think it's my turn to write. You see we have to destroy all letters after reading them, as we cannot leave them lying about and mustn't take them over the lines in case we get brought down.

Things out here are going on "spiffingly." Raining like blazes now, so have nothing special to do except test machine guns and study trench map. The mechanic boys here are good lads—work hard and generally contented. I'm trying to organise a string band among them, as there are several who play fiddles. I shall want some boots very soon, although not while I'm here. Some with good "uppers."

I understand that the sword has been forwarded on to you. Don't be under a wrong impression, old boy, over that matter.

The usual routine carries on from day to day, except when bad weather blesses us by its presence. I went over to Béthune (raining) with a few of the lads in a tender the other afternoon. The town is more or less under shell fire, but they left us alone during the evening. The Canadian Infantry Officers we met there were tremendously anxious to treat us royally, and the party would have been drinking there now, had it not been for one sober airman—your humble servant. It seems that they were in the front-line trenches when we went over on the balloon strafe, and saw the whole show. I was horribly proud over that business at the time.

Regards to all at home and I hope Derek is quite well.

Drop a line when you can.

Yours,<br>PAT."

The diary continues:

25.5.17.—Morgan got the M.C. on the 23rd, and was brought down by one of our own shells on the 24th. It appears that a shell struck his machine at 6,000 ft. (he was flying too low) and knocked the engine out, broke his right thigh and left ankle. The undercarriage was also blown away. Notwithstanding this, he kept his head and planed down into our lines, but the machine—or what was left of it—broke up in touching earth. He crawled unaided from the wreckage and was immediately taken to hospital. He said that the only thing that worried him when coming down was that he might faint before reaching the ground! Some lad!

Received a parcel from Wellingboro' yesterday (birthday). Very nice. Someone thinks about me, apparently.

Went up this morning, patrol leader. Met two Huns—one too high, but managed to "put the wind" up him with some long-range shots. The other was absolute "cold meat." A big two-seater painted like a beetle. I got about 30 rounds into him from close range—distinctly saw the tracer going into the body of the bus where the pilot sits. Still he went on and put his nose down. Just my luck. The others didn't notice him until too late. Better luck next time.

Very hot weather here now. Had a good game of tennis last evening. Anzac and I beat the C.O. and the Padre. Next job at 5.0 p.m.

A letter to Eyles brings out again his keenness on looking after his own guns.

"SAME PLACE,
*May 31st*, 1917.
11 *a.m.*

DEAR JIM,

Many thanks for your letter and parcel dated 21st. It came as a very welcome gift. I appreciate it very much. I noticed that the good lady managed to put some of my name plates on the things, which was a great 'stunt' indeed.

I regret that I did not acknowledge receipt of the Photograph which you sent along, but it came to hand all right. I am pleased with it, and the worthy old chaplain here begged it off me.

Very little news out of the way here, except for the usual everyday excitement—scraps and narrow shaves and much 'wind up.' The General Officer Commanding the Army came down here a few days ago and shook hands with all those who took part in the balloon stunt. He was awfully bucked, don't you know.

I went over and landed at Reeves' aerodrome last evening.

1.45 *p.m. same day.*

Was interrupted in this letter to go on patrol and have just come back. As I was saying, I saw young Reeves and had a chat and drink. He seems to be getting on all right, although he's dissatisfied with the machines they fly. Slow ones which do observation for the artillery, photography, etc. No fighting! He thinks that the machines we fly are wonderful. As you say, they're 'French.' He is going to write to you soon.

I have had one or two scraps since I wrote to you last— very exciting, and one of the scoundrels chased me. I had to break off the engagement owing to my ammunition running out. Talk about 'wind up,' I had a scare attack I may tell you.

Well, old sports, I could chatter away all day like this, but I cannot leave a gun job that I've got in hand. Send us a line when you can.

Love to Derek and I hope he is keeping well.

PADDY."

The diary continues:

2.6.17.—A beautiful morning, with more than a handful of cold wind from the N.W. Am "standing by" to escort Sopwiths over the lines on photography. No signs of them yet—thank God.

Had several exciting moments since writing the last notes. Led the patrol yesterday (5 machines) and had a scrap. Emptied a full drum of rounds into a big coloured two-seater Hun from about 25 yards. Must have riddled the bus, but nothing untoward happened. She put her nose down and went straight. "Melbourne" Bassett got hit in the leg in this scrap. Made a good show by flying all the way back to the' drome and landing, and this with a shattered leg! It was just bad luck that this shot was the only shot on the machine.

I tried my hand on a balloon N.E. of La Bassée just after the above scrap. Fired about 25 rounds of Buckingham, but couldn't set the darned thing alight. In the meantime clouds of "Archie" all round me, but managed to zigzag away. Later, was "Archied" by our people at 7,000 ft. Felt very mad.

MacKenzie came back from leave on the 31st and was promptly ordered to Home Establishment again. Lucky dog! Capt. Keen, my Flight-Commander, went into hospital yesterday with "flu." I hear that our Capt. Gregory—just gone back to H.E.—has been awarded the "Légion d'Honneur" for specially good service. He deserved it!

Saw Archie Reeves at No. 2, the day before yesterday. I landed there in the old bus. Had to do a few spins, turns, and leaps before I left to show the boys that the "circus" hadn't it all its own way. Very nice letter from Mrs. Dunn yesterday.

I had almost forgotten to record the visit of the G.O.G. Army on the 28th last. He came specially to congratulate us on the success of the last balloon stunt. He was very pleased indeed, and advised us to shoot at the observers as well as the balloons. He shook hands with the "'eroes." Our C.O. was very pleased, I imagine. Two days later Gen. Trenchard came to see us.

At last a victory! But as there is some doubt as to the enemy's ultimate fate, Mannock in his official combat report modestly claims an "out of control." His diary, however, is more definite, and reveals what he really thought.

As the British fighting pilots were engaged in almost all their fights over the enemy's lines, Headquarters classified their victorious results under the headings:

Destroyed.
Driven down out of control.
Driven down.

*Destroyed* meant that the enemy was either seen to go down in flames, in pieces, or actually crash.

*Out of control* meant that the enemy appeared to be hit, and that by the manœuvres of the machine the pilot was dead or had lost control, but that the machine was not seen to crash. This manner of result was the most frequent in our air fights, as usually the fighting began at any height between 15,000 and 19,000 feet. Owing to this high altitude and the general engagement which normally took place when formation fought formation, it was impossible for a pilot to concentrate on the fall of a tumbling enemy. If he did so, he would probably find himself soon attacked at a disadvantage.

*Driven down* meant that an enemy was seen to "force-land" but not to crash.

All three forms of results had to be confirmed before being officially acknowledged, except on those comparatively rare cases when an officer's word was accepted for a victory while on lone patrol. This privilege was unfortunate, as it led to nasty rumours being circulated which reflected gravely on the integrity of some of the pilots concerned, but Mannock's good name was never in question and remained unsullied to the end of his career.

This problem of results, in other words "victories," has always been a bone of contention among fighting pilots when attempting to assess the merits of the various famous pilots in the war. After a close study of this controversial

subject I have come to the conclusion that it is not possible
to declare accurately how many victories any pilot on either
side definitely gained, as often the pilot was not aware of his
victories, while some made false claims. The Germans were
lucky to have their enemies over their aerodromes most of
the time, so that their victories were easier to gauge. In spite
of this fact, we do know that, our machines often landed
safely in Hunland, and that in the case of a victory, the victor
was often unknown. This was because the prisoner had been
simultaneously attacked by a formation. It is understood
that the leader was in such circumstances officially given the
kudos; hence (so I have been told by several German pilots)
arose the legend of many of Richthofen's victories! Again,
many of our machines which landed in Hunland with
ordinary engine trouble were claimed as victories.

Victorious British pilots often had to be satisfied with an
"out of control" or a "driven down," when actually the
enemy had crashed or the occupants had died after landing.
A typical instance is recorded in Richthofen's own memoirs,
*The Red Air Fighter*, pages 114-15. The Baron's father is
paying a visit to his famous sons at Douai aerodrome, and
Richthofen writes:

"In the meantime, an aerial fight took place above our
aerodrome. My father looked on and was greatly interested.
We did not take a hand in the fight, for we were standing on
the ground and looked on ourselves. An English squadron
had broken through, and was being attacked above our
aerodrome by some of our reconnoitering aeroplanes.
Suddenly one of the machines started turning over and over.
Then it recovered itself and came gliding down normally. We
saw with regret it was a German machine. The Englishman

flew on. The German aeroplane had apparently been damaged. It was quite correctly handled. It came down and tried to land on our flying ground. The room was rather narrow for the large machine; besides the ground was unfamiliar to the Pilot. Hence the landing was not quite so smooth. We ran towards the aeroplane and then discovered with regret that one of the occupants of the machine, the machine-gunner, had been killed."

This machine would have come under the category of "driven down." Is it not a more definite victory now that we know its fate? The question even arises, should it be considered a victory at all?

I wonder how many machines crashed in their own lines and the occupants lived to fight another day? They must have run into hundreds! If observed, these crashes would have been accepted as "enemy destroyed." Yet the pilots might have been in the air again on the same day: I have known of such cases. Again, I wonder how many wounded pilots by grim determination landed their machines safely on an aerodrome and later died of wounds? There could have been no possible chance whatever of their being claimed as victories, yet victories they were.

We now know that both the Richthofen brothers were shot down and wounded: that a similar fate befell Guynemer; and also many of our successful air fighters; yet they recovered and carried on to achieve more destruction of their opponents. In Manfred von Richthofen's case, twenty-two more victims were claimed. If any of these aces was seen to crash, his successful opponent would naturally have claimed a victory. Yet, was it a victory? When Manfred and Lothar von Richthofen were wounded, they both eventually crashed, but as neither their victors nor any of our pilots saw them crash, no claims for a victory were made.

From these few examples it can easily be appreciated how difficult it is to say which fighting pilot gained the greatest number of victories. It is not difficult, however, to decide whether a fighting pilot was a real fighter or whether he was a modest one. It will be seen by his diary, letters, combat reports, and general behaviour that Mannock was both. He is always hunting the enemy over their aerodromes and attacking their fighters at every opportunity, whilst he never makes a claim of a doubtful nature. Here is a copy of his first combat report:

*Army Form W.3348.*

### COMBATS IN THE AIR

Squadron No.: 40.                    Date: 7.6.17.
Type and No. of Aeroplane:      Time: 7.10-7.15.
Nieuport Scout B.1552.           Duty: Escort.
Armament: 1 Lewis Gun.          Height: 13,000 ft.
Pilot: Lieutenant Mannock.     Locality: North of Lille.
Observer: Nil.
RESULT:     Destroyed.............................................Nil.
                 Driven down out of control.................One.
                 Driven down....................................Nil.
Remarks on Hostile machine: Type, armament, speed, etc.:
Single-seater Scout.

*Narrative*

When escorting machines N. of Lille one H.A. attempted to dive on one of the leading F.E.s but turned before diving. Nieuport engaged H.A. at very close range and fired approx. 30 rounds into pilot's position, and engine of H.A.

H.A. turned upside-down, nose-dived and spun, obviously out of control.

Nieuport endeavoured to watch H.A. crash, but was unable to do so.

Signed.............................. E. Mannock, 2/Lt.
      This was witnessed by 2/Lt. Blaxland and
                               2/Lt. Lemon.
Signed.............................. G. W. Beer, R.O., *Captain*
                           *for O.C., No. 40 Squadron, R.F.C.*

His diary records the fight in a few words:

7.6.17.—Either Wednesday, Thursday, Friday, or Saturday. Lots of things have happened lately. Capt. Keen O.C. "C" Flight, in hospital for about 5 days, and in the meantime I have led the Flight patrols. Many scraps, and I brought my first dead Hun down this morning—over Lille—North. Have been up to 21,000 early in the morning (3.30 a.m.) looking for the early birds. Got 50 rounds into a fat two-seater the other morning over Lens—Liétard. Sure I smashed him up, he went straight down without turning and I had to swing away to get out of the line of friend "Archie." Lost Capt. Allcock on the 5th. He attacked a Hun and two more got on to his tail. Sorry I wasn't there, although I couldn't have made much difference. Two Huns this morning for "C" Flight. One for Hall, Godfrey and Redlar got one each also. Four today.

The push on Armentières-Ypres sector commenced this morning. We escorted F.E.s over Lille on bomb-dropping business—and we met Huns. My man gave me an easy mark. I was only about ten yards away from him—on top—

so I couldn't miss! A beautiful coloured insect he was—red, blue, green, and yellow. I let him have 30 rounds at that range, so there wasn't much left of him. I saw him go spinning and slipping down from 13,000. Rough luck, but it's war, and they're Huns.

There is nothing more depressing for a fighting pilot than to be for weeks in a squadron where other pilots are shooting down enemies and he is not. His feelings are akin to those of a rugger player who, although exceedingly energetic, never scores a try. There is plenty of vigour and dash about him, but his technique is a little out, and he fails to finish off any movement successfully, although often within easy reach of the line. Most depressing. So it is with an unsuccessful fighting pilot. He may get close to his enemy and victory may seem to be within his grip, yet nothing happens.

After a while depression sets in, and the pilot decides he will never make an air fighter. Then the end comes as far as his sphere of usefulness as an air fighter is concerned. Mannock, in spite of his slow progress, never allowed himself to get into this state of fatal depression. By sheer will-power he resisted depression.

He never forgot this early experience of his, for later in his career he often gave credit of a personal victory to one of his pilots for the purpose of raising his *moral*, and simultaneously that of his Flight. Hence one reason why the number of enemy machines he actually shot down will never be known.

Having now in his own opinion gained a victory, his *moral* took a vertical jump. The technique of the game was slowly and unconsciously revealed to him, and the result of his next flight left him with feelings like those of the victor of a cock-fight.

14.6.17.—Easy time lately. Only one job a day, with the result that I have a lot of time on the aerial range. Had another scrap the other evening with five Huns N. of Douai. Scalped two of them. Both went down nose first, although nothing definite as regards their absolute destruction could be vouchsafed. I felt like the victor in a cock-fight! Poor old Shaw went West a few days ago.

Had an accident the other evening. Going about 120 m.p.h. near the ground, when a small piece of grit went into my right eye. The pain was intense, and I don't know how I landed. Got up to the mess somehow or other, and after some attempts at first-aid, I promptly fainted. Hospital, where the P.M.O. injected cocaine, and extracted the foreign body. Eye painful afterwards. Today, had to go down again, and through the same ordeal. A piece of grit had been left in the eye. Over-looked. More teeth-gritting and profanity. My eye feels now like a bell tent!

Several new pilots lately.

Went over to Nos. 10 and 43 with Godfrey the other day. Stunted and otherwise "put the wind" up the boys. C.O. at 10 invited us over at any time we cared to accept it.

Went over to Omer to fetch a new machine, and was chased and beaten by a "Camel" when returning. They are wonderful buses and will make the Huns grovel. The Spad Squadron has left for somewhere up north. Very decent fellows, but they did not seem to have much luck. Lost three on the first day of the Armentières push.

Feeling nervy and ill during the last week. Afraid I am breaking up. Parry rejoined us yesterday. Capt. Keen very decent. Let me off flying for today. I think I'll take a book and wander into the woods this afternoon—although it rather threatens rain. Oh, for a fortnight in the country at home!

Mannock's narrative in his combat report of the fight mentioned just stated:

"Pilot saw H.A. formation when N. of Douai. Nieuport engaged two of these, firing one drum. Hits were observed, observed, but with no apparent effect."

A typical Mannock report: devoid of any form of exaggeration or attempt to deceive Higher Authority. To down an enemy was sufficient compensation to his nature. Decoration and promotion to him were merely fruits of conceit, and the methods which some officers adopted to achieve this end he openly despised.

We can hear more of Mannock's keenness in practising air gunnery when he is not on patrols. Major J. L. T. Pearce, who now lives at Ealing, and who was the Chief Armament Officer in the field to the R.F.C. and R.A.F., writes of Mannock:

"I cannot remember my first acquaintanceship with Mannock, but I was employed from February to May 1917 as itinerant Armament Officer to the Royal Flying Corps in the field. My especial task was to visit fighting squadrons and assist pilots in making their guns function in the air. Whenever a new invention as regards armament was introduced from home, it was always sent to me first, and I visited squadrons and explained the functions of the gadget.

It was during this time that I first remember Mannock very well. He showed the keenest interest in anything that might help to increase fire power in the air, or make it more accurate. By the insertion of a washer on the front of a Vickers gun barrel, the rate of fire was increased and made the gun more effective. It was to Mannock I first gave this out, and regulated his gun accordingly. It was so successful with him that he was my disciple amongst other fighting squadrons for the introduction of any new gadget I might introduce. From September'17 until the armistice I was employed as chief Armament Officer in the field, and each time I visited No. 40 Squadron I always found Mannock full out for any recommendations I might give as regards guns or bombs. So much so that he was instrumental in making me lecture to himself and the younger officers in the squadron, in order that they might be efficient in the latest improvements in armament. At the same time, Capt. McElroy was also a Flight-Commander in the squadron, which was in my time commanded by Major Tilney and later by that delightful Australian, Dallas; Mannock was one of those lovable types who made one go full out to help him in every way. I am quite sure that in many cases, especially where there was any doubt, he always gave the credit of a dead Hun to one of the younger officers in the squadron.

I later met him when he was in Nos. 74 and 85 Squadrons, and he showed the same enthusiasm in armament, in order that his flight and squadron should be, if possible, first in the field. I did not see very much of him in No. 74 Squadron, but I remember quite well shortly after his squadron came out, he compelled me to give a lecture to the pilots of the squadron on the theory of gunnery in the air; how to increase fire volume and how to avoid stoppages with the guns when they occurred; and how to overcome them.

His loss in those days, when some of my best friends were 'going West,' and some of the finest types in the R.F.C., left a very great blank in my life."

16.6.17.—Yesterday had to see the doctor again about my eye. Had some cocaine and he extracted another piece of steel from the membrane. No flying for me again today. Capt. Keen got a Hun last night in flames over Vitry. Awfully hot weather. Went to Lillers with the Padre today. Brought plenty of tobacco back, and strawberries and cherries for the Mess. Nothing doing in the air line today at all.

Expect my leave in about three weeks' time. Roll on! I think I've got a prickly heat rash breaking out on my face—never handsome at the best of times! Don't sleep very well o' nights. My sins, probably!

Capt. Napier came back today, although he's still not quite fit.

Major Tilney (later killed) was a discerning CO., and he arranged that Mannock should proceed on leave at once. He left the squadron the next day and remained the usual fourteen days in England, dividing his time, as he usually did, between visits to his mother at Birmingham, Mr. Eyles, and the R.F.C. Club in Bruton Street. While on leave, he completely forgot the war, and enjoyed himself in a quiet manner, except on the occasional evenings when he met his comrades in the R.F.C. Club—then he had a good old "jolly." As a member of the R.F.C. Club, he was a tremendous favourite; his mixed nature of sincerity, modesty, and boyish revelry captured all hearts. No greater popularity has ever been achieved by a member of the Club unless perhaps by Flight-Lieutenant S. M Kinkead, who was killed in the Solent in March 1928, when attempting to break the world-speed record.

Bidding farewell to his mother was always a distasteful business to him, and his sister Jess relates how he never said "good-bye" when returning to France. He would kiss them "au revoir" as he parted from his home, on the pretence that he would be returning, and then with a boyish chuckle would say, "I'll be back the day after to-morrow to say 'good-bye.'" But the "day after to-morrow" never came.

While on this leave, he called to see his favourite cousin, Patrick Mannock, a son of the late J. P. Mannock, the famous billiard player, who taught King Edward the game. His cousin narrates a story which indicates most strikingly Mannock's complete indifference to the sight of aeroplane crashes, which is symptomatic of sound nerves. Further, the narrative confirms Mannock's strong aversion to anyone connected with "Society."

"On June 26th, 1917, I was at Hanworth Aerodrome, where I had a job with Whitehead Aircraft. There had been a crash when a Sopwith was being tested by the firm's pilot, named Sykes, who was injured. On the scene I suddenly saw Edward, with his friend Eyles—a surprise visit. Edward, who asked me when Whitehead was going to make some really up-to-date machines, laughed a lot at the crash. Somehow it was obviously amusement at the mishap, not callousness; for he made it his business to ask after Sykes. He stayed with me some days at Barnes. On the 29th, with my father, dining out, we met a certain sporting baronet, and I recall Edward expressing contempt for him, saying what a pity it was that such people mattered because they had a handle to their names. The next day he went back to France."

His brief rest in England completely cured his troubles, and he returned to his squadron full of fight and the offensive spirit—a new man. While on leave, he gave a lot of thought to tactics, and he opened his heart to his friend Eyles. He told him how he felt his age was against him in this new and intensive form of warfare. "But," he said, "I think there is room for brains in this game, and, I hope to balance the weakness of the flesh by formulating tactics. I've spent hours thinking out schemes of catching the wily Hun (since I've been home). Watch me bowl them over, when I return." And bowl them over he did, for soon after his return he commenced to realise his theories with conspicuous success. After each success he evolved new tactics, until he became the supreme air fighter tactician—pre-eminent and unchallenged.

On his return from leave, he found the enemy fighters shyer than ever, and after chasing them out of the sky for a few days, he was fortunate to find on July 12th an enemy two-seater on our side of the lines. He promptly shot it down. The next day he was victorious over another two-seater. Whatever deficiencies there had been in his marksmanship, he had now perfected, and his stock was rising in the squadron. Mannock, the once-despised airman, was coming into his own. He relied on accurate deflection shooting and surprise for his victories. His C.O., who had all along recognised his soundness and keenness, recommended him for promotion and award.

A letter to Eyles reads:

"40 SQUADRON, R.F.C.,
B.E.F., FRANCE.
12.7.17.

DEAR JIM,

Yours of the 6th to hand. Glad you have received parcel O.K. and not much the worse for wear.

I had a nice quiet time at Staines on the river, and feel as fit as a fiddle now.

So the good lady and D. have gone to 'Sloshport.' I hope the weather is favourable and that Derek will show the beneficial effects of the sunshine.

'Some' raid on London, eh! We chuckle like blazes out here about it. The way the papers at home are whining and whimpering makes us all sick. Poor old France and Belgium and Servia and Rumania and a few others have had to stick it for over two years. The majority of people at home don't realise we're at war!

Regarding Sykes, I hear that he is progressing very favourably, no bones having been broken after all, and he expects to be on the job again in two months.

I have drawn a few diagrams on the back of machines, which you may be able to identify. The important thing about them and the easiest way to find what type is to note the kind and make of engine.

Had one or two great scraps since I've been back. And very nearly done in by 'Archie.' Struck my top-plane main spar with a lump of shell, but luckily it did not break. Had to have a new one fitted of course.

We are now on special work about two miles behind the line. We got shelled often, and have to dive for the dug-outs.

13.7.17.—I was interrupted in this letter to get out after a Hun. That was yesterday morning at 9.50 a.m. At l0.20 a.m. I was lucky enough to get a big two-seater Hun down in our own lines. I shot the pilot in three places and wounded the observer in the side. The machine was smashed to pieces and a little black-and-tan dog which was with the observer (a captain) was also killed. The observer escaped death, although the machine fell about 9.000 feet. The pilot was horribly mutilated. I am sending you herewith a piece of the fabric from the Hun machine. This was put on by the Germans. I've got some other souvenirs, which I will send along later, when the opportunity crops up. I also send along a cheque which you might cash for me, please, and give the 'splosh' to Mrs. E., who will send me some things out, as arranged. Some films for the cam., etc.

No more now, old boy. My boots will be wanting renewal very soon, and I want some shoes for the *seaside* almost at once. Write soon.

Yours,
P."

The "special work" which he refers to in this letter concerned the enemy artillery co-operation machines. Our infantry and artillerymen used to get very worried whenever a solitary German peeped over our lines, and in order to keep them in a good humour, the R.F.C. decided to have special fighting machines at hand to shoot down or drive away the enemy. It was found that the best way of combating the enemy's activities during this period was by having an Advance Landing-ground within easy striking distance of the lines. It was while working from these advance landing-grounds that Mannock caught the three victims which he destroyed on our side of the lines.

Another letter to Eyles gives an idea of the fighting in which he was engaged:

"SAME PLACE,
ONLY HOTTER.
17.7.17.

D.J.,

It's horribly hot out here, almost as bad as little old Turkey. And the new push has commenced and we helped it on by bringing down 4 Huns in one morning. The G.O.C. Army congratulated us by special telegram. We've had bags of aerial scraps, and I am getting quite a seasoned warrior. I acted as Flight-Commander for a week while the Captain was ill in hospital.

I was out with a patrol four days ago and we had a scrap with 3 Huns. Two of us dived on them and my chum got shot in the leg. He flew back to his own aerodrome (27 miles) landed safely and went direct to hospital. Stout man.

If I described to you all the battles we've had, I'd be writing for a week and not tell you half. I expect to get ten days' leave in another month's time, and shall run along to little old W'boro'—on condition that Mrs. Brown doesn't abuse me too much! Anyhow, I have another month to live yet before talking of leave. In the meantime I will try and get some more pieces of prop. for you.

Love to Derek, regards to the 'Missus.'

Yours,

P."

His diary records the fight with the two-seater:

20.7.17.—After over a month of negligence and laziness, I again turn to the diary.

Lots of things, interesting and otherwise, have taken place since my last entry. We've lost poor old Davis (some weeks ago now) over the lines.

Walder and Blaxland have gone home, and new pilots have arrived. Capt. Keen and Godfrey have both won the M.C. for stunt work and Huns, and Bond has won an extra bar to his Cross. Fights galore and thrilling escapes. The King paid a visit to the squadron and was of course pleased with everything he saw.

Went over the lines a few mornings ago with Hall and Crole. Very cloudy and misty. Ran into 7 or 8 Huns south and east of Douai. Had an exciting 20 minutes playing hide and seek with them, and noticed a new type of enemy machine. Crole lost us on the return journey and didn't report until late in the day. I thought he had gone under. Pleased to hear that he was O.K. He landed at Amiens, having lost his way.

Had the good fortune to bring a Hun two-seater down in our lines a few days ago. Luckily, my first few shots killed the pilot and wounded the observer (a Captain) besides breaking his gun. The bus crashed south of Avion. I hurried out at the first opportunity and found the observer being tended by the local M.O., and I gathered a few souvenirs, although the infantry had the first pick. The machine was completely smashed, and rather interesting also was the little black-and-tan terrier—dead—in the observer's seat. I felt exactly like a murderer. The journey to the trenches was rather nauseating—dead men's legs sticking through the sides with puttees and boots still on—bits of bones and skulls with the hair peeling off, and tons of equipment and clothing lying about. This sort of thing, together with the strong grave-yard stench and the dead and mangled body of the pilot (an N.C.O.), combined to upset me for days. I got another Hun the next morning a little further east. He went down on the other side though. An hour later, I got right over another two-seater, but held my fire a fraction too long, with the result that I had to bank away to prevent collision. Turned again and fired 40 or 50 rounds into him, and he steered straight for Douai in a dead line. Probably wounded or the engine hit. I did feel mad.

The next morning, I went over the lines and got on top of

a Hun well east, when a tappet rod on my engine broke—ripped the cowling off, and I had to glide down from 15,000 without an engine, absolutely helpless. Luckily the Hun didn't follow or didn't see. I landed on our side, in a field of tall corn, and promptly turned over. Goodbye bus. Yesterday evening I fired a drum of ammunition into one of our own machines south of Lens. The old bus was being "Archied" by our own guns, and being very dark (9.0 p.m.) I couldn't distinguish the markings. Luckily no damage was done. Not much of a compliment to my shooting.

This morning we went out north as far as Armentières, Keen leading a 6 patrol. Ran into three of the finest Hun pilots I ever wish to meet. Had quite an exciting and enjoyable 10 minutes' scrap. These Huns were artists. Do what I would, I couldn't get a line on them, and it was 6 against 3.

Eventually they drew off, apparently none the worse for the encounter. I shall always maintain an unsullied admiration for those Huns. The aircraft battery people reported the battle as one of the most splendid exhibitions of tactics they had ever seen. We did nothing but swear. Likewise the CO.

I hear officially yesterday that I have been awarded the M.C.

Met young Buck of the R.E. Sigs. a few days ago. He's at the Corps H.Q. here. Brings back old times.

Ran down to Arras to try and see Gent. Just a day late, as he had left with the division the day before, for the north—or south, so I wrote him.

On the 22nd, Mannock was officially awarded the Military Cross, promoted to Temporary Captain, and made a Flight-Commander. His entry regarding the M.C. is another example of his modesty, for although he knows his diary is private, he does not go into ecstasies over the award. He was proud of being awarded decorations, but he treated them as quite impersonal, and in confirmation of this statement it is only necessary to point out that he had not applied to receive any of them at the time of his death, although he had ample opportunity of doing so whilst home on leave. "I'm fighting for a Cause, not decorations," he often told his comrades. And they believed him. Bond, writing of the award, said: "He is absolutely without fear and does his job always."

The citation in the *London Gazette* in recording the award read:

"In the course of many combats, he has driven off a large number of enemy machines, and has forced down three balloons, showing a very fine offensive spirit and great fearlessness in attacking the enemy at close range and low altitudes under heavy fire from the ground."

A letter to Eyles further indicates his modesty:

"SAME PLACE.
23.7.17.

DR. JIM,

Just a short note this time. Got yours of the 17th O.K.

Secret: Got the M.C., old boy, and made Captain and Flight-Commander on probation.

*Don't tell anyone* and still write me as the usual Lieutenant.

Had some more luck, only bad this time. Busted two buses during the last three days. Engines broke in two places in mid-air. Got down all right. Some pilot! The Old Man congratulated me. 'Damn good work, Mannock you did well!' Hurt myself a little bit on the second occasion, but not much: Send Mrs. E.'s letter on if she's not yet returned.

Bags of fighting in the air now. Every day. One day I had five scraps of my own and fired off 470 rounds of ammunition. Got one.

Lost some fellows during the last week. Rotten. Hit by 'Archie' direct. Went down in a spin from 7,000 feet.

No more now. I haven't sent off that parcel yet, but will do so within the next 24 hours. No time, old son.

Thanks for the French quotation. As you say, there is a good time coming.

Yours,
PAT."

In his enthusiasm for his work, he augmented the normal duty patrols with additional flights, usually accompanied by a comrade or two. Many miles over Hunland he would go hunting, and any enemy who offered himself as a reasonable target was unceremoniously attacked after a little preliminary manœuvring to get into a favourable position. It is an interesting and significant fact to note that most fighting pilots who were successful showed exceptional keenness for the job, and were not content to laze about between patrols, but busied themselves practising air gunnery and sighting guns, or carrying out extra patrols. Some pilots carried out extra patrols "just for fun," as in the case of those who looked on air fighting as "only a dangerous sport"; others, like Mannock, Guynemer, and most of the best French pilots, whose war outlook differed from that of their more light-hearted comrades, went out on additional patrols in order to "do some more killing." Mannock and Guynemer quivered like falcons poised ready for the attack at the sight of a German aeroplane, and they hovered over their opponent, watching and waiting for the joyous moment to swoop down and destroy it. When they failed in their mission, they flew back to the aerodrome to reload their guns, and swiftly they returned to hover once more over enemy territory like sentinels of the sky.

War weariness causes him to ignore his diary; continuous high flying made him very sleepy and lethargic, and the desire for writing ceased. Consequently we have to jump a month before we come to his next entry. In the meantime he has had several thrilling and successful combats. Among these were two notable ones: the first, when he led his Flight on July 28th on to a formation of highly coloured Albatross scouts, and gave a simultaneous taste of his mettle as a leader to both his Flight and the enemy; he surprised the Albatrosses by attacking them from the east when over Henin-Liétard, and forced them down from 10,000 to 2,000 feet, bowling one over himself on the way. The second interesting fight concerns an Albatross Scout which he spotted attacking one of our balloons. He was standing-by at an Advanced Landing-ground and promptly took to the air and shot it down in our lines after an exciting duel and before it had succeeded in its mission. His combat report reads:

### Narrative

"Hostile machine observed at 3.10 p.m. crossing our lines south of Thelus.

E.A. attempted to attack our balloon west of that point and descended to low altitudes for that purpose. Nieuport engaged E.A. at approximately 1,000 feet over Neuville St. Vaast and fired 70 rounds during the course of a close combat. The hostile machine was observed to be hit, a glow of fire appearing in the nacelle, and glided down under reasonable capable control south and east of Petit Vimy, landing down wind and turning over on touching the ground. Prisoner: Lieut, von Bartrap, sustained fracture of left arm and flesh wounds in right arm and leg, and was taken to hospital immediately on landing. Machine was in very good condition, although upside down, but was unfortunately affected by eventual hostile gun fire."

This victory has a significance, for the reason that it makes one wonder how many victories Mannock would have won had he been able to meet enemies every day on his own side of the lines. This is the second German that he had been able to engage over our territory, and he made no mistake about shooting him down. There is every reason to believe that the records of other aces (most certainly Germans') would have paled into insignificance when placed alongside Mannock's. While shooting down these machines, he displayed the qualities of the great air fighter—skill in manœuvre, the instinct for taking the enemy at a disadvantage and straight shooting. He now proved his ability to destroy enemies, provided he could force them to fight.

With his personal victories mounting in number, his popularity in the squadron as a leader increased rapidly, and pilots (even those who were his detractors) were anxious to follow him on patrols. Their sluggish mentalities awoke, and they realised that the new pilot who appeared to be wasting time practising air firing and fought with caution was, after all, apparently only following a preconceived plan of progress. After months of tedious and careful practice, positive results were beginning to justify the course he had adopted. Since he became a Flight-Commander, the pilots in his Flight found it a pleasure to follow him on patrols. He attacked with superb skill, never for a moment losing his head, even under the most trying circumstances. His presence inspired confidence, and made his comrades courageous, often in spite of themselves. He proved that he had all the qualities of a great leader, and with his successes mounting, the *moral* of his pilots rose like that of soldiers commanded by successful generals. And in the same way, as great generals depend for success on hard thinking and careful calculation, so did Mannock's tactics depend upon the preparatory discipline he had grounded himself in, aided by the Goddess of Fortune. It was for the same reason as that to which Napoleon attributed his famous successes: "If I always appear to be prepared," he said, "it is because before entering on an undertaking I have meditated for long and have foreseen what may occur. It is not genius—it is reflection and meditation."

On August 1st, he found time to write to Eyles:

"SAME PLACE,
*August 1st,* '17.
Raining like H—l.

DEAR JIM,

Received yours of the 28th today, and your previous one yesterday. Thanks for your congrats. I have been decorated with the M.C. officially, and have also been made a Flight-Commander (acting). This means that I get my captaincy in about another fortnight or three weeks—if I live long enough.

*THE AUTHOR, 1918.*

FAMOUS GERMAN AIR FIGHTERS AND "MR." FOKKER
*Top Row:* Myn Heir Fokker. Capt. Ernst Udet.
Hpt. Ritter Eduard von Schleich. *Centre:* Baron Manfred Freiherr
von Richthofen. *Bottom Row:* Lieut. Max Immelmann. Capt. Oswald Boelcke.
Lieut. Werner Voss.

*BALLOON STRAFFING*
*From the painting by Geoffrey Watson.*

FAMOUS BRITISH AIR FIGHTERS
*Top Row:* W/Cdr. Stewart Maxwell. G/Capt. LW.B. Rees, V.C.
Sq. Ldr. Mulholland. *Centre:* Major Hawker, V.C. *Bottom Row:* Major
"Zulu" Lloyd. Capt. Windsor. Lieut. C.B.R. MacDonald.
W/Cdr.B.E. Baker.

FAMOUS BRITISH AIR FIGHTERS
*Top Row:* Gen. Sir H.A. van Ryneveld. Capt Rhys-David.
Air-Vice-Marshal C. Longcroft. *Centre:* Capt Albert Ball, V.C.
*Bottom Row:* Flight-Lieut. Kinkead. Col. Keith L. Caldwell.
Lieut.-Col. Louis Strange.

H.M. THE KING CHATTING TO PILOTS OF No. 74 SQUADRON
*Roxburgh-Smith, the Author, and Carlin (in slacks)*
*The group includes General Plumer, General Horne, and*
*Brig-General Webb-Bowen (commanding 2nd Brigade, RAF).*

*FAMOUS BRITISH AIR FIGHTERS*
*Top Row: G/Capt. F. Sowrey. Capt. Beauchamp-Proctor, V.C.*
*Colonel Barker, V.C. Centre: Major J.B. McCudden, V.C. Bottom Row:*
*W/Cdr. G.H. Bowman. Major C.M. Corwe. Major Dallas.*

FAMOUS FRENCH AIR FIGHTERS
*Top Row:* Capt. Georges Guynemer. Lieut. Charles Nungessor.
Lieut. Dormé. *Bottom Row:* Lieut. Georges Madon. Capt Foncke.
Capt. Coppens.

VOSS'S LAST FIGHT
From the painting by Geoffrey Watson.

*THE AUTHOR.*

I saw Archie Reeves a few days ago over at his place. He has also got his M.C. for good and stout work, and is also in charge of a Flight. We very often go up and protect his machines when they are on the lines spotting for our artillery. Great fun it is diving all around and under and over his heavy slow old buses. He wants very much to get into a scout squadron. He is a very good pilot.

Plenty of scrapping in the air now. Every day without fail. Three of us went slap into 9 Hun machines a few mornings ago and had a glorious 'shemozzle.' They gave us a hell of a time, although we held our own. I made the old bus do some horrible things on that occasion. Talk about Hucks on the little old Caudron. Nothing like it. I believe the whole front from Lens to Arras was looking at us. They hopped it in the end, and I hadn't a bullet-hole anywhere on the machine. They set fire to one of my chum's planes, but it went out after a few minutes and he carried on. Another bullet went less than an inch from his head, cutting through his coat collar! Some joy that was! I shall never forget it.

I sent the parcel off to you yesterday. Pilots' boots which belonged to the dead pilot. Goggles also belonged to him. The cigarette-holder and case was given to me by the Captain Observer. The piece of fabric with the number on it is from the Hun two-seater. The bayonet is one I pulled out of the body of a dead Hun who was lying near the crashed bus. It is one of our own bayonets. I had to crawl out on my stomach to get it and there was not much cover. The other little brown packet is a field dressing carried by the Hun observer for dressing wounds when in the air. I got it from the crashed bus. I have several other things which I cannot send home, they will do later.

That blooming old swab Archie Reeves has just blown over to see me (really to get a drink). He is in the pink and waiting for us to bring down some of his pet balloons! I shall want some more boots very soon—within the next week—for work here.

Mrs. E.'s parcel came to hand. Thank her for me, only tell her to send me anything but what I ask. Really she is very kind. I hope she has enough left over to buy a packet of hairpins or a hair net. Glad to hear that Derek is in good health. Cheerio.

Yours,<br>PAT."

On the 15th he sent an Albatross down out of control, and two days later crashed one two-seater and chased another as far as Douai, when he had to return to our lines owing to engine trouble. His next entry reads:

19.8.17.—Almost a month since my last note. True laziness. Things have happened. Plenty of scrapping in the air, and much glory. Brought my ninth Hun down yesterday morning.

Had a splendid fight with a single-seater Albatross Scout last week on our side of the lines, and got him down. He proved to be Lieut. von Bartrap, Iron Cross, and had been flying for 18 months. He came over for one of our balloons—near Neuville St. Vaast—and I cut him off going back. He didn't get the balloon either. The scrap took place at 1,000 feet up, well within view of the whole front. And the cheers! It took me five minutes to get him to go down, and I had to shoot him before he would land. I was very pleased that I did not kill him. Right arm broken by a bullet, left arm and left leg deep flesh wounds. His machine—a beauty, just issued (June 1/17) with a 220-h.p. Mercedes engine, all black with crosses picked out in white lines—turned over on landing and was damaged. Two machine guns with 1,000 rounds of ammunition against my single Lewis and 300 rounds! I went up to the trenches to salve the bus later, and had a great ovation from everyone. Even Generals congratulated me. He didn't hit me once.

Brought three Huns down during the Lens push. Great luck.

Ran into my old friend the "purple man" again a few weeks ago.

No luck. He's a marvel. For ten minutes I was 300 feet above him, and he manœuvred so cleverly that I was unable to get my gun on him once. He got away in the end.

Congratulated yesterday by General Home, G.O.C. Corps.

Went up this morning at 5.00 a.m. (in the dark) and only 1,000 feet above the trenches to try and trap the early birds. Nothing doing. Climbed to 18,000 feet eventually, and whilst over Sallaumines, my petrol pipe broke. Landed on Advance Landing-ground without mishap. A peach of a landing!

Poor old Pender is missing since Wednesday, also is Cullen. I hope both are all right. Poor old Bond is gone and I see they have awarded him a posthumous D.S.O. Cold comfort!

My nerves seem better lately, for which I am glad.

Engine failures and aerodrome crashes were again dogging his flights, and, as must be expected, he was eventually hurt, although not seriously. Pilots who learn to fly nowadays do not have to worry about forced landings as the war pilot was forced to, and consequently the mere strain of flying is not so pronounced, particularly at night.

Crashes, forced landings, "Archie," and "dog fights" had by this time no terror for him, and he recorded them as only of casual interest, and no longer in a manner signifying danger or affecting his nerves and *moral*. The shadow of Mannock, the victorious air fighter, disappeared as the real figure showed itself at last in clear outline.

31.8.17.—Rather a long time since my last entry. We've had some bad weather just recently, and plenty of spare time, so I have no excuse for my laxity. Had plenty of fighting and many mishaps. On the 19th (evening), my engine gave out again at 16,000 feet (the second time during that day), and I managed to reach our lines only to crash the old bus and my head as well. Felt rather rocky for a bit, but soon got over it. On the 22nd, three of us met a bunch of Huns east of Lens— 5 above us and 7 below. I thought we were in for a rough time, but the cowards didn't attack us. This sort of thing just proves to us how much on top of them we really are, and does a wonderful lot of *moral* good to our new pilots (I had one with me that morning). On the same evening, I took a big patrol (10 machines) well over the lines, with orders to visit 5 Hun aerodromes. We met trouble half-way through the programme in the shape of 7 Huns coming home east. I saw them first and had first blood. Got a lovely burst into the first machine from about 25 yards range. He immediately went over on his side and went down in a beautiful wide spiral. I hadn't time to observe him hit mother earth, as things were happening. A glorious mix-up for about two minutes. One of my boys got another one down, and they got poor old Kennedy. We finished up by driving them to ground to the safety of their anti-aircraft guns, but we ought to have got the lot. It was really a disappointing show.

During the last few weeks, we have been issued with a new type Nieuport machine. The tail-plane and rudder are shaped very like a Hun's scout, also the body is fish-shaped. These similarities are a source of great concern to our other machines in the air, as we are often mistaken for Huns, and consequently get fired at.

The boys have rigged up the two top wings of my Albatross, down in the flight hangar, with my name and the date and place at which the machine was brought down painted on. Mighty proud they are of the trophy. So am I really!

Three American paper men came to visit us the other day, and the C.O. insisted on my telling the story of the fight. They were frightfully interested, and took voluminous notes, and begged for pieces of the wing as mementoes. I am having a model of the Hun made out of the woodwork of one of the wings.

Just as there is a "knack" in bird-shooting, so there is a "knack" in air-firing. To some it comes easily, and to others not at all. I am satisfied that good shooting in the air can never be achieved by practice alone (practice is of course of vital importance) ; it is necessary to have the "knack," which is a precious gift of the gods. It was this gift which lifted the star air fighter out of the groove of mediocrity. And it is for this reason that Mannock did not agree with the award of decorations merely for downing Huns, a view with which many other successful fighters heartily agreed.

From now on the Goddess of Marksmanship showered her favours upon him, and he proceeded to shoot down the enemy at intervals, the frequency depending on their willingness to fight. And it was only their timidity which prevented him piling up his score to unchallengeable heights. Unfortunately, the enemy fighters, who were faster and always flying over their own territory, often proved too elusive to be drawn into combat; and so he had to transfer his attentions to the unprotected two-seaters. One of this family he caught over our lines and promptly shot it down in flames; again proving his outstanding ability to destroy any enemy when the opportunity reasonably offered itself.

5.9.17.—The end of a fairly hard day. Went over to Petit Vimy and Thelus in a side-car this morning in an endeavour to pick up some relics of the last victims, downed yesterday afternoon in flames. Regret that nothing remained of the machine. I met this unfortunate D.F.W. at about 10,000 feet over Avion coming south-west, and I was travelling south-east. I couldn't recognise the black crosses readily (he was about 300 yards away and about 500 feet above me), so I turned my tail towards him and went in the same direction, thinking that if he were British he wouldn't take any notice of me, and if a Hun I felt sure he would put his nose down and have a shot (thinking I hadn't seen him). The ruse worked beautifully. His nose went (pointing at me), and I immediately whipped round, dived and "zoomed" up behind him, before you could say "knife." He tried to turn, but he was much too slow for the Nieuport. I got in about 50 rounds in short bursts whilst on the turn and he went down in flames, pieces of wing and tail, etc., dropping away from the wreck. It was a horrible sight and made me feel sick. He fell down in our lines, and I followed to the ground, although I didn't land. The boys gave me a great ovation.

The same evening I got another one down east of Lens, confirmed by the A.A. people. Capt. Keen had previously engaged it, but broke off combat in order to renew ammunition drum. I got quite close up and let him have a full drum, and he went nose-down east. Owing to the haze, I couldn't see him crash.

Prior to that—at 9.40 a.m. I had a beautiful running fight with another two-seater at 17,000 feet, from Bruay to east of Lens. This one got away, notwithstanding the fact that I fired nearly 300 rounds at close range. I saw the observer's head and arm lying over the side of the machine—he was dead apparently—but the pilot seemed to be all right. He deserved to get away really, as he must have been a brave Hun. This fight was watched from the Advance Landing-ground by the mechanics and caused great excitement. Anyhow, two in one day is not bad work, and I was today congratulated by the Colonel.

Had a scrap this evening with 6 Hun scouts E. of Lens, but had to retire early owing to gun trouble.

This is the first gun trouble I've had for months.

The C.O. bet me to-night 10 to 1 that I don't bring down a two-seater to-morrow (if fine) on this side of the lines. I've taken him on, so I am going all out to-morrow to win my bet.

This entry was unfortunately his last, and it is full of interest.

We see our hero getting well into his stride along the rocky road of fame as a successful air fighter, his star each day increasing in brilliance.

In shooting down the two-seater he displayed cunning as

well as good flying and shooting. This was the first of many machines that he shot down in flames, and the horrible sight as the flaming wreck floated and disintegrated in the air sickened him, as it sickened most airmen the first time that they were witness to this most fearsome form of human destruction. A burning machine is a glorious and yet a most revolting sight to the victor; but there is no question as to the completeness of the victory. To watch a machine burst into flames after its petrol tanks have been pierced by incendiary bullets is a ghastly, hypnotising sight. At first a tiny flame peeps out of the tank as if almost ashamed of what it is about to do; then it gets bigger and bigger as it licks its way along the length and breadth of the machine; and finally, all that can be seen is a large ball of fire enveloping in a terrifying embrace what was a few minutes before a beautiful bird of wood and metal flown by a probably virtuous youth who loved flying and life. After the wreck has long reached the ground, a coiling tell-tale trail of ominous black greasy smoke mounts high in the sky as a disappearing monument of heroism and self-sacrifice.

This particular victory had an interesting sequel. A few months later a note was dropped by a German airman and picked up by our infantry. It read:

"To THE BRITISH FLYING CORPS.
The 4th September I lost my friend Fritz Frech He fell between Vimy and Lievin. His respectable and unlucky parents beg you to give any news of his fate. Is he dead? At what place found he his last rest? Please to throw several letters, that we may found one. Thanking before,

His friend,
K.L.

*P.S.*—If it is possible, send a letter to the parents: Mr. Frech, Königsberg i. Pr. Vord Vorstadt 48/52."

Mannock received this letter while on leave in England, and wrote to the parents as requested. He felt compassion for the stricken parents in their loss, so he told his mother.

What little chivalry there was left in modern warfare was shown by the Knightly ones of the Air, by the dropping of notes asking for information about prisoners, as in this case. Much balderdash, however, has been talked and written about chivalry in its broadest sense as far as it affected air warfare, and in particular air fighting. Personally, I think it has been grossly exaggerated, for I doubt if any genuine chivalry was ever shown by rival airmen during combat. A gladiatorial farewell of hand-waving, resembling the parting of lovers, as has often been alleged, was altogether an inconsistent ending to a fight of life and death when fear had taken temporary command of the will and the only desire of the body was to leave the presence of the enemy as quickly as possible, when the ammunition had been exhausted or the guns had jammed. That a spirit of good fellowship was often shown when an airman was taken prisoner is admitted, and it was only natural, because of the outlook of many airmen who regarded air fighting as a cheerful if somewhat dangerous sport. To treat a captured and defeated rival generously was considered to be a part of the game. Further, the normal risks of flying bred a common spirit of comradeship among those who braved the perils of the air. Fighting airmen on the whole regarded each other with a peculiar mixture of hatred and personal esteem. It was not a strange scene in a British or German mess to see pilots toasting the health of some opponent who, although hated for the cause for which he was fighting, was greatly admired for his valorous deeds. When the Royal Flying Corps heard, for instance, of the death of the great Oswald Boelcke, who was much admired and respected because of his achievements and his kindness to prisoners, the R.F.C. dropped a wreath on the enemy side to be placed upon his grave as a mark of esteem. I cannot, however, imagine any British pilot allowing chivalry to interfere with the destruction of Boelcke in the air, nor can I believe that any Britisher had his life saved in an air fight because an enemy allowed chivalry to interfere with his duty.

Unable to find an enemy on his side of the lines, Mannock lost his bet to the C.O., but whilst patrolling the next day at 14,000 feet east of Lens, he spotted Lieutenant Harrison of his squadron attacking a two-seater at 8,000 feet over the Métallurgique Works. Harrison was in turn being attacked by two Albatrosses, one of which was sitting close on his tail. He dived to his comrade's rescue and poured a drum into the Albatross, which immediately dived steeply away. It was later reported by C Battery Anti-Aircraft to have forced-landed apparently under control near the trenches. This fight is officially recorded as a "driven-down" victory, but it looks as if the Albatross engine was put out of action or the pilot was wounded, since otherwise there would seem to be no reason for the forced landing.

From now on, Mannock devoted his spare time to training his Flight in air gunnery and flight tactics. On actual patrols, his genius for leadership emphasised itself as time went on: his Flight was never attacked by surprise, although he frequently mystified and surprised the enemy.

On October 14th he was awarded a bar to his Military Cross. The citation in the Gazette reads:

"He has destroyed several hostile machines and driven others down out of control. On one occasion he attacked a formation of five enemy aircraft single-handed and shot one down out of control. On another occasion while engaged with an enemy machine, he was attacked by two others, one of which he forced to the ground. He has consistently shown great courage and initiative."

He wrote to Eyles to inform him of the "news":

"SAME ADDRESS.
14.9.17.

DEAR JIM,
Your last letter was on the 28th ulto., I think. Sorry I've been remiss in replying thereto, The snaps are all O.K. You all look quite well. I have not sent that souvenir parcel on because I can't. See. Plenty of very valuable stuff to get across, and I cannot trust the gentle postmen. The things might get broken. Got another one down in flames this side of the line on the 4th inst. Horrible sight. Came down from 9,000 feet with streams of fire and smoke behind him. Not many souvenirs from that one. Two more in the last 10 days, making 13½ in all. I'll explain the half when I come over on leave (some time during the first week in 'October').

Sorry to hear of all the 'dud' pilots at home. They should first test the engine.

Very nearly got it in the neck a few days ago. Two Hun scouts caught me napping, but they were rotten bad shots. May have better luck next time. Archie Reeves has gone home on leave, and is in W'boro' by now, so have a chat with him and he'll tell you probably some of the news.

Derek looks well, I'm glad to see, and I hope the Missus is still keeping fit. I am glad also that all the boys think of me occasionally. It cheers one up so. Good old Parrot!

Just been called to the telephone. News. Just been awarded a bar to the M.C.

Must leave now, as the General wants a machine.

Love to all,
PAT."

In early October he enjoyed his second spell of leave; and on returning to his squadron he found the enemy not only scarcer but more timid than ever. His bag of Huns consequently progressed at a depressingly tedious rate, and we find him writing to Eyles that "business is very slow since I returned from leave, and nothing doing in the Way of increasing the total."

The Battle of Cambrai, which commenced on November 20th, when our tanks made their first surprise attack in massed formation and crushed big gaps through the enemy's wire, and then roamed about behind the enemy's lines attacking targets which obstructed their paths, added to the excitement of the squadron routine work, for they were given a new type of duty, commonly known in the R.F.C. as "ground-strafing." This duty consisted of bombing and attacking with machine-gun fire enemy ground forces from the height of tree-tops; it was a very dangerous duty, and casualties were heavy, but our pilots carried it out with the utmost vigour and determination, as they felt they were really helping our tired troops on the ground to overcome the opposition. For good work which Mannock carried out during the battle, he received a mention from the G.O.C., R.F.C.

By the first week in December, the squadron had been re-equipped with the S.E.5a, which was a single-seater biplane armed with a Vickers gun, firing through the propeller, and a Lewis gun mounted on the centre section like the Nieuport. It had a speed of about 125 m.p.h. near the ground, and was consequently faster than the Albatross. It was heavier on controls and more sluggish on turns than the Nieuport, but its extra speed, armament, and strength made it into a vastly superior fighting machine, especially above 15,000 feet. And as far as my investigations go, it was the most feared and respected of all our war machines by the enemy. The result of this change of machines in the squadron caused Mannock to write on December 9th: "We chase the Huns out of the sky with our new bus. They won't stand up to it at all. Rather rotten luck." A week later he wrote: "Had a few (very few) scraps since last leave, but my guns have let me down badly. Had one a few days ago, and drove an Albatross down from 11,000 feet to 3,000 feet, then my guns jammed and he got away. Very annoying!"

Although the guns were lubricated with anti-freezing oil, it was noticeable that stoppages were more frequent during the winter than the summer months. Such failures were most annoying and aggravating; for often the pilot took great risks in order to attack a German at a low height, and many miles over his lines. To find when he had got into a favourable position to destroy his enemy that his guns did not respond to the pressure on the triggers, he felt was the act of a Judas. Many pilots, of course, lost their lives or were taken prisoners as a result of such circumstances.

On January 1st, 1918, he won his last victory in the squadron, when he destroyed a two-seater by shooting it to pieces. This was the twentieth combat report which he submitted for official recognition, and his characteristic tendency to understate rather than exaggerate his claims is proved by the fact that he only claimed six as having been destroyed. Knowing his capabilities as we do by the expeditious and definite manner in which he destroyed the only aircraft which he came across on our side of the lines, it is fair to assume that at least twenty enemies were rendered *hors de combat*. It is now known that there were several other victories which he might have justly claimed, but his selflessness and modesty combined prevented him from doing so.

The next day he returned to England for a well-deserved rest. His departure was regretted by the whole squadron, for he was a tremendous favourite in the Mess, of which he was the life and soul, while the squadron concerts depended for their success upon his enthusiasm.

W. G. Soltau, a Canadian, who was a close friend of Mannock's while in No. 40 Squadron, relates:

"I also recollect some small incidents of his great popularity among men, both mechanics and other ranks, as well as junior officers. How he made them sing sometimes during the concerts and sing-songs, and how they always responded to his leadership in all things! ... In January 1918, I was ordered to the south of France for a rest, and at the same time Mannock was ordered back to England. Four of us decided to make the trip to Boulogne in one car, Mannock, McCudden, McElroy, and myself. I am the only one left of the merry party—all three flying men were eventually killed with a large number of Huns to their credit.... As we left No. 40 Squadron, the car was loudly cheered by the officers outside the mess, and we found the road lined with cheering mechanics. I then realised Mannock's influence over the men.... Mannock was one of the most lovable men I have ever known, always cheery, witty, courteous, daring, brave, and resourceful. He personified the best type of Irishman.... On the way to Boulogne we stopped at a hospital, as there was an Irish sister, named Murphy, who wanted to say au revoir to Mick. His popularity in this Sister's mess staggered us as much as it embarrassed him."

When Mannock left the squadron, the Commanding Officer recorded his services as a Flight-Commander in these terms:

"His leadership and general ability will never be forgotten by those who had the good fortune to serve under him."

# IV

# *Second Tour of Duty in France With Nos. 74 and 85 Squadrons*

Mannock was home exactly three months before he was allowed to return to the war. This long rest proved its value, for he returned to the fray with such a determined spirit of offence that his comrades marvelled at his fierceness and keenness to kill Huns, whilst his enemies must have wondered what fiery dragon had arrived over Flanders, for he traversed the Ypres Salient like a meteor, leaving a trail of flaming, smouldering wreckage.

After a month's leave, he was posted to the Wireless Experimental Establishment at Biggin Hill. From here, on February 4th, he wrote to Eyles, "I don't think I shall be able to remain satisfied at this delightful spot, and I am trying to get out to France as soon as I can." A week later he wrote:

"Just got my instructions. As you know, I have been trying very hard to get out to France again. Well, I have been posted to No. 74 Training Squadron at London Colney, and we are proceeding overseas next month. Hooray! I feel horribly glad about it. We shall be flying the same machines as I flew in No. 40 Squadron—S.E.5S."

His posting from Biggin Hill came about in rather an interesting manner. Eyles relates how one day, in the R.F.C. Club, Mannock happened to meet General Henderson:

"The General asked Mannock how long he had been home. Mannock replied, 'A month too long, sir.' The General informed him that he would have to remain at home for at least a couple of months, if not more. Mannock then rather staggered the General by saying, 'If I can't get back to France soon with permission, I shall return without permission. I shall take a machine out of the hangar one day and fly back to my old squadron.' Whereupon the General replied with a twinkle in his eye, 'If you do that, Mannock, you will be court-martialled and shot.' Whereupon Mannock promptly replied, 'Death is better than dishonour, sir! 'General Henderson, taken aback by this swift repartee, laughed out loudly and said, 'You win, Mannock, I will see what can be done.' The conversation then changed to air raids. Mannock wanted permission to have 'a go' at night, flying an S.E.5 against the Gothas. Henderson, however, thought that the S.E. was too difficult to land by night."

I first met Mannock when he arrived at London Colney. His tall, lean figure; his weather-beaten face with its deep-set Celtic blue eyes; his unruly dark-brown hair; his modesty in dress and manner appealed to me, and immediately, like all the other pupils, I came under his spell. He had a dominating personality, which radiated itself on all those around. Whatever he did or said compelled attention. It was obvious that he was a born leader of men.

When he gave lectures on air fighting they were delicious dishes of the offensive spirit. He was a forceful, eloquent speaker, who had the gift of compelling attention. He had the ability to convince the poorest and most inoffensive of pilots that they could knock hell out of the best Hun. From his experience he gave valuable details of air fighting, without discussing the nerve-wracking combat, and he instilled into his listeners an offensive spirit which stood them in good stead when they had to pass the acid test of fighting.

I well remember his first lecture on single-seater fighting. He commenced and ended it with a motto which he had invented, and to which he religiously adhered. "Gentlemen," he said, "always above; seldom on the same level; never underneath."

No. 74 Squadron lived up to this motto, and the fact that in eight months of war its record of one hundred and forty enemy machines destroyed and another ninety sent down apparently out of control, against a loss of fifteen killed and five prisoners of war, appears to justify Mannock's claim to its infallibility.

During one of his lectures, he told us that the enemy had produced a good Fokker triplane fighter, and that this machine was much superior in manœuvrability to the aircraft with which we were equipped, the S.E.5, but that the S.E. was much faster. Furthermore, the triplane was not very strong, and several had broken up in the air owing to excessive diving speed, whereas the S.E. was stronger and delighted in a steep dive.

"When we get to the war," Mannock said, "don't ever attempt to dog-fight a Triplane on anything like equal terms as regards height, otherwise he will get on your tail, and stay there until he shoots you down. Take my advice, if you ever do get into such an unfortunate position, put your aircraft into a vertical bank, hold the stick tight into your stomach, keep your engine full on, and pray hard. When the Hun has got tired of trying to shoot you down from one position, he will try another. Here is your chance, and you'll have to snap it up with alacrity. As soon as your opponent commences to manœuvre for the next position you must put on full bottom rudder, do one and a half turns of a spin, and then run for home like hell, kicking your rudder hard from side to side in order to make the shooting more difficult for the enemy, but—still praying hard."

A short time later, on April 12th, about 06.30 hours, "C" Flight did its first offensive patrol over the area where the Portuguese were retreating; and as the whole of the enemy air force appeared to be massed to witness the occasion, "C" Flight was soon attacked. Eventually one pilot was cut off from the formation by a black Triplane, assisted by eight Pfalz. For fully ten minutes the triplane sat within fifty yards of the S.E.'s tail, firing short bursts at it, whilst the Pfalz dived, fired, and zoomed at intervals.

The S.E. pilot, however, remembered Mannock's advice, and put his "aircraft into a vertical bank, held the stick tight into his stomach, kept his engine full on, and prayed hard." The Triplane pilot, who was the leader of the enemy formation, from his tactics, was obviously an old hand at the game. By various tricks of the trade he tried to compel the S.E. pilot to get out of his vertical bank, as the bullets were obviously going behind him. The British pilot, however, kept cool, and stuck to Mannock's advice, and at no time did he think he was going to be shot down, although the staccato bark of the enemy's machine guns at so close a range did not increase his confidence. Eventually, as Mannock predicted, the enemy got fed up at his lack of success in the position which he was keeping in relation to the S.E., and decided to try another. Our pilot was anxiously awaiting this moment, and as soon as his opponent commenced to change position, he put on full bottom rudder, and whether he did one and a half turns of a spin or one hundred and a half he cannot say, but he does remember, so to speak, putting one foot on his throttle and the other foot on his joy stick, while "with his other two feet" he kicked the rudder from side to side. The enemy had given the S.E. fully 200 yards start before he spotted him running away. When he did, he and his comrades immediately opened fire and gave chase, and it was a joy to behold how that S.E. said "Good morning "to the outraged Huns.

When the pilot returned to his aerodrome, the S.E. was examined for bullet-holes, and none could be found. Mannock was proud of his pupil, and in an impromptu talk after breakfast he gave praise to him, and stressed the importance of not trying to fight a Triplane at a disadvantage, or to dive away from an enemy in a tight corner. Those who followed his advice lived to fight again.

This is one instance of the value of Mannock's lectures; dozens of others were equally instructive.

Lots of other useful advice was given in this way by him. He explained how to effect surprise by approaching the enemy from the east (the side he least expected) and how to utilise the sun's glare and clouds to achieve this end. Pilots must keep physically fit by exercise and by the moderate use of stimulants. Pilots must sight their own guns and practise as much as possible, as targets are usually fleeting. Pilots must practise spotting machines in the air and recognising them at long range, and every aeroplane must be treated as an enemy until it is certain it is not. Pilots must learn where the enemy's blind spots are—that is, the parts of their machines which obstruct the pilot's view. Scouts must be attacked from above and two-seaters from beneath their tails. Pilots must practise quick turns, as this manœuvre is more used than any other in a fight; practising stunting is a waste of time. Formation flying at twenty-five yards apart must be practised. Pilots must practise judging distances in the air, as they are very deceptive, just as objects across water are. Decoys must be guarded against—a single enemy is often a decoy—therefore the air above should be searched before attacking. If the day is sunny, machines should be turned with as little bank as possible, otherwise the sun glistening on the wings will give away their presence at a long range. Signal lights should not be fired except when absolutely necessary, as they attract attention. Pilots must keep turning in a dog-fight and never fly straight except when firing. Pilots must never, under any circumstances, dive away from an enemy, as he gives his opponent a non-deflection shot—bullets are faster than aeroplanes. Pilots must keep their eye on their watches during patrols, and on the direction and strength of the wind.

His fighting tactics, he told us, varied with circumstances. There were rarely two identical situations; enemy personnel, type of enemy aircraft, meteorological conditions, and the position of the enemy continually varied, and consequently, adjustment of tactics had to be made to suit the occasion. However, the main principle of his tactics remained the same: the enemy must be surprised and attacked at a `disadvantage, if possible with superior numbers, so that the initiative was with his patrol. To achieve this objective it was sometimes necessary, he said, to spend over half the time of the patrol manœuvring the enemy formation into an unfavourable position. Having got it there, pilots must dive to the attack with zest and must hold their fire until they get to within one hundred yards of their target: the closer the better. The combat must continue until the enemy has admitted his inferiority, by being shot down, or by running away.

He told us that he did not believe that it was possible to dictate hard-and-fast rules for combats. He considered that it would be pernicious to attempt to carry out attacks according to plan. Certain principles, he admitted, demanded respect, but even these were not absolute. They were not to be regarded as finger-points indicating the only path to be pursued, but rather as warnings of the dangers that generally follow certain courses of action. He based his tactics on rapid decisions. Mannock did not believe information or spear-head attacks. In the former case he considered that pilots would fear collision and so neglect their target: in the latter, he considered it a waste of personnel merely to allow the leader to do all the attacking.

Apart from this, young pilots should have as much individual fighting as possible, so that they would in time become leaders themselves. The theory that any pilot could become an efficient leader through flying practice only, without any experience of fighting, he contended, was a fallacy, and he supported his contention by examples of inefficient leaders who had been promoted by favouritism or seniority. For a leader to sacrifice a pilot's life through brainless attacks was to him an unforgivable sin: a pilot who followed an enemy down to earth he thought worthy of severe censure.

In matters of sport, Mannock would join in any game that was going. He revelled most in Rugger, although he was not an adept at the game, but he said that he preferred it chiefly because "he could lose his temper without losing his self-respect!"

As an after-dinner speaker, Mannock was very popular and accomplished. His fluency, wit, and sincerity of speech were most fascinating to listen to. Never a week passed but at some time or other he would delight us with a brief but sparkling impromptu speech on some topical subject. It may have been to congratulate some pilot on some worthy deed of valour; to lament the loss of a comrade; or to decry the social activities of certain aristocrats whom he considered would have been better employed on war work than having their photographs taken for the leading pictorial papers and soliciting popularity and fame at the expense of the wounded soldiers. Mannock always revelled in making speeches. At times he made them for the sheer amusement of his listeners, at other times he was quite serious.

"Mick" Mannock, as I knew him, had indeed an intriguingly complex nature. It fluctuated so. When he thought of or met an enemy, he was cruel and ruthless; when he was out with a party, or on most occasions in the Mess, he was full of boyish pranks and fun; when he considered that a person should be reproved, he was harsh and cynical, for he never spared his tongue in reproving anyone, although he never reproved without cause; when a person deserved praise, he was generous to a degree; if sympathy was called for, he was gentle and kind; when he was worried, he was depressed and morbid; but at all times he was unreservedly unselfish. In fact—typically Irish!

On March 1st, No. 74 Training Squadron ceased to exist, and from its personnel No. 74 Fighter Squadron was formed, under the command of Major A. S. Dore, D.S.O., M.C., a gallant officer who had seen much active service. There was tremendous keenness among the forty-odd instructors and pupils who were competing for the twenty vacancies in the new Squadron; and on the 7th, the Squadron was selected. The Flight-Commanders chosen were Captain Mannock, who was allotted "A" Flight; Captain W. E. Young, a pilot who had had fighting experience in the famous No. 19 Squadron at a time when it could boast of such redoubtable fighters as John Leacroft, Fred Sowrey, Oliver Bryson, Pat Huskinson, and Harvey Kelly, was given "B" Flight; Mannock's friend of Joyce Green days, Captain Meredith Thomas, who had just returned from a tour overseas with No. 41 Squadron, was given "C" Flight.

The chosen pilots were: "A" Flight—Lieutenant Roxburgh-Smith, one of the instructors; Lieutenant Dolan, an artillery officer who had won the M.C.; Lieutenant Hamer, who had had previous experience as a war pilot; Lieutenant Howe, a South African; Lieutenant Atkinson, and Lieutenant Clements, Canadians. "B" Flight—Lieutenant Kiddie, who had seen service in West Africa; Lieutenant Savage, a South African; Lieutenants Piggott, Richardson, Bright, and Stewart-Smith. "C" Flight—Lieutenant Giles, who had been badly wounded during the Somme Battle when serving in the Somerset Light Infantry and who had subsequently served as an observer in No. 43 Squadron when the machine he was flying in was badly damaged by "Archie"; Lieutenant Begbie, who had already done one tour in France as a pilot and claimed to be a distant cousin to Richthofen; Lieutenant Birch, one of the instructors; Lieutenant Skeddon, an American; and the author. Lieutenant Harry Coverdale, the famous English and Blackheath Rugby half-back, was the Gunnery officer; Lieutenant C. Mansfield, the equipment officer; and Lieutenant James VanIra, a Welsh-South African, the spare pilot.

The selection of the pilots could have been slightly improved upon here and there as the future proved, but on the whole the selectors may be well proud of their choice, for the Squadron passed the acid test of battle in a truly wonderful manner.

The chosen pilots were immediately attached to the Fighting School at Ayr, Scotland, for a course in air fighting. This School was commanded by the gallant Welsh V.C., Colonel L. W. B. Rees. Among the instructors were the famous Captain James McCudden, V.C., and Captain Maxwell, late of No. 56 Squadron; Captain Dover Atkinson, late of No. 29 Squadron; and the one-eyed Captain Foggin. The course consisted of the pupil being shown by the instructor what to do and what not to do during an air fight. It was an excellent course, and later its teaching saved the life of many a pilot on more than one occasion. During fighting practice pupils were encouraged to throw their machines about with abandon in order to gain the maximum confidence.

The course lasted one week, and when we arrived back at London Colney, we found a new Commanding Officer. We were all distressed at the departure of Major Dore, whose charm of manner and war record appealed to us. He relates how surprised and almost disgusted Mannock was when he informed him of his impending departure.

"Surely," said Mannock, "you don't really mean to say that you would rather stay at home on a staff job than be commanding this Fighting Squadron in France."

"But I am going to be promoted," replied Dore,

"What!" yelled Mannock, as he pulled his hair and jumped round the Mess, "that's worse than ever." It was only when

Dore pointed out to him how long he had been in France that he reverted to normal.

Another great loss to the Squadron was the departure of Captain Thomas, who, owing to his short period of rest in England, was compulsorily relieved by Captain W. C. Cairns, a pilot who had three Huns to his credit whilst serving with No. 19 Squadron.

Major Keith Caldwell, the new C.O., was a New Zealander from Auckland. He was about five feet eleven in height, heavily built, had jet-black unruly hair, swarthy complexion, deep-set blue eyes, a protruding chin, and a personality which expressed extreme determination. He was famed as a great fighter and a dashing patrol leader, a reputation which he built whilst fighting alongside Ball in No. 60 Squadron. He wore the purple and white ribbon of the Military Cross. His fame as an air fighter was such, that Colonel Jack Scott, an astute judge of a genuine air fighter— he being himself a brilliant exponent of the art—considered that Caldwell would have been the British ace of aces had he been capable of shooting straight, for he considered that none of our pilots had fought so many air fights as he had done for the number of times which he had been on patrol. "Grid" Caldwell commanded No. 74 Squadron throughout its war career, and he more than fulfilled expectations. As a straight, honest, hard-fighting air fighter, irrespective of results, he has had no peer. For sheer gallantry in the air no Victoria Cross has been won more truly than by this worthy son of New Zealand. To his personal example and encouragement Mannock owes much; in fact, he alone knew how much.

As soon as Caldwell (who had the sobriquet of "Grid," for by such a name he called all aeroplanes) took over command, he immediately commenced intensified training for the war. Apart from the daily practice of air fighting on a target in the Elstree reservoir and formation flying, he instituted lectures on air fighting which were given by himself and Mannock. These lectures proved of infinite value when we met the enemy. Whilst Mannock taught all about the tactics of air fighting, Caldwell instilled into us the spirit of comradeship and esprit de corps. In his final talk before the Squadron left London Colney for France, he expressed the view that he was certain we would be a very happy family, and that when we met the enemy each one would fight like hell, and that it must never be said that a pilot of No. 74 Squadron had ever failed to go to the rescue of a comrade irrespective of the odds. Finally, he told us that never must a patrol of his Squadron leave the ground late, and that at all times pilots must remember that they were playing for their Squadron and not for themselves. The subsequent result was that No. 74 developed into a Squadron with a Soul. And Mannock played no small part in achieving this happy state.

Mannock and Caldwell immediately became inseparable friends and they pulled one another's leg unmercifully; occasionally the leg-pulling revealed the grim humour of war, for often Mick would faithfully volunteer to describe Grid's descent in flames to his mother, not sparing any detail. In retaliation, Grid would bet Mick that he would be the first to "sizzle," and would give a demonstration of the noises that would emanate from Mannock's machine as it floated a burning mass to earth! It is strange, but ever since Mannock shot down his first machine in flames in our lines, he has unconsciously from time to time revealed how the ghastly sight affected him mentally. His continual references to flames, often jokingly, is a positive proof of this. And as time went on it developed into an obsession, and eventually it was obvious that he suffered mental torture from the effects of a premonition of death by being shot down in flames. In his diary he put this question to Cairns:

"What do you imagine would be your first conscious thought, in the event of your aeroplane being set on fire in mid-air?" The reply was: "My thoughts would be confused between whether I could put the fire out and what my fate was going to be." Mannock's reply to Cairns's answer was: "My reply would be—a bullet in my head."

And Mannock always carried a revolver in his machine in case of such a contingency arising.

His diary had many questions and answers which are of interest, as they reveal his thoughts. One to Caldwell reads:

"Tell me why you take a delight in fighting and beating the Hun in the air?" The reply was: "I think an air fight is quite the most thrilling sport there is; apart from doing one's duty, and in beating the Hun, one realises the same satisfaction as in winning a keenly contested game of tennis or golf."

A question to Mannock from Caldwell reads:

"Do you think that you can have your heart in France and England at the same time?" The answer was:

"Thank you, Major, I will acknowledge and accept your warning. There's a job to be done, an example to set, and above all, an atonement to make on my part. The least that

I can hope for, in my second venture, is to play again the good old game in the air."

To Captain Everard, our Adjutant, who was an Irish Guardsman, Mick put this question:

"What do you think of the average Irishman (excluding the Orangeman) as a pure fighter in comparison with any other European nationality, and why?" Everard replied: "Mick, darlin'—excluding the grim, determined stalwarts of Ulster, 250,000 strong before the declaration of war, fit to fight the fully trained continental troops according to The Times Military Correspondent's opinion early in 1914—the average Irishman, a mixture of Celtic and Norman blood, is essentially, under such a combination, not only a gifted but a natural fighter. 'Blood is blood and breed is breed and ever the twain will tell.' It is sometimes forgotten that the Irish are volunteers, not conscripts. *Cela va sans dire.*"

When Begbie was later shot down in flames, Mannock wrote in his diary: "I hope he blew out his brains first."

Towards the end of March, the Squadron were stamping their feet impatiently on the tarmac as they waited for the order to fly to the war, to assist their hard-pressed and gallant comrades who were exhibiting unparalleled bravery whilst resisting the avalanche of enemy hosts which had commenced on the 21st. These were depressing days, waiting to leave for the Great Adventure, which all were anxious to undertake. On the 27th the glad news was received and the Squadron flew as far as Goldhanger Aerodrome in Essex. From here Mannock wrote to Eyles:

"Ordered here at the last moment after all our baggage and transport had been despatched to France. Shall be here probably a week until they can find an aerodrome for us in France.

I suppose this big Hun attack has thrown them somewhat off their balance. Anyhow, I am sick of waiting and want to get out. There must be lots of fun out there now, in view of the scrap."

Actually our three days at Goldhanger were due to an air-raid scare, but we neither saw nor heard any enemies. Our brief stay in this cheerless spot was enlivened the night before we left by a little excitement caused by the great big chief of the village who objected to the Squadron singing some of the renowned R.F.C. songs in one of the hotels. Mannock resented the intrusion, and offered to throw out the "big noise" or give him a drink. The Arm of the Law fortunately saw the funny side of the offer and chose the drink.

The Squadron landed safely, with the exception of Lieutenant Jones and the Squadron mascot (a black puppy of doubtful pedigree), at St. Omer Aerodrome on the 31st. It moved the next day to Tetengham Aerodrome, near Dunkirk. Here it remained for a week, while pilots sighted and got their guns in fighting order by daily practice on targets which were floating in the sea near by. Line patrols were carried out to accustom pilots to the sight of trenches and anti-aircraft fire—which, by the way, was very good in this area, Lieutenant Jones's machine being written off the first time "C" Flight got within reach of the enemy's "Archie" over Nieuport.

The long-awaited German offensive was eventually launched against the British Front between St. Quentin and Cambrai at dawn on Thursday, March 21st. This sector was lightly held by Gough's Fifth Army with fourteen divisions against forty, and it was doomed to defeat because of inadequate defences and reserves. This sector was so lightly held because the British Front had been extended from St. Quentin to Barisis in order to shorten, and therefore strengthen, the French Front where the German attack was expected. By skilful use of the advantage which the possession of the interior lines gave Ludendorff in the St. Quentin-St. Gobain Salient, he massed troops in that angle without disclosing which side he was going to attack. He thus neutralised to a considerable extent the information obtained without much opposition from the enemy Air Force. Further, the transportation by night of large numbers of troops who were concealed in woods in the daytime also assisted him in his secret concentrations.

The attack was facilitated by the abnormally dry season, which reduced the strength of the water defences on the British right, and further, as on the first day of the Cambrai Battle, a favouring fog assisted the attackers to effect a surprise advance on their opponents' forward positions.

After being compelled to retreat owing to force of numbers, Gough, by collecting a miscellaneous force, consisting of all sorts of combatant and non-combatant details, succeeded in preventing the Germans from breaking through: this last-gasp effort eventually had a decisive bearing on the failure of the attack. The Allied fortunes during this battle so darkened that on the 25th Marshal Foch was appointed Commander-in-Chief of the Allied Forces on the Western Front.

The failure of this battle from a German point of view did not deter Ludendorff from launching a second assault on April 9th. It was a desperate effort to break through in the

Lys-La Bassée area in order to reach the coast of the Straits of Dover—and so enable the Germans to shorten their line— to capture the Belgian Army and half of the British, as well as harass the Port of London with long-range guns.

This attack was anticipated, and it was decided to relieve the two Portuguese divisions which were holding the part of the Front between the Lys and LaBassée. Unfortunately, they could only be relieved by tired British divisions; and when the attack was opened on the misty morning of April 9th, the change over had only been partially effected. Our Allies retreated, and the British flanks on either side were turned by the masses of attackers who filed through the gap caused by the retreating Portuguese. By that night the Germans had advanced to Fleurbaix, Laventie, Neuve Chapelle, Lacouture, and were on the Lys from Bac St. Maur nearly to Lestrem. By the 12th they had reached Merris and Merville and advanced to the La Bassée Canal, but were held up between the canal and the Forest of Nieppe, so they turned to continue their advance north of Bailleul. It was on this day that No. 74 commenced active operations; and on the morning of this day, the squadron received General Haig's famous "Back to the Wall" order which read:

"To all ranks of the British Army in France and Flanders.

Three weeks ago today the enemy began his terrific attacks against us on a fifty-mile front. His objects are to separate us from the French, to take the Channel Ports, and destroy the British Army. In spite of throwing already 106 divisions into the battle, and enduring the most reckless sacrifice of human life, he has, as yet, made little progress towards his goals. We owe this to the determined fighting and self-sacrifice of our troops. Words fail me to express the

204     KING OF AIR FIGHTERS

admiration which I feel for the splendid resistance offered by all ranks of our Army under the most trying circumstances. Many amongst us now are tired. To those I would say that victory will belong to the side which holds out the longest. The French Army is moving rapidly and in great force to our support. There is no other course open to us but to fight it out. Every position must be held to the last man: there must be no retirement. With our backs to the wall, and believing in the justice of our cause, each one of us must fight on to the end. The safety of our homes and the freedom of mankind depend alike upon the conduct of each one of us at this critical moment."

With this exhortation ringing in their ears, No. 74 sallied forth to assist their indomitable comrades on the ground, by fighting with equal determination and tenacity the enemy in the air.

H. A. Jones, the British Official Air Historian, states that April 12th was a critical day of the battle, and that every Squadron was used unsparingly from dawn to dark, with the result that many new records were set up. The air fighting, which was continuous throughout the day, had a ruthless and bitter quality. Included amongst the records made was the amazing effort of Captain H. W. Woollet, of No. 43 squadron, who equalled the record of Captain John Trollope of the same Squadron by destroying six enemies in one day—records which have remained unbroken.

There had been great competition among the Flights as to who should carry out the first patrol, so lots had to be drawn for the honour. Cairns won, so we in "C" Flight hoped to shoot down the first Hun for the Squadron record. Mannock was crestfallen.

In order to describe this eventful day in the life of the Squadron, I can do no better than quote from a diary entry of Vanlra's:

"The day of days has arrived, and is now almost over. Butler, my Cockney batman, called Skeddon and me (we are sharing a hut) at 5.30 a.m. The sky was cloudy, but the visibility was particularly good. After a cold sponge down and a hot cup of tea and some biscuits, we donned our sidcot suits and strolled across to the aerodrome, which is about 200 yards away. Butler came with us to wish us luck. Cairns, Giles, Jones, and Begbie were already standing by their machines. As there was ten minutes to go, we were not late. Cairns told us that he was going to cross the line at Merville and work up towards Ypres over the Salient. Everyone was bursting with keenness, each thinking of the Hun he was going to down, and no one of the possibility of death, or worse still—a breakfast of black bread and sausages in the enemy's lines. The C.O., Mick, and Coverdale were also present to see us off: the former and latter for obvious reasons, but Mick turned up to ask us not to disturb the Huns in case they were not there when his Flight went on patrol.

We were off the ground punctually at 6 a.m., and twenty minutes later we were crossing the lines between Forest Nieppe and Merville, which is now the front line of trenches. As we crossed, I looked at my altimeter, and was amazed to find we were only 6,000 feet. This was a ridiculously low height, I thought, as the clouds were quite 10,000 feet. From my observer's experience I knew that the enemy's 'Archie' was fairly good at this height, while there was every prospect of Huns attacking us from above. It was not long before the 'goods' arrived—and it was not wrapped up in brown paper either—it arrived well cooked and on a plate!

'Archie' bursts soon bounced our machines all over the sky, while two miles away and about 2,000 feet above, there was approaching a large flight of biplanes led by a Triplane. I watched them for a second or two, and wondered whether they were our machines or Huns'. As we were approaching one another rapidly, I dashed up to Cairns, waggled my wings to attract his attention, and then pointed at the approaching aircraft. He signalled back O.K., so I returned to my position at the tail of the Flight, on the right flank. We were flying in the customary 'V' formation, with Skeddon and Jones on the immediate left and right of Cairns, then behind them were Begbie and Giles, and behind Giles was myself. This position of honour was given to me owing to my exceptionally good eyesight. It was my duty to warn Cairns of any approaching Huns sneaking up from the rear, or from any other angle. Eyesight plays an important rôle in air fighting.

When Cairns continued to fly towards and underneath the approaching machines, I naturally assumed they were comrades, but the Triplane puzzled me, and as I couldn't recognise the type of the others, I became more and more anxious. I remembered Mick's advice about fighting Tri-planes. Through my mind flashed the thoughts—Are they Huns? No! Yes! No! Yes! I couldn't make up my mind, but as we were fast approaching, the black Maltese crosses on their wings soon settled the question. For a moment I was fascinated by those little black crosses. It was months since I had seen any. How pretty they looked! And what pretty machines! They were all colours of the rainbow! Black and red, bright blue and dark blue, grey and yellow, etc. It never struck me that they were aeroplanes flown by men—possibly by the crack pilots of the German Air Force. Men whom I knew as Huns. Death-dealing gentlemen, possibly smothered with Iron Crosses and Orders *pour le Mérite*. I looked on them for a moment as rather a pretty flock of birds. But I was soon rudely awakened from my reverie.

Cairns, as soon as he had seen the black crosses, turned sharply left to get away and improve his tactical position, as they were diving to the attack. Skeddon and Jones could easily turn tightly with him, and Begbie and Giles, by crossing over positions, could turn fairly quickly. But I, being so far behind, was left standing, so to speak. The enemy leader soon took advantage of the gap between me and my Flight, and brought his formation into it, ignoring the remainder of the Flight, and soon he was on my tail, firing sweet bullets of welcome to No. 74 Squadron. Wisely I kept my head, and immediately put my machine into a vertical bank, held the stick tight into my stomach, kept my throttle wide open and prayed hard! According to Mick's advice.

It did not take me long to realise that the gentleman who was doing his best to kill me was an old hand at the game. A sure sign of an old hand is that he reserves his ammunition and only fires in short bursts; if he is aiming straight he knows that a burst of twenty is as good as a burst of 200 and much more economical. Having only about 1,000 bullets in all, it is foolish for a pilot to use them up when he knows that his aim is not good, on the off-chance that an odd bullet may hit his opponent. Once he has used up his ammunition, he then becomes defenceless himself. Mick had warned us that we had to be careful of a Hun who fired in short bursts; on the other hand, if the Hun is firing long bursts at you, he said, you can be sure that he is frightened and probably a beginner. 'Fight him like hell, he should be easy meat.' This Hun on my tail was so close that I could easily discern his features. His machine was painted black with a white band round his fuselage just behind his cockpit, and he was flying it superbly. It seemed to slither round after me. Round and round we waltzed, in what was no doubt, to my opponents, a waltz of death, but this morbid aspect of the situation fortunately never occurred to me. Of course, I could see the big idea. The leader was to shoot me down while his eight companions prevented anyone coming to my assistance, or myself from getting back to my lines. Some of them kept above and on the north side (the side that Cairns and his Flight were climbing), and the remainder kept on the west side of me at various heights, so that I would have to run their gauntlet of fire if I chose to quit. As we waltzed around, I kept on repeating to myself, 'Keep cool, Vanlra, he can't hit you. His bullets are going behind.' I could see the track of his bullets as he was using tracers, and this fact encouraged me to keep cool. I had no desire to have a burning bullet roasting my intestines, especially before breakfast! So keep cool I did.

Occasionally I shouted at the top of my voice at him, telling him to do his damnedest. I also used most indecent language. Of course, he could not hear me, but it gave me satisfaction and temporarily acted as a stimulant to my sorely tested courage. While he flew close to my tail but did not fire, I did not mind very much, but whenever I heard the Kak-Kak-Kak of his Spandaus and saw the spurting sheets of flame close behind me, I felt a little anxious of a stray bullet hitting me. Every now and then my attacker would zoom up, and a couple of his comrades would make a dive and zoom attack, hoping that I would get out of my vertical bank—but

I wasn't having any, as I knew of this old trick from past experience. Once they got me out of the vertical bank, the gent on my tail (he may have been Richthofen, Udet, or any of the other Hun star-turns as far as I know) would no doubt have soon put paid to my account. After a while I feared, unless I got out of the mess that I was in quickly, the fickle jade Fate might step in and stop my engine, or worse still put a stray tracer bullet through my petrol tank, and send me down to Hunland in a blaze of glory—a glorious death for an airman, but not one that I wanted on my first patrol. I wanted to kill a couple of Huns myself first. As we waltzed around one another sparring for an opening, I kept my eye on the big green mass of trees about five miles away—the Forest de Nieppe. I knew that those trees were in our territory anyway. It was a consoling thought. But I could not make up my mind when to make my dash, the Triplane kept on nagging me with his bullets—so did his companions, and the longer I stayed as their guests, the more attention they paid me. Occasionally two or three would have a crack simultaneously. I would sometimes fire for *moral* effect only.

The seconds passed like years, and the minutes like eternity. The tension grew as the minutes rolled by, until eventually in desperation I decided to make a bid for home as soon as the Triplane did his next zoom. I watched my opponent carefully, as he was then only about 25 yards behind and he seemed to be grinning as I looked at him over my left shoulder; as soon as I saw him commence to zoom up to change his position I obeyed Mick's instructions and 'put on full bottom rudder' and my machine did a turn of a spin. When I came out of it, I found I was facing east instead of west, so another spot of bottom rudder to turn her round westward was quickly applied, and there in front, a few miles away, was my landmark—the Forest de Nieppe. Between me and my objective were half a dozen Huns, hungry and angry Huns, just waiting for me to come their way. So their way I went, accepting their challenge like a mad bull charging a toreador. I knew this was my only chance. It was now or never. So, barging through the middle of them—neither looking to left nor right, as I had often done before through a rugger scrum when cornered, I went for home like Hell kicking my rudder from side to side to make the shooting more difficult for the enemy—and praying hard. It was a grand thrill, that run for the lines—I knew by the incessant angry barking of the enemy's guns that there were hundreds, if not thousands, of death-dealing bullets chasing my little machine. Occasionally during my mad careering, I looked over my shoulder to see whether I was gaining on my enemies; to my joy I could see I was—but the bullets, I realised, were still faster, and it was not until I was well clear of the enemy—half a mile away, that I knew I was safe. It was a joy to see my little S.E.5 gaining ground on the Triplane and the Pfalz, and to listen to the fading rattle of the staccato barking of the enemy's guns as my machine gradually outstripped her opponents. I crossed our lines just to the north of the forest, right down close to the ground and fortunately my enemies feared to follow me owing to the approaching of Cairns from a higher altitude. Cairns then chased them miles over their lines.

The feeling of safety produced an amazing reaction of fear, the intensity of which was terrific. Suddenly I experienced a physical and *moral* depression which produced cowardice. I suddenly felt that I was totally un-suited for air fighting and that I would never be persuaded to fly over the lines again. For quite five minutes I shivered and shook while my aeroplane careered about the sky almost uncontrolled. Had I been attacked at that moment by the rawest of Huns he would have had no difficulty in shooting me down, as I had temporarily completely lost control of myself and my *moral* resistance was at its lowest ebb. This depressed state of mind disappeared after a tremendous mental battle, and as suddenly as it had appeared, it left me. The air fighter had triumphed over the coward.

The patrol ended without any victory or loss, and when my machine was examined for bullet-holes, there were none. Mannock was proud of his pupil, and after breakfast, he made an entertaining little speech on the value of listening to good advice and keeping cool in a tight corner. The C.O. whispered a little word of praise which made me happy.

Mick and his Flight were delighted to hear that we had not destroyed a Hun, and they went on their first patrol at 8.25 a.m., full of the offensive spirit. Before taking off, Mannock gave his final instructions, which ended with the remark: 'Remember, to fight is not enough. You must kill.' An hour and a half later the Squadron awaited their return with bated breath, and we breathed a sigh of relief when we counted the full number as they appeared in the distance, approaching from the direction of Cassel. We soon realised that they had been up to some dirty work, for they commenced firing all colours of Very lights as they flew over the aerodrome. Every one was very excited when they got out of their machines. We rushed up to Mannock, and his face was wreathed in smiles as he greeted us with his slogan: 'Always above. Seldom on the same level. Never underneath.' It appears that the air was still full of Huns when they got over the lines. Mick decided to get into a position between the enemy formations and their aerodrome before attacking. Eventually he led his Flight on to a formation of Albatross Scouts over Merville at 13,000 feet. Mick and Dolan each succeeded in crashing an enemy. The first Hun to go down was persuaded to do so by bullets from Mick's guns, and so to him goes the honour of having destroyed the first enemy credited to the Squadron. Later in the day his Flight attacked another formation of Albatross Scouts, coloured black and yellow, one of which was shot down and fell near the Bois de Phalempin. Although all the other members of his Flight say that Mannock was the victor, he himself has put in a report which states that 'The whole Flight should share in the credit of this enemy aircraft.' He has done this to encourage his Flight. What wonderful unselfishness!

The C.O. and Young also destroyed an Albatross Scout apiece during the afternoon. 'C' Flight tried hard to destroy a two-seater over Ploegstreet Wood on our second patrol, but we had no luck, although most of us tried our damnedest to sock him one. I managed, however, to force one to land, but he did not crash. I came home on the carpet and Jerry gave me a lively time with his flaming onions and 'Archie.'

All Flights did three shows each, and we felt pretty tired at the end of it. Clements has had to go to bed with a splitting headache due to the sudden change of atmospheric pressure during dives. Dolan tells me that Mick swoops on the enemy formation like a hawk on its prey. On my last patrol, my crankshaft broke when we were about ten miles over the Hun lines. As the propeller slowly stopped so nearly did my heart. I was escorted back by the Flight, who protected me until I crossed the lines. It was an uncanny business. There was my machine gliding gently towards our lines without any power of propulsion, while all around were dozens of enemies who had not the temerity to attack. It was an eerie flight. I could hear the roar of the cannonade below while the 'Archies' burst with a violent detonation which sorely tested my nerves. Eventually I landed in a ploughed field and turned a somersault, but am feeling O.K.

Five Huns destroyed and one forced down without any loss augurs well for the success of our Squadron. We had champagne at dinner in honour of the occasion, and afterwards speeches of encouragement and praise from the C.O."

VanIra confessed his mental reaction after the fight to Mannock, and was comforted by him with a narration of his own similar early experiences. "Most pilots have this reaction at some time or other," he said; "it is just a question of fighting resolutely against the desire to give in. This is the test of a MAN—whether he be a fighter or a coward." It is a tribute to the spirit of the pilots in the Squadron who experienced similar reactions that they never allowed them to interfere with their work. The Britisher's incalculable ability of hiding his feelings under a cloak of gaiety and humour often deceives friends and foes alike, and transforms him into the invincible fighter his foes have learnt to respect.

Thirteen years later VanIra dined in London with the pilot of the Triplane—Hpt. Ritter Eduard von Schleich, an enemy ace with thirty-five victories to his credit. He is a charming man; tall, fair, blue eyes, and possessed of a smile and a laugh which reveal his joyous spirit. He could easily be mistaken for an Englishman (he is a Bavarian), and has a spirit akin to those gay pilots of the Royal Flying Corps. They are now very great friends, and after their first meeting, Von Schleich informed a friend that he would have been "very sad if he had killed VanIra!" Discussing the fight, he said that he made a great mistake in attacking VanIra instead of the whole Flight which was at a tactical disadvantage. "VanIra looked such 'easy meat'!" he said laughingly. VanIra told him of his reaction, and with a broad smile Von Schleich replied: "I always feel like that!" "The stupidity of war," says VanIra, "I never realised so acutely until this pleasant meeting. It seems so silly, for we liked one another at sight."

A letter from Mannock to Eyles reads:

"74 SQUADRON,
R.F.C., B.E.F.
13.4.18.

DEAR JIM,
    In the thick of it. Two more pieces of propeller for you, although I gave one of the two to the Flight just to buck them up.
    Things are a bit funny at the moment, and I am not at all content. Maybe it's O.K.
    Much work, much fighting, and much 'wind up' at times, but O.K. at present. Drop me a line when you can. Hope all O.K. at home.

Cheerio,
PAT."

In this letter we have the proof-positive of his great selflessness. "I gave one of the two to the Flight just to buck them up." No other ace has the proud reputation of shooting down enemies and crediting the victory to someone else for the purpose of encouragement. Richthofen's reputation in this connection, for example, is the antithesis of Mannock's. He is reputed to have claimed victories which were really his formation's, and I must say that many of his combat reports give this impression. Some of his war comrades to whom I have spoken on the subject are most definite in their accusations.

To me, for some not understandable reason, flying men as individuals appear to be secretly very jealous of one another's achievements, and the greater the triumphs of a pilot the more secret opposition and contemptuous rumours of a vicious nature he has to contend with. Of all the famous war aces, no air fighter's reputation has weathered the storm of jealousy and prejudice without some form of battering, except Mannock's. His has remained untouched and unsullied, as it must be now to the end of time.

Next day the Squadron was visited and congratulated by the Wing-Commander, Colonel H. A. Van Ryneveld, a South African of Dutch extraction, who, as a boy, assisted his race during the Boer War. Van Ryneveld was loved and admired by everyone who came in contact with him. Never has there been a more deservingly popular Wing-Commander ; he was a friend to all his subordinates, while his personal example as an airman holding high rank may have been equalled by a few but never surpassed. He was ever encouraging and sympathetic to tired officers, enabling them to carry on often in spite of themselves. Pilots knew that whatever Van Ryneveld asked them to do was necessary, and that it was not a mission which he himself had not at some time done, or would not have done. Mannock adored Van Ryneveld, and his kindly encouragement and understanding meant much to a man so highly strung. One day Mannock said to me, "If it were not for Van Ryneveld and Grid, I would ask for a month's rest. My nerves are beginning to fray."

The value of a sympathetic and encouraging senior officer was never better illustrated than on the occasion when our Brigadier-General visited the Squadron after a couple of months' hard fighting. He spoke only to the C.O. and to a few mechanics to ask them technical questions. He passed by and completely ignored Mannock and all the other pilots. This lack of recognition and encouragement so upset Mannock that he applied for a couple of days' leave, and went off to Boulogne. His highly strung and impetuous nature could not withstand such an affront. He did not desire decorations, but he expected praise and encouragement. Mannock on this occasion reacted the petulancy of Lannes, Napoleon's famous Marshal, who left the field of Marengo to sulk in his village home because he felt himself slighted by Napoleon's report of the battle which historians now agree was successful largely owing to Lannes' personal bravery and skill.

For the next week or so the weather was usually misty in the morning with low clouds during the rest of the day, and air fighting was at a discount. In order to keep fit we had stirring Rugby football matches with No. 54 Squadron, who shared the Clarmarais North Aerodrome with us. These matches were played in the spirit that the game demands— very hard, almost fierce, but absolutely clean. On our side, Coverdale and Caldwell were irresistible, and played with scintillating brilliance. These games were the first of eighteen victories which the Squadron won during its period in France. No match was lost. Thirteen out of twenty-one officers played in these games. The spirit of determination and team work which is so essential for success in Rugby is the same spirit necessary in a squadron of successful air fighters. Mannock played Rugby with the same determination and almost with as much fierceness as he fought in the air! The next best thing to shooting down a Hun, he contended, was "a low, hard, flying tackle!" "The sound of the thud when your opponent bumps his nose on the ground," he used to say, "gives me a kick almost as much as when I see a Hun go down in flames!"

No. 54 was equipped with Sopwith Camels, a single-seater fighter, which was famous for its quick manœuvrability, and was commanded by Major (now Wing-Commander) Stewart Maxwell, M.C., D.F.C. During this period its activities were chiefly confined to shooting up enemy ground troops—a dangerous duty which called for exceptional courage—at a very low height many miles on the enemy side. Among the prominent and gallant members of the Squadron at this time, and one who was decorated with the Military Cross for ground-straffing, was a slim and very boyish youth named Roy Royston, who nowadays is an accomplished actor of great repute. Their casualties were so heavy that at the end of the month they were withdrawn from the line for a well-deserved rest.

The next Squadron victory was not until the 21st, when, largely owing to the agency of Mannock's leadership, Dolan destroyed another enemy. On the same day, the squadron suffered its first casualty, when Begbie was shot down in flames during a dog-fight in which "C" Flight was engaged with about fourteen enemies. VanIra's diary entry of this fight is so typical of a dog-fight that it is worthy of being quoted in full:

"We took off for our last patrol at 5.30 p.m. When we crossed the lines we noticed an unusual number of Huns knocking about. After a while Cairns led us to the attack on four Albatross Scouts over Armentières at 15,000 feet. Begbie and Giles remained above to protect us from surprise, whilst Skeddon, Birch, and I followed our leader. After a little waltzing and sparring, Cairns and Skeddon sent a couple down out of control. I had a crack at one of the boys, but to no purpose.

Having re-formed after this scrap, we had another a little later. This one started against four Albatross Scouts, but our enemies were soon reinforced by about ten others, and a real dog-fight ensued. Fourteen to six are rather long odds, but we held our own valiantly for some minutes. These Huns were, as usual, highly coloured and pretty to look at. They fought with a spirit which was quite unusual; probably they were out to revenge the death of Richthofen, who was killed this afternoon. The fight continued for about five minutes, and was fast and furious while it lasted, We waltzed around one another as if in a vicious unbreakable circle, machine guns spitting lead in blazing streams. Every now and then Death's black wing brushed passed me as my machine missed friend and foe alike by hairbreadths. First Giles, then Begbie, then a scarlet and black Hun would rush past in mad confusion, each sweeping through the stringy smoke of tracer bullets, making it curl as if in a whirlpool. The staccato barking of the jibbering machine guns at close quarters was obliterated by the rushing imminence of a terrifying collision. It was an awe-inspiring sight of hurtling machines smashing through the sky at one another. It developed into a game of snap-shooting. There was no time to aim and no time to stick on anyone's tail. Try as I would I could not bring down a single bird; yet some of them looked for a second as if my bullets had gone home. But the sudden erratic movement which I hoped portrayed injury was only the quiver of the heart as the brain conveyed to it the nearness of Death. Every now and then an enemy would spin away or drop in a drunken stagger from the fray, and I would wonder if it was hit, but the battle was too hot to worry any more about it. We were there to kill Huns, not to trouble about claiming victories. Through the corner of one eye I could see my comrades taking pot shots at fleeting targets as they passed across their path. Suddenly I spotted a machine commencing to smoke—then, burst into flames. Quick as thought, I wondered if it was a comrade. It was. I recognised by the marking that it was poor old Begbie. A sudden feeling of sickness overcame me, and I felt I was about to vomit. A shiver of horror passed through me. Fascinated with horror, I momentarily forgot the fight, but the vicious barking of a couple of Spandaus soon brought my mind back to realities, and I had to fight for my life again. Poor old Begbie had to leave us without a wave of farewell. I had a final peep at him as I flew near by. Thank God he looked as if he was dead. Immediately after, a Hun started shooting at him again, and while he was gloating over his victim, Giles came roaring down at him and poured lead into his machine, and he spun away into the mysterious depths below. Gradually the Huns left the battle scene one by one, and as I returned helter-skelter to our lines, chased by 'Archie,' there was sadness in my heart and a void in my stomach as I looked back over my shoulder and saw the long trail of black smoke which marked the last flight of a brave comrade and a lovable companion."

Skedden had a remarkable escape in this fight. A bullet actually passed through his flying cap and singed a groove in his hair! Amazing luck. His engine was so badly hit that it eventually "seized." He had to land at Marie Capelle, and his machine bore the following scars of war: three bullet-holes in the elevator; the oil tank pierced in several places; wings hit; and one of the centre section struts badly splintered. In spite of all this, the Huns let I him get away! His nerves were badly shaken.

At dinner that night we drank to Begbie's memory, and, led by Mannock, we sang the appreciative ditty, "For he was a jolly good fellow." The C.O. made a neat little speech, the main theme of which was that Death must never affect our *moral*, and that everyone must cast sorrow aside. When casualties later occurred the Squadron showed no sorrow to the casual visitor, although often a member would secretly retire to his room to shed a silent tear in the seclusion of his hut. To the visitor we were always a sporting crowd, full of the joy of life.

Mick brought the news to the mess that Richthofen had been killed. He was delighted. Most of the pilots were secretly sorry that he was dead, and when one of them, voiced his feelings, Mannock told him that he had better send home for his petticoats! At dinner, a member suggested drinking, "To the health of the dead Baron." Some drank to the toast, but Mannock wouldn't. He had as poor an opinion of Richthofen as he had of all other Germans, except Voss and Boelcke, whom he admired.

It is strange that when for the first time Richthofen had crossed our lines for months and months, if not years, that he should be shot down. The story of his death has so often been told that I do not propose to tell it here, but I must say that from a close study of all the numerous reports, both written and unwritten, I favour the opinion that he was shot down from the ground. The only bullet that pierced his body killed him, and it passed through in an upward direction. This being so, I cannot imagine in what position Richthofen's machine was, at the time he was hotly beset by Captain Roy Brown's, so that a bullet from the latter's machine guns could have penetrated Richthofen's body as it did. Brown's combat report does not give the impression that he was at any time below him. I am of the opinion that the two greatest air adversaries of the war, Mannock and Richthofen, died by the ironical hand of Fate, which directed a bullet from the barrel of a lone infantry man "firing for fun." I am not suggesting that Richthofen was invincible as an airman, for we know that he was shot down twice on his own side of the lines. Anyway, whether he was shot down by Captain Roy Brown, flying a Sopwith "Camel," by an Australian machine-gunner, or a lone infantryman, his death had a demoralizing effect on his Service. His cunning tactics of only attacking "cold meat" gave the Germans a false impression that he was invincible, and his death came as a terrific shock.

It was most noticeable from now on that the enemy's aggressiveness subsided into almost a cowardly channel; rarely did one meet a formation which would stay in a fight, let alone attack of its own initiative. As a result, patrol leaders had to use their brains in order to force an engagement. This necessity made plain the need for applying tactics to formation-leading. For reasons which one looking in retrospect cannot understand, formation leaders as a whole did not bother about tactics, they led their formations anywhere over the enemy's lines, and trusted to luck that they would stumble across some Hun in a suitable position for attack. They did not, as Mannock did, spend most of their time on the ground thinking and scheming of how best to trap timid enemy formations. Mannock the air fighter, as No. 74 knew him, was fearless, ferocious, and cunning; he possessed all the essential qualities which go to arm the ideal air fighter. As an individual, he was a killer; as a patrol leader, he was a schemer and a fox. It is as a patrol leader that posterity will remember Mannock's brilliant record; and it is in this rôle that I am best able to pay tribute to him, for it was in this capacity that I had most opportunity of witnessing and appreciating his unrivalled skill and determination in attacking enemy formations.

Mannock the individualist ceased to exist after his tour with No. 40 Squadron. He now lived for his Flight; and although he gained a large number of successes for himself, it was due to his tuition and agency as a leader that the enemy suffered most of its casualties as the result of the Squadron's aggressive activities. In just over two months, he and his formations obtained over 70 victories with only one casualty, and that one was through excessive zeal and lack of self-control.

What fights he and his formations fought in No. 74! Some he reported, others he did not trouble to. On the 22nd he crashed a Pfalz. The next day he destroyed another. This was the first dead pilot that VanIra had seen at close range, and he writes:

"I saw a dog-fight going on between a number of machines east of Merville at about 14,000 feet, so I went along to join in the fun, although I was at a lower altitude. As I was climbing towards the scrap, I suddenly saw a machine falling away from the whirling mob and come tumbling down in my direction. I awaited its approach with a considerable amount of anxiety, as I suspected a ruse, and that he was going to attack me. However, as he approached my level, the Pfalz, which was highly coloured with a black body, white-tipped tail, silver and black chequered top planes, suddenly assumed a position on its back, and I noticed that the propeller was stopped. I flew close up to it, and to my horror I saw the body of the pilot partially dangling out of the cockpit as if he were dead; in addition, the machine began to smoke badly."

Apparently Mannock had expedited this enemy's soul from this to the next world with three short bursts at close range. On the 29th, he shot down a Scout in flames after only firing 40 rounds with a right-angle deflection shot. This machine was one of a formation of ten, flying in the vicinity of Dickebusch Lake at 5,000 feet. Two others were destroyed by members of his Flight after a glorious dog-fight on the same patrol, Dolan getting one and Roxburgh-Smith the other. This was the latter's first of sixteen victories which he gained in the Squadron. In civilian life Roxburgh-Smith was a bank clerk and hailed from Bromley, Kent. He was over thirty years of age, and, considering he was a married man with a family, he fought with a spirit and audacity which reflected greatly on his personal courage and on the example set him by his Flight-Commander. The majority of successful fighting pilots were unmarried, and observations proved that marriage was a definite handicap, domestic ties increased the sense of responsibility. Some hardy souls like Smith succeeded in controlling their mental outlook and prevented a condition of nervousness arising which eventually caused a complete loss of nerve. The married man had always the knowledge of what death would mean to his wife and family, and unlike the unmarried man, risks were carefully weighed before taken. Smith's spirit of abandon equalled that which was displayed by the young and unmarried members of the Squadron, and he proved that the will can overcome matter even in connection with marriage in war-time. When Mannock was killed, this gallant veteran wrote: "Those of us who had done any good work in the Squadron, owe a tremendous lot to his example and advice!" Those were indeed words of truth.

Roxburgh's victim was an L.V.G. two-seater. On returning from the big fight, Mannock saw this machine near Dickebusch Lake apparently carrying out artillery co-operation duties, so he dived with his Flight to attack it. His gun jammed after firing a few rounds, so he pulled away. Dolan and Smith then swooped on the enemy. Just when Smith was getting his sights on to his target, Dolan swung across his bow and put him clean off, apart from frightening the life out of him. Dolan in his eagerness was diving too steeply, overshot, and missed his target badly. The Hun pilot was flying his machine very well, turning with steep bank and enabling his observer to have a good field of fire. Smith, however, zoomed up under his tail, and with his first burst apparently put the gunner out of action. The pilot then spiralled earthwards with his engine off, but Smith stuck to him, firing the whole time. Finally, the Hun crashed into a shell-hole and Smith, who had followed him down to the ground, momentarily quite forgot in his excitement that he was now a few miles over the lines. The noise of "Archie" and the crackle of machine guns soon brought home to him the necessity of making a bee-line for our lines. Fortunately, he had kept his bearings and looking westwards he saw a red light dropping gently in the distant sky; it was a signal to re-form fired by Mannock. After a thrilling zigzag flight a few feet off the ground, he eventually crossed the lines and rejoined Mannock and Dolan. His machine on landing was found to have a fair-sized hole in the left lower plane, a bullet hole in the left-hand spar, the bomb lever was nearly shot away, and three bullets were in the fuselage. The efforts of the enemy were not Smith's only escapes, for Mannock nearly blew his head off for following an enemy down to the ground over the enemy's lines. To do this was a crime in the Master's eyes.

On the 30th, while on patrol with Mannock, Dolan shot down on our side of the lines, near Ypres, a two-seater. Mannock on this occasion gave a display of his hatred for the enemy which startled even his own comrades. Caldwell, who witnessed the fight, writes of the incident as follows:

"Mannock and Dolan were up together, and on seeing British 'Archie' bursting on our side of the lines, they chased along to see what could be done. They spotted a Hun two-seater beetling back towards the lines, and got down just in time to prevent this.

The Hun crashed, but not badly, and most people would have been content with this—but not Mick Mannock, who dived half a dozen times at the machine, spraying bullets at the pilot and the observer, who were still showing signs of life. I witnessed this business, and flew alongside of Mick, yelling at the top of my voice (which was rather useless), and warning him to stop.

On being questioned as to his wild behaviour after we had landed, he heatedly replied, 'The swines are better dead—no prisoners for me'!"

Mannock's hatred for the Germans had by now reached an intensity which I think was never exceeded by any other airman during the war. This display of hatred is quite beyond the imagination of his mother and other relations, who believe that it is inconceivable that a boy with such a quiet and kindly nature could ever develop a hatred for anyone which was so bitter and unmerciful. This hatred was intensified no doubt by the fear in his soul that Might might triumph over Right, and that the British Empire would be segregated and held in bondage by a tyrannous. and bullying victor. Mannock could only see one way in which he could help to defeat this menace, and that was by killing every German he possibly could.

On May 3rd, while accompanied by Dolan, Kiddie, and Clements, Mick, unable to find any enemy scouts to engage, led an attack on an Albatross two-seater south of Merville at 3,000 feet. After a brief attack the Albatross was shot down. Mick in his report states, "As several members of the patrol took a close part in the destruction of this machine, the credit for such, in my opinion, cannot easily be given to any individual member of the patrol." Everyone swore that Mick had undoubtedly shot it down. How great was his selflessness, only he knew. Young pilots had to be encouraged!

His tactics when attacking these low-flying two-seaters were those of a hawk. He would hover about the sky thousands of feet above his prey, pretending that he was not watching, then, when he was quite satisfied that his enemy was off his guard, he would go swooping down at a terrific speed, to effect a complete surprise. He would flatten out about a mile east of his opponent, and throttling back to steady his machine, he would approach from beneath his victims, having in the meantime reduced his speed to about 100 miles per hour. His favourite shot at a two-seater was a right-angle one, which is the most difficult shot of all. It used to amaze everyone who witnessed these right-angled attacks of his, how easy it all seemed. His tactics were to compel the enemy to fly into the bullets by aiming a short distance ahead of his target, and holding his fire until the enemy's engine appeared in his sights. If his first burst failed, he would repeat the attack. It was a lucky enemy who did not fall a victim to Mannock's guns once he got his sights trained on him. Mannock invariably sighted his own guns, and invented a pet sight of his own. He placed gunnery before flying as a means of gaining victories: "Good flying has never killed a Hun yet," he used to say to his pilots; "you just get on with sighting your guns, and practise spotting Huns. Then shoot them down before they shoot you." Spotting Huns quickly was a gift to some pilots. Without the ability to spot an enemy many miles away, a patrol leader was unfit to lead, and many were the war casualties due to the blindness of a leader.

Mannock had wonderful long eyesight, in spite of the defect in his left eye. He was never surprised during his whole career as a patrol leader. This was one reason why every pilot felt so secure when following him on offensive patrols many miles over enemy territory. During patrols, he not only mystified and surprised the enemy, but also the formations he led. Once over the lines, he would commence flying in a never-ending series of zigzags, never straight for more than a few seconds. Was it not by flying straight for long periods that formation leaders were caught napping? As he tilted his machine from side to side, he scanned the sky above and below with the eye of an eagle. Suddenly his machine would rock violently, a signal that he was about to attack—but where were the enemy? His companions could not see them, although he was pointing in their direction. Another signal, and his S.E. would dive to the attack, the red streamer attached to his rudder fluttering faster than the heart-beats of those who followed it with taut nerves. A quick half-roll, and there beneath him would be the enemy formation flying serenely along; the enemy leader with his eyes no doubt glued to the west—the result was a complete surprise attack.

Mannock would take the leader if possible in order to give his pilots coming down behind him a better chance of an easy shot at someone before the enemy formation split up, and the dog-fight began. Having commenced the fight with the tactical advantage of height in his favour, Mannock would adopt dive and zoom tactics in order to retain the initiative. Woe betide a pilot who lost the initiative and got himself into such a mess that his comrades had to forgo their tactical advantage in order to extricate him from his perilous position! Whilst the fight was in progress, Mannock, in spite of being in the thick of it, would be summing up the situation the whole time, and, as often happened after the commencement of a battle, an enemy, having sneaked away and climbed to a height above our pilots, would return to the fight hoping to effect a surprise. Mick, however, would be keeping an eye on the wily bird all the while, and when he returned, Mick would give him a burst and that was the end. When the enemy had been demoralised and defeated, Mannock would give the signal to re-form, and would not leave the battle ground until he was satisfied that all the machines had seen his signal.

During these formation attacks, the machines were spaced about fifty yards apart as they dived to the attack, and as soon as the fight began, each pilot fought for himself, attacking any enemy who presented itself as a favourable target. Mick, on a few occasions, tried a concentrated fire attack, but the crackle of machine-gun fire from behind coupled with the fear of collision so frightened everyone, that no one took deliberate aim, so he decided against any further attacks of this description. As it is imperative to concentrate on aiming, the main object of the attack was destroyed. Captain Beauchamp-Proctor, of No. 84 Squadron, I understand, was more successful with his formation attack experiments. This great diminutive South African air fighter was perhaps, next to Mannock, the most constructive and progressive of our patrol leaders, and no pilot was more worthy of the Victoria Cross which was awarded him.

From now on, by brilliant tactics and resolute attacks, Mick and his Flight commenced to pile up its record score, but Mannock lost his most promising protégé—Dolan. The Squadron received a stunning blow on the morning of the 8th, when "B" Flight was caught napping by a flight of triplanes between Ypres and Menin several miles over the lines. I must pay tribute to the cleverness of the leader of the Hun formation, for I witnessed the whole tragedy. Whenever a flight went on patrol during this period we used to carry a few 20-lb. bombs with us, and drop them on some town behind the enemy's lines. On this occasion, the objective for the bombs was Menin, and "B" Flight, which had taken off before "C" Flight by about 10 minutes, crossed the lines at Ypres at about 12,000 feet, which was rather low in view of the possibility of enemy aircraft patrolling at higher altitudes. When "C" Flight got to Ypres we were only at 11,000 feet, so we continued flying northwards to gain more height. On looking eastwards, however, we spotted a flight of Triplanes manoeuvring for a position west of "B" Flight, who appeared not to have seen them. The enemy leader was at least 3,000 feet above "B" Flight, and was obviously pretending he had not seen them by flying S.W., but when "B" Flight turned to come back after dropping their bombs on Menin the Huns whipped round and made a dash for them. Within a few seconds Stuart-Smith and Bright were going down in flames, while Piggott was going down at high speed eventually to crash in No Man's Land, uninjured but badly shaken. Young was shot up to the extent that he had to land at Marie Capelle Aerodrome, while Kiddie's machine, which was the only one of the Flight to return to our aerodrome, was well plastered with bullet-holes.

I have never seen a better example of the value of wireless telephony in air warfare. Had "C" Flight been able to Warn "B" Flight of the enemy's whereabouts, they could easily have outraced the Huns by steering a N.E. course, for the S.E.5 was much faster than the triplanes. This was a black day for the Squadron, for on the same morning, Skeddon, the Squadron's best acrobatic pilot, was killed on the aerodrome after a wing had collapsed following a half-roll on the top of a loop. This crash made us realise the folly of stunting after an offensive patrol; we suspected that the wing had been weakened by a hit from a piece of shrapnel or a bullet. This set-back did not lower our *moral*; Caldwell and Mannock saw to that. In fact, all that day pilots carried out extra patrols in an effort to seek revenge; revenge being the finest incentive in war to fight and kill. Before nightfall we crashed in flames a two-seater, which was a little consolation, but not "good arithmetic" as Mannock used to say when a Squadron lost more machines than it shot down.

Caldwell, by personal example, incited the Squadron to greater efforts during the next few days, and on the 12th, while leading a squadron patrol in the absence of the C.O., Mannock surprised a formation of eight Huns over the Salient by masterly tactics which resulted in the enemy formation being routed. The Squadron was flying in tiers, each being about half a mile apart and about 1,000 feet above one another, Mannock leading the foremost lower flight. After a short time on patrol he spotted a flight of eight Albatross and Pfalz about 4 miles over the lines and flying north. He decided to fly south for a short while and then east, pretending he was not interested in them; then gradually he changed his direction to north. After a while he had manoeuvred his flight into a safe attacking position; and quicker than the swoop of a hawk, he was down among his prey wreaking havoc; Dolan and Clements were by his side and Roxburgh-Smith and Howe not far off. In less than three minutes his guns had sent three enemies to their doom, while the remainder of the Squadron were dealing with the others; Giles, Roxburgh-Smith, and Young each gaining a victory. Unfortunately, this decisive victory was robbed of much of its joy by the death of Dolan, who was seen to go down out of control and crash near Wulverghem. Dolan's death was a great blow to the Squadron, for he was developing into a first-class fighting pilot; he had already destroyed six enemies without having any bullet-holes in his machine. His brief and splendid life was ended by the most glorious of deaths—struck down in the heat of combat, 11,000 feet above the earth, His loss was an irreparable one to the Squadron, for he was a rare fighter of the Caldwell-Ball type, who attacked the enemy regardless of position or numbers, and the closer he could get to them before firing the happier he was. Had he lived he would no doubt have developed into a great air fighter and destroyed innumerable enemies because of his natural ability to shoot accurately.

Dolan was a great friend of Mannock, and his death was a blow which added considerably to the bitterness of his fighting. When it was confirmed by another member of the patrol that Dolan had actually crashed, Mannock retired to his hut, where he wept like a child for some time. That evening, however, in the Mess, he gave little sign of his sorrow, and in the revelry which followed the dinner, he as usual was the life and soul of the party. This cloak of his real feelings he cast aside when the party was over, and when he found himself again alone with only the companionship of his thoughts, sobbing was heard coming from his hut.

From this day until the end of the month, he fought with such relentlessness that he himself gained an average victory of one enemy per day. He would on occasions lead his patrol as far as 20 miles over enemy territory in an endeavour to make contact with pusillanimous enemy formations. When he found it impossible to get on the east of such formations in order to compel them to fight, he would sweep the sky for the unprotected two-seater. Many of his victims were shot down in flames, and when he returned from such victories he would come bounding into the Mess whooping loudly and shouting, "Sizzle, Sizzle, Sizzle, wonk, wooff!" He always gave vent to his pent-up nerves by similar outbursts, the blood-lust of his spirit was momentarily appeased.

However, he was never satisfied, he never fought enough battles, or burned or destroyed enough Huns. When he could not find any enemies during official patrols he would go out accompanied by anyone who was anxious to carry out an extra patrol, or occasionally alone. Lone patrols however, did not appeal to him, as he considered that solo flying was unsatisfactory for lack of confirmation. He wished to avoid any suspicion that he was making unjust claims and gaining decorations thereby.

"The only time," writes Major Caldwell "I can remember Mannock got a Hun when alone, happened when he attacked a Fokker scout just east of Ypres one afternoon in June. He attacked at short range, did a climbing turn to keep height in case the Hun zoomed, and never saw the Hun again. When he landed on the aerodrome he told me that he thought he could not very well have missed from such close range. So I rang up the 'Archie' battery near Ypres and asked for a description of any combats between 7,000 feet and 10,000 feet just east of Ypres between 3 p.m. and 4 p.m. The reply came straight back that an S.E.5 had shot down a Fokker in a vertical dive at the time Mannock reported."

On such occasions as he was accompanied he would not take more than two with him, as he used to make these flights into one of personal instruction as well as an offensive patrol. Often after spotting an enemy formation he would hand over the reins of leadership to one of his comrades in order to see what sort of a job he would make of a surprise attack on the enemy. After the patrol was over he would point out to the potential patrol leader his mistakes; in this way Mannock gave confidence to young pilots and trained new leaders.

May 21st was a happy day for Mannock, for on this day he destroyed four enemies: three Pfalz scouts and a Hannoveranner two-seater. Vanlra describes these fights:

"In his first fight, which commenced at 12,000 feet, there were six Pfalz scouts flying east from Kemmel Hill direction. One he shot to pieces after firing a long burst from directly behind and above; another he crashed; it spun into the ground after it had been hit by a deflection shot; the other, a silver bird, he had a fine set-to with, while his patrol watched the Master at work. It was a wonderful sight. First, they waltzed around one another like a couple of turkey-cocks, Mick being tight on his adversary's tail. Then the Pfalz half rolled and fell a few hundred feet beneath him. Mick followed, firing as soon as he got in position. The Hun then looped—Mick looped too, coming out behind and above his opponent and firing short bursts. The Pfalz then spun—Mick spun also, firing as he spun. This shooting appeared to me a waste of ammunition. The Hun eventually pulled out; Mick was fast on his tail—they were now down to 4,000 feet. The Pfalz now started twisting and turning, which was a sure sign of 'wind up.' After a sharp burst close up, Mick administered the *coup de grâce*, and the poor old fellow went down headlong and crashed.

This was a really remarkable exhibition of cruel, cool, calculating Hun-straffing. A marvellous show. I felt sorry for the poor Hun, for he put up a wonderful show of defensive fighting. His effort reminded me of mine on April 12th. The only difference was, that he was miles over his own lines and had a slower machine. Had he only kept spinning down to the ground, I think he would have got away with it.

I asked Mick after we landed why he fired during the spin. He replied : 'Just to intensify his wind-up.' And a very good answer, too! This was the first occasion that I have seen a machine loop during a fight. It was obvious to us watching that to loop under such circumstances is foolish. Mick managed, however, to keep behind him, though, and did not lose contact with him, although it was obvious by his manoeuvres after he came out of the loop that the Pfalz pilot was all at sea, for he twisted and turned his machine in a series of erratic jerks, just as if he was a dog stung on his tail!

Mick says he only looped as well for a bit of fun, as he felt his opponent was 'cold meat.' He says what he should have done instead of looping was to have made a zooming climbing turn as the Pfalz looped, then half-rolled and come back on his tail as he came out of the loop. By this means he would have been able to keep the Hun in sight all the time, while he would not have lost control of his machine as the Hun did while coming out of the loop.

Mick's other Hun was a Hannoveranner two-seater, which he shot down after a burst at right angles. The old boy crashed into a tree near La Couronne, south of Vieux.

Four in one day! What is the secret? Undoubtedly the gift of accurate shooting, combined with determination to get to close quarters before firing.

It's an amazing gift, for no pilot in France goes nearer to a Hun before firing than the C.O., but he only gets one down here and there, in spite of the fact that his tracer bullets appear to be going through his opponent's body! Mick on the other hand takes an angle shot and—Hun in flames."

His combat report gave no inkling of the thrill which the fight must have given him, and was written with characteristic modesty and terseness.

### Narrative

"Observed Pfalz machines (about 6) flying east from direction of Kemmel. Attacked from the south-west and above. Fired long burst at dark-coloured E.A., which went to pieces. Engaged another dark-coloured E.A. and fired remainder of Lewis drum and proportionate number from

Vickers. This machine spun and crashed. Engaged another Pfalz (silver) which was diving north for some unknown reason and a close combat ensued. E.A. looped and S.E.5 followed, firing Vickers when opportunity occurred. Followed E.A. down to 4,000 feet, and watched it side-slip occasionally. At about 100 feet from the ground the machine spun and crashed.

Two of these machines are confirmed by other members of patrol."

When the weather was unsuitable for offensive patrols, as it was for the next couple of days, pilots would go and pay calls on other squadrons or visit St. Omer or Boulogne. There was a wonderful spirit of comradeship between squadrons and every Mess was an open house to any visitor. This *spirit of extreme comradeship* must be the outstanding memory of anyone who served in the Royal Flying Corps overseas. Such enthusiasm and cordiality permeated the entire Corps: it was fostered, no doubt, by the instinctive knowledge of men in daily contact with death that they could rely on one another's help when the occasion arose and circumstances permitted. These men lived for the day, and the future played an insignificant part in their calculation: as the strain increased, so jealousy and pettiness of mind disappeared, a canker which so often destroys *esprit de corps*, the foundation of unity and strength in war or peace. Pilots and observers of all ranks greeted one another with open arms and on the same footing of equality.

Those who by achievement had gained decorations and had won fame received the hero-worship usually associated with schoolboys. Heroes of the calibre of Mannock were fussed and petted wherever they went; and the modesty of these supermen was severely put to the test. Some succumbed to the flattery, and by so doing neutralised to a large extent the spirit of adoration which was fermenting in the bosoms of their comrades. Others trod those difficult paths with ease and grace: Mannock belonged to this enviable company. His great-heartedness, sincerity, joviality, and supreme modesty won for him the hearts and admiration of everyone he met. He was a model hero. I well remember a visit he and I made to No. 7 Squadron. We were persuaded to remain to dinner, and he was afterwards called upon to make a speech. The theme of his speech was that two-seater pilots and observers had to do all the dirty work, while the fighting pilot gained all the decorations and fame. When he sat down the applause was loud and prolonged, and followed by musical honours. Wherever Mannock went it was the same—even in Sisters' messes!

On May 24th, General Plumer, under whose command we served, visited our Squadron to congratulate us on our work. The visit of this great and much-loved General is well described by Vanlra:

"This afternoon General Plumer, who commands the Second Army, came and gave us a surprise. He is a quaint little man to look at, but very charming to speak to. He is about five feet eight in height, corpulent, has a podgy red face, white hair and moustache, a twinkle in his eye, wears a monocle, and stands like the grand soldier he is, very stiff and erect. He flattered us with his praises of our fighting efforts, but I have suspicions that he did not approve of either the cleanliness or the mode of our dress. Naturally when off duty we are not particular about our dress, as we believe in being comfortable today, as tomorrow we may be dead.

Mick, who had just landed, was the most disreputable of all. As he approached the group where the General stood, he was hatless, without a collar, his tunic open, his hair ruffled; in fact, he looked a typical bush-ranger! The General said to the C.O., 'Which is Mannock?' Mick was duly pointed out to him. When he set eyes on him, I really thought he was going to pass right out. By a masterly effort, however, he pulled himself together and literally seemed to stagger up to Mick with his arm outstretched. Mick's dirty paw clutched the gloved hand and squeezed it in his usual hearty manner. Plumer's face twitched, and for a second I thought he was going to give a shout. 'Mannock,' he stammered, 'let me congratulate you on your D.S.O.' This was the first official intimation of Mick's well-deserved award which we've been expecting for some days. Later he said to Mick: 'Further, let me congratulate you on your first day's work.' Mick replied, 'We expected that, sir,' meaning that, having a lot of good fellows in his Flight, he naturally thought that they would shoot down some Huns. But, of course, it did not sound like this to General Plumer, and he departed with a puzzled expression in his face no doubt wondering what sort of a fellow Mick might be, and possibly thinking that he is spoilt by success. Quite wrong."

Mannock's D.S.O. was celebrated in no uncertain manner. That evening the Squadron entertained freely at dinner and after Richardson, the Squadron's cocktail king, made everyone happy before dinner with his famous concoction, "the 74 viper." Roxburgh produced a feast worthy of the Ritz *maître d'hôtel*. Coverdale, who was in charge of the wine cellar, introduced champagne of a vintage which sealed the success of the evening. The guests included many great warriors of the air. Cobby was there, the greatest of Australian air fighters, with his fighting partners, King and Watson; Clayson and Owen of No. 1 Squadron; Nigger Horn, McGregor, and Longton of No. 85 Squadron; Ventor, Ross, and Harrison of No. 29 Squadron.

VanIra's diary thus recounts this hectic evening:

"There were many speeches during and after dinner, mostly incoherent and full of ribaldry against the Hun. What we are not going to do to him is not worth doing! The Hun Air Force is going to be wiped out! Mick made by far the most sensible speech, it was prominent for its modesty. He started off by saying that he apologised for having the D.S.O., as he felt we should all have got one—or none at all. This went down well and the cheers were loud and prolonged! He went on to say that as he had had the D.S.O. we must expect to hear at any moment now that Grid had won the V.C. Air V.C.s, he said, have been given to less worthy pilots than he. Thunderous and very prolonged cheers. He finished up by enthusing over the wonderful spirit of comradeship which existed among fighting pilots. 'Gentlemen,' he ended, in his most passionate and rhetorical manner, 'the sky must be cleared of Huns. And we are the boys to do it. United we stand—divided we fall.' Thunderous applause, intermingled with cat-calls, whoopings, and rattling of crockery. Several members slid exhausted under the table!

After dinner we sang popular songs to the accompaniment of Roxburgh on the piano. Mick in a solo effort sang, 'Mother Macree,' with great pathos, much to the delight of everyone. When we got tired of singing we played *high-cock-alorum* and other rough games, ending up the party with a rugger scrum—the coloured troops versus the rest (the 'coloured troops' being the nickname which Grid gives to all Colonials). In this case the coloured troops were much too rough for the delicate British Islanders, and many were the scars of battle after the 'rough house.' It was a glorious evening."

A letter to Eyles dated the 25th indicates for the first time his interest in the number of machines which he was shooting down purely from a numerical point of view. It had suddenly occurred to him that his record as a destroyer of Huns might even eclipse that of his friend McCudden, who had 56 victories to his credit. But to achieve this end he admitted he must have "luck," for perhaps he realised that Death comes often swiftly and quite unexpectedly to the Knights of the Air. If he beat McCudden's record, he could see no reason why he should not "oust old Richthofen." To refer to the Baron as "old Richthofen" indicates how his hatred for the German ace was mellowing as he reflected on him in death.

"DEAR JIM,
    Your last letter to hand. Glad to hear that all at home are well and in good fettle.
    I regret to say that poor old Dolan is gone. We have no definite news from the other side yet, but I have not much hope, as I saw him go past me in a spin about five miles the other side of the line. There were six of us and I attacked eight Hun scouts; the remainder of the Squadron was in echelon some distance away. We got six together and I got three of them. Dolan must have received chance shot, as we had height and position on the Huns. He was a good fighter, and I am sure that it was a chance shot which brought him down. Clements is getting on O K., no Huns yet, but he is

coming on. We have only lost six of our original squadron and have brought down about 45 Huns. My total is now 41, although you may not believe it, and they have given me the D.S.O. I'm expecting the bar at any moment, as I have brought down about eight since I was recommended for the D.S.O. If I've any luck, I think I may beat old Mac. Then I shall try and oust old Richthofen.

I've still got Derek's mascot on the old bus! It smiles at me continually and cheers me up lots, although I haven't been very well lately. Too much flying, I think.

Talk about stunting over Wellingboro'. My God! If you saw what we do out here in a scrap, your eyes would drop out.

Give my kind regards to all the good people at home.

> Cheerio,
> Yours,
> PAT."

Mess life—in our large wooden hut with its feeding-table at one end; leather lounge chairs, piano, and Decca gramophone at the other—was a very happy one in the Squadron. Drinks were pooled by special agreement, although several members were teetotalers; this arrangement ensured, not only that all guests were well looked after, but also that the burden of upholding the good name of the hospitality of the Squadron did not fall-on the shoulders of a few generous hearts, as so often happened in a unit where similar co-operation was lacking. Superstition we decided to flout: we lit three cigarettes from the one match, walked beneath ladders, carried mascots one day and not the next; We even had our photographs taken before flights, because we heard that this superstition was strong in the Richthofen "circus." Badminton and swimming were the favourite summer pastimes, while a lot of light reading, particularly magazines, was indulged in. Mannock was often to be found reading Shakespeare and Tennyson. He loathed the weekly illustrated papers which advertised society pets "on war work." It is certain that had he survived the war he would have been a Socialist M.P.; his forensic powers and great personality would have made him a force to be reckoned with, for he would have effectively combined vigorous and penetrating criticism with popularity. Popular Labour leaders and he would have assuredly linked arms, for he naturally sympathised very deeply with the proletariat; his own personal experience of the hardships borne by the masses from whom he was sprung remained ever uppermost in his mind.

The gramophone worked overtime: Violet Loraine and George Robey singing "If you were the only girl in the world," Elsie Janis singing "Give me the moonlight," and José Collins singing "Love will find a way," were the records which had to stand up to the greatest strain. Mannock had a passion for Irish airs, in particular "The Londonderry Air." Often he would play this record before going on the dawn patrol, much to the annoyance of the other members of his Flight who were feeling like anything other than listening to a gramophone. During these early morning periods whilst awaiting the first streak of dawn, the usual combination of laziness and drowsiness reproduced a feeling of great irritation against the Kaiser, who was held solely responsible for these unpleasant circumstances. As a result, many were the vulgar oaths heard; but as soon as pilots got over the lines and were stalking the enemy, all were happy again and the Kaiser was forgiven for the grand sport he offered.

Mannock was always full of pranks; his favourite one was to enter a comrade's hut in the early hours of the morning after returning from a "night out." He would enter, usually accompanied by Caldwell, who would be carrying a jug of water; once inside Mick would pretend that he had dined and wined too well (in fact, he was a very moderate drinker), and would make gurgling noises if he were going to be sick; as each "retching" noise was made, Caldwell would splash an appropriate amount of water on the wooden floor. The poor lad asleep would suddenly wake up and jump out of bed to the accompaniment of roars of laughter, as his legs would be splashed with the remaining water. This was a rag which all newcomers had to go through in order to be initiated as a member of the Squadron. Mannock once ragged in this manner a certain C.O. of an adjoining squadron who was famous for his poor sense of humour, much to the annoyance of the victim, although to the great delight of the angry Major's pilots.

If the weather was too poor for offensive patrols against the enemy, Caldwell and Mannock would often organise "bomb raids" on friendly aerodromes. One raid on No. 1 Squadron proved most sensational, for we dropped two hundred oranges on their Mess and huts at Clarmarais South! One orange obtained an O.K. on a pilot's head and momentarily stunned him! A retaliatory raid was carried out with bananas as missiles. The umpires eventually decided that honours were easy. Declaration of peace between the Squadrons resulted in a memorable evening at the popular "George Robey" café in St. Omer. What days! What memories!

Many authors of books describing the war in the air have given a distinct impression that pilots used to drink to excess. This reflection is entirely unjustified and the stigma a cruel one. The author being a teetotaler at the time can speak with confidence about his comrades. It must be obvious to anyone with only a little imagination that excessive drinking seriously impaired the judgment and therefore the efficiency of a pilot, and that pilots fighting daily for their very lives would naturally avoid such intemperance On special occasions, such as the award of a decoration or the birth of a beautiful daughter to the armament officer, a "beano" was naturally arranged—this, of course, is acknowledged—but such occasions, as one can imagine, could only happen at specified intervals. A war pilot had to be perfectly fit, physically and mentally, other wise death or injury came sooner or later.

Richthofen, we are informed, was extremely hard with all new pilots. A famous German pilot tells the story that one day he was chatting with Richthofen on Douai Aerodrome, when a flight of S.E.s circled overhead. Richthofen called a newly joined pilot to him and in a harsh manner said: "You see those enemies up there? Go and kill them, or be killed." The poor lad went up, and was promptly shot down. Richthofen was not in the least perturbed—he just felt it was one way of training his flock. How different was Mannock's manner to a newcomer. J. F. Hunt, a Hampshire lad from Whitchurch, tells how he was received when he joined No. 74:

"I arrived at the Squadron late at night, rather shy and frightened. Mannock was in the Mess, and he looked after me just like a big brother. I was posted to his Flight, and he did not allow me to cross the lines for over a week; during this time he took me up twice on a line patrol and we had several practice fights. His advice to me was to always follow my leader, keep my eyes and ears open and keep a silent tongue. It was wonderful to be in his Flight; to him his Flight was everything and he lived for it. Every member had his special thought and care."

The training which Mannock gave Hunt made him into a pocket edition of himself, and he soon won the D.F.C for destroying Huns and balloons; had it not been for the armistice, "Mike" would have become an air fighter of undoubted fame.

"One of Mannock's greatest characteristics as a commander was the equal treatment which he meted out to all. He treated everyone alike. He had no use for slackers, but until he found them hopeless he gave them endless encouragement. When he caught a member of his Flight deliberately leaving his formation, as on one occasion, after he had given the signal 'Prepare to attack,' his anger was such that the coward was lucky to escape with his life."

So writes H. G. Clements, of Leicester, who flew on Mannock's left on almost every patrol that he led while in No. 74, and gained many victories as a result. On one occasion he caught a Rumpler on our side at 20,000 feet and shot it down in flames, the occupants both falling out.

Although they possessed similar natures, the contrast between Grid and Mick in the air was as the poles apart. Grid resembled Ball and Voss—a warrior. He never worried about tactics or orders—where the enemy were, there lay his orders. Tactics just meant to him getting as close to the enemy as possible; whether they were above, on the same level, or underneath, made no difference to Grid's plans. He always led squadron patrols when possible, and when we returned most of us trembled for many minutes after landing, including Mannock on occasions. Will anyone who was present ever forget the epic occasion when he, because there were no enemy fighters to be found in the air, led the Squadron round and round and round the enemy aerodrome at Roulers at only 8,000 feet? We were being plastered by "Archie" while we challenged the Huns on the aerodrome to come up and fight. Come up they did by dozens from aerodromes all around, but not to fight. We were eventually escorted back to our lines by what appeared to be the whole German Air force, but cowardice prevented them from coming nearer than about 400 yards, from which distance they fired. Every now and then Grid would turn the Squadron round to fight them, but as soon as he did so, they would turn tail and scuttle. It was very funny. When we all landed safely, Caldwell could not stop laughing, while the rest of the patrol struggled to restore their normal composure.

Mick, on the other hand, was a mixture of Ball and McCudden; he had the bulldog tenacity of the former and the cunning and marksmanship of the latter, plus the personal touch of a tactical genius which was lacking in all other patrol leaders. His aim was to kill as many enemies of his own calibre without suffering any casualties; to achieve this he would stalk his prey until he got them into a position of tactical disadvantage, and then he would lead his formation to the attack with the dash and enterprise of a born leader.

Losing height quickly was very necessary in order to effect surprise on enemies patrolling at a much lower altitude; so in order to increase the efficiency of his Flight when executing this manoeuvre, Mannock often after a patrol would circle over the aerodrome at 18,000 feet, and on a given signal from him all the machines would tumble earthwards in a series of falling vertical side-slips, which was the quickest way in an S.E.5 to lose height. The first machine to fly low over the sheds was the winner. Occasionally the whole squadron after a patrol would execute this manoeuvre, and the mechanics used to love watching the thrilling spectacle. As a matter of fact, we really did it as much for the mechanics' benefit as for our own practice, for they were all such fine fellows and they did not get much kick out of the war. It was just a round of hard exacting work for them, and they were mighty good about it. The pilots respected the men and they admired their pilots, admiration was reciprocated a hundredfold, with the result that No. 74 was a unit of 100 per cent. effort, everyone putting in the last ounce in an endeavour to maintain its high standard of efficiency. One could do no more. The fact that one pilot was more successful than another did not matter: it was the honour of the Squadron that was uppermost in the minds of all. Caldwell and Mannock set the standard and the others followed.

May 26th was a day of exceptional activity so far as the Hun was concerned. In the course of it Mannock had his Flight engaged in six fights. The last fight of the day was the most notable that the Squadron had been engaged in since its arrival in France. It took place at dusk, and 18 S.E.s and 12 Bristol Fighters (of the famous No. 20 Squadron) fought what appeared to be about 40 Triplanes, Pfalz and Albatross for about ten minutes. Machines, friend and foe, were so close to one another that pilots had to concentrate on avoiding collision rather than on firing. It was a hair-raising affair.

Suddenly you would see one of your own machines coming straight for you; turning sharply to avoid it you would find yourself confronted by a highly camouflaged Albatross apparently charging you; turning again quickly you would find yourself in a hail of tracer bullets fired by a Triplane which had momentarily got on your tail; bullet holes would appear in the fabric of your wings to the accompaniment of the frightening staccato barking of the Triplane's Spandau guns. Next, a Hun would come hurtling past with a Bristol Fighter tight on his tail, firing hard, and on the Bristol's tail would be a couple of Huns spraying him, while the Bristol observer peppered them in return. After a while Huns started leaving the battle ground, some because of their faint-heartedness, some no doubt because of engine trouble; others because they were dead or wounded, or their machines were on fire. It was thrilling to see these machines go tumbling out of the fray—defeated and demoralised. All our machines returned. Mannock, as usual, was in the thick of the combat, but only claimed one Albatross, although many others went scurrying away from his tracer bullets; the fight was too furious to bother any more about them.

It was after this fight that Mannock first displayed signs of nerves. He kept on referring to a Hun who had passed close to him going down in flames and saying, "God, I'll blow my brains out rather than go down roasting." Further proof of nerves was the frequency with which he crashed his aeroplane after an exciting combat. These crashes were a sure sign of an impending cracking up of the nervous system. It was about this time that H.Q. became alarmed at the number of crashes, and a letter was received in the Squadron drawing pilots' attention to the number of "unnecessary write-offs," and charging them with carelessness; it was further hinted that disciplinary action would have to be taken unless they were more careful. The result of this letter was that pilots returning from hairbreadth engagements were so keyed-up for the landings that the combination of both excitements resulted in more crashing than ever. In one week the Squadron crashed seven machines; Mannock turned two over on their backs, and stood one on its nose! Unfortunately for the Hun, no disciplinary action was taken. This crashing business was a source of much concern to H.Q., as in some squadrons more machines were crashed by our pilots than there were enemies shot down by them. One pilot in No. 74 crashed almost as many of our machines as he destroyed of the enemy's. Mannock included his efforts in the "bad arithmetic" column.

In a letter dated May 26th, he reveals his competitive spirit coming to the surface once more. He again declares his desire to beat McCudden's record, even if he has to "die in the attempt":

> "74 SQUADRON,
> R.A.F.
> 29.5.18.

DEAR JIM,

Your letter today and wire on the 27th. Thanks for your congrats., old boy. I am going to try and beat old Mac's score or die in the attempt.

What price now for the old men? Everyone out here is delighted with my future and is prepared to follow me wherever I go. Old Clements is coming in O.K. and I expect him to do great things.

Well, I hope all are quite well at home. I'm well, but feeling the strain slightly.

Has Johnnie come out here yet? If so, let me have his address and I'll endeavour to call on him.

Weather has been dud for the last few days and no Huns. Shall want some new boots very soon again. I'll let you know.

Oh, a little note of interest. No. 74 has the record now for Huns in a given time. No. 56 had it for the first 50 brought down. We beat them by some ten days. We are well in hand for the 100 now. The Huns think that Mac is with No. 74 Squadron, according to their prisoners' statements.

Well, cheerio!

Love to D., etc.,<br>Yours,<br>PAT."

No. 74 also beat No. 56's record for the 100 Huns, for on the day that Mannock went on leave, nearly a month later, the Squadron won its 100th victory. These two records, which remained unbeaten, were almost entirely due to Mannock's wonderful leadership and coaching. Some day, no doubt, the Squadron number will again be revived in the Royal Air Force. When this happens, its members will have a tradition of which they will be proud.

For some reason, the enemy became more numerous and slightly more aggressive during the next few days, and the Squadron had an enjoyable time. Mannock and his Flight were in daily engagements, and VanIra describes interestingly some of his adventures:

28.5.18.—The C.O. saved Giles's skin to-night. Giles very carelessly allowed a black Albatross to pounce on him while he was concentrating on the destruction of a silver-grey two-seater. Giles has had his leg pulled unmercifully; we declare he was decoyed. Pilots hate admitting that they have been taken in as a sucker!

Clements tells me that Mick saved his life to-night, too. Appears to be a lot of saving lives going on today. But this is a part of the air-fighting game.

Mick and Clements went up for a bit of fun after tea. They each got what they wanted. First they dived on a couple of scouts east of Kemmel, but had to scurry away when they heard the kak-kak-kak of enemy guns behind them, and saw a formation of Pfalz diving on them. Back to our lines and climbing again, they were soon after some more, this time over Ploegstreet Wood. On the way to cut them off, Clements spotted a large formation of Huns obviously making a bee-line for them. Clements put on full throttle and his nose down to catch up Mick, who as usual was wasting no time in getting at his enemy. Mick had seen the Hun formation all the time, and was just going to have a snap-shot at the isolated Huns. Seeing that he just could not manage it without being properly trapped, he turned west quickly and dived, the Huns following and firing. Mick saved Clements by losing height directly beneath them and so drawing them on to him, while Clements got clear. Clements says it was a rotten sight to see one S.E. being attacked by such a bunch, and that had it been anyone except Mick, he would have been anxious about his safety. (We all believe that no Hun will ever shoot down Mick.) One Pfalz followed him very closely, and suddenly Mick went down apparently out of control; on his back— spinning—and doing everything imaginable from 8,000 feet to 4,000 feet. At 5,000 feet, the Hun, completely fooled, flattened out to watch the crash. Mick then decided he had had enough, and flattened out too and made for our lines— diving hard. The Pfalz dived after him, but in doing so got

below Clements, who was waiting for Mick over Dickebusch
Lake. Clements then joined in the fun and crackled at the
Hun, who now left Mick and turned round to fight Clem. A
stout Hun this, a breed we don't often meet. The other Huns
now came down on Clements, so he and Mick decided to
clear off towards Ypres, accompanied by the whizzing of
bullets. The Huns must have decided that Mick and Clements
were hopeless cases, as they then left hem and returned to our
lines surrounded by haloes of "Archie" bursts.

Mick and Clements having got clear, climbed once again
to 10,000 feet, and there they were joined by the C.O. (who
was also on a joy flight). They then went over the lines
together and attacked the first Huns they saw—a couple of
Albatross scouts. No sooner had they done so than a
phalanx of Huns swooped down upon them from nowhere.
They fought their way back again, eventually getting clear
by sheer speed of the S.E.5. Their wires screaming; their
engines roaring with bursting energy; and their nerves taut
as their speedometers registered 200 miles per hour. Oh,
boys, what a game!

29.5.18.—Cloudy most of the day, but cleared up towards
the evening.

Did two shows, one after lunch—when there was nothing
doing; and another late this evening, when we had lots of fun.
Mick took Clements and me up at 7 p.m., and after climbing
with great patience for a long time, we eventually came
across a dark camouflaged Albatross two-seater flying east
from Kemmel. Mick pointed it out to us when we were over
Armentières at 19,000 feet, the Hun being a couple of
thousand feet below. It looked to me as if it was gaining
height before crossing our lines on a late reconnaissance.

Anyway, Mick did not take long before he put paid to its account. Manoeuvring to the south-east, he gradually approached it and eventually made his attack. The Albatross saw the S.E.s coming and hastily dived north-east, but it was too late. We did not take long to catch it up and Mick's S.E. was soon tight on its tail, and his incendiary bullets were penetrating its fuselage. A few minutes later all that remained of it was charred and beyond recognition. Rotten sight! Ugh!

We re-formed at 10,000 feet and proceeded to climb again—looking for more trouble. We soon found it; after a while we came across a formation of six S.E.s; Mick flew close to them, and we recognised by their markings that they were No. 85 Squadron—newly arrived from England. The leader turned out to be "Nigger" Horn. Mick waggled his wings, as an invitation for Nigger and his flight to follow him. This they did like lambs being led to the slaughter. And here begins my big fight story.

Just after 8 p.m. Mick spotted about a dozen Huns coming from the direction of Roubaix; we were then over Lille. As we had not too much time for a fight, having already been up for over an hour, he decided to go straight at them, as we had a slight advantage of height. The Huns, who were Albatross Scouts, were of the stout variety, and they accepted our head-on challenge. Both Mick and the Hun leader opened fire at one another as they approached from about 300 yards' range, but nothing happened. This burst of fire was the signal for a glorious dog-fight—as fine and as frightening a dog-fight as I've ever been in. Friend and foe fired at and whistled past one another at a tornado pace—it was a real stunner. I have never been so frightened in my life. Of late I have been able to keep very cool during the actual fight, but to-night I became so flustered that occasionally I fired at my own pals in an effort not to miss a chance—thank God, my shooting was erratic. How terrible it would have been if I had, say, shot Mick down! The thought gives me the very creeps. I'm afraid that I completely lost my head. It was an experience worth having once, and having come through it O.K. I must try and benefit by it. I got so worked-up during this fight that I have not yet fully recovered. I must make a supreme effort to keep cool next time. Mick sent two slate-blue Albatrosses down out of control, and Clements crashed his first Hun. He is very bucked about it. It is wonderful how cheered a pilot becomes after he shoots down his first machine; his *moral* increases by at least 100 per cent. This is why Mick gives Huns away—to raise the *moral* of the beginner. No. 85 Squadron claim an out of control, too. The main thing, however, about this fight is that we did not suffer a casualty.

Nigger telephoned Mick during dinner to say that his patrol were drinking double brandies, and could they please follow him again to-morrow!

VanIra's next entry gives a vivid description of a busy Hun-strafing day when the weather was perfect and the enemy was not shy:

1.6.18.—Poor old Cairns was shot down this afternoon, and is no doubt dead, as one of his wings came off.

It has been a hell of a day for fighting.

I led a dawn patrol, leaving the ground at 4.30 a.m. It was a dawn which attracted the eye; there was no cloud, and gently the eastern sky lit up, gradually waking the warriors of the war area to activity. The air was crisp and had a bite in it. I got up at 3.45 a.m., had my cold sponge bath to help me to wake up, and then went into the Mess to have the usual cup of tea and biscuit. Giles, Jones, Battel, and Richardson were the others. As we were a little early, Jones and Richardson continued to slumber, as they were suffering from a slight headache. I thought this continued sleep was bad for them, so I put on the Decca Violet Loraine singing "College Days." This song woke them up immediately, and simultaneously books and magazines were flying at my head and at the gramophone. This was just what I wanted, for there is nothing better than sudden violent exercise to wake a man up. As we put on our flying suits in the Mess before going over to the aerodrome, we could hear the distant explosions of our "Archies," which informed us of the presence of an enemy two-seater or balloon-straffer over our trenches; so off to our machines we hurried. On the way the Kaiser and his ancestors were volubly abused in no uncertain manner, and we worked ourselves up to such a state of hate that our one aim in life was the desire to kill one of his airmen.

When we got to the aerodrome, our machines, as well as "B" flight's, were ticking over all ready for being flown. The mechanics looked very tired and almost fed up. They had been up since 2.30 a.m., as they are now sleeping out at "Brighton." We took off punctually to time, and climbed towards Ypres at about 65 m.p.h.—which is the best climbing speed for the S.E.—I turned east just north of Ypres and crossed the line at 15,000 feet. Flew over to Menin (accompanied by "Archie" bursts), where we each dropped our six Cooper bombs. Where they fell, God only knows, but let's hope He is on our side!

At 5.15 a.m., I spotted three Albatross scouts over Armentières, so I led my Flight to the east and above them, *à la Mick*, before attacking. They were completely surprised, but due to bad shooting we failed to bag one. Personally, I forgot to load my guns during my initial dive, and so lost my opportunity. We only engaged these fellows for about half a minute before they dived away towards Berlin!

After leaving this fight we re-formed quickly, and I made for Dickebusch Lake (which is a favourite landmark of mine), where I could see some of our white "Archie" bursts trailing a black speck, which was a dark camouflaged Pfalz scout returning from an expedition of balloon-straffing at 3,000 feet. I had to take a right-angle shot at it, and this time, having made sure that my guns were loaded, I was more successful. I did Mick's trick of traversing, and almost immediately we had the joy of seeing the Hun go spinning down and crash a mile and a half south-east of the lake. We foolishly followed him down to the ground, and Battel and I gave him a parting shot into the wreckage. We had to pay the penalty for being so reckless, as on our way back to our lines many bullet-holes perforated our machines, and Battel's machine, having been hit in the engine, had to land in a field behind the trenches. As Mick has always told us, to follow a machine down to the ground is to ask for trouble, but I find the urge irresistible. I get so excited once I find that I have hit my opponent that I become fascinated and cannot resist following him down, unless I am in a dog-fight.

Re-forming after this fight we flew south, climbing towards Hazebrouck. Here we came across "B" flight going home, so we joined them. On landing, everyone in "B" flight rushed up to Young's machine. At first I thought he must be hit, as he was slow in getting out of his machine, but when I saw everyone slapping him on the back and heard the loud laughter, I knew that he had been up to some dirty work. He had shot down two two-seaters in flames, one of which fell in our lines Great show!

Three Huns before breakfast is not bad, and everyone is very bucked. It is a pity we cannot get single-seaters for breakfast, though. Their pilots are suffering from cold feet.

As I am going home on leave to-morrow, Grid suggested that I did not do another patrol, but when Mick started teasing me that I would get shot down if I went up with him in the afternoon, I decided to go, as we had a bet of a hundred francs on my sage return. As he was leading, I knew this bet was as easy one for me, for his leadership is fool-proof. My scrap with a Triplane has given me infinite confidence in my own ability to hold my own with any Hun. This patrol with Mick in the afternoon led to a dog-fight which was the hottest that I've been in for a few days. Mick led "A" and "C" flights on to seven Pfalzes, camouflaged dark blue with white tails, over Estaires at 13,000 feet. For five minutes the ten S.E.s fought the seven Pfalzes almost down to the ground, and when the battle was over one enemy had been shot down in flames, one crashed and one sent down out of control, all by Mick. We lost poor old Cairns, who was seen to; leave the fight with the right wing of his machine breaking away from the fuselage. It spun towards the ground at a terrific rate, and as I watched him disappear into the depths below, a feeling of sickness overcame me. It is a terrible sight to see a pal going to his death. I then saw red and went for everything I saw, but my aim was bad and I got nothing in revenge.

The reference to the mechanics "sleeping out at Brighton" indicates the village about 4 miles away from the aerodrome where pilots and mechanics were compelled to go and rest at night because of the attention which night-flying Huns were paying to our aerodrome and its vicinity. One night a bomb actually fell on the aerodrome, but did not explode. The aeroplanes were spaced at intervals around the hedges with their noses well inserted into the bushes. This bombing was sufficiently harassing to cause the High Command to issue an order compelling us to make out nocturnal moves. Although the idea was sound enough, the pilots and mechanics hated the arrangement, as we had to get up so much earlier for the dawn patrol. Further, the pilots were mostly all fatalists, and cared little for the activity of the night marauder; in fact, we invariably used to go out on the aerodrome in order to have a better look at him as he flew overhead. On one occasion we could distinctly see the observer leaning over the side of his cockpit. This particular machine was flown by a very gallant pilot who cruised about at 1,000 feet and eventually blew up the ammunition dump at Arques, near St. Omer. His observer also had his bit of fun by firing into every searchlight beam that he came across. Mannock asked permission to go up after him, but as S.E.s had not been flown at night in France, permission was not granted. Major McClaughry, who commanded the fiery fighters of No.4 Australian Squadron, went up after him in a Sopwith Camel, as he had had previous experience of night flying in England. His efforts to destroy the Hun were frustrated by out searchlights and anti-aircraft, who kept attacking him, as they thought he was an enemy. No doubt they did not know that he was in the air, and it was an instance of the necessity of co-operation between night-flying aeroplanes and ground defences. It was a stout effort of McClaughry's because he flew without any night-flying equipment, and landed safely on out very small and sloping aerodrome.

Aeroplane crashes often used to result in casualties, and Mannock's flight suffered in this respect on two occasions. Replacements were normally received from a Pilot's Pool, but Caldwell as he had been an instructor at the Central Flying School, had an arrangement with Colonel Jack Scott ad Major "Zulu" Lloyd, who were holding positions of authority at the School. When Caldwell wanted a replacement he would send a wire to one of these officers, and a pupil selected by Scott or Lloyd would be on his way out to the Pilot's Pool on the next boat. Colonel Van Ryneveld, of course, had to be consulted for his approval in order to withhold a posting from the Pool until the right man had arrived. In this way Caldwell arranged that the Squadron was reinforced by the right type of pilot.

Occasionally, when there was a rush for more than one pilot at a time, he had to accept a Pool replacement, and the first of these was a complete failure. This pilot was posted to Mannock's Flight, and as usual Mannock took a great interest in him. He told him what he must expect if he did not follow his advice, and for fun faithfully recorded the sight of a machine going down in flames, hoping that such a description would ensure that he did not "dive straight away" from a Hun when he heard the rattle of a machine gun behind him. Mannock's well-meaning tuition had an amazing effect. One day, before he had carried out a single patrol, this pilot went to his Flight-Commander's hut, and with tears streaming down his cheeks told him that he could never brave a fight in the air. Mannock pointed out to him that he could not refuse. Refuse, he did, however, and ultimately he was "invalided" home with "nerves." Once in England he was posted to a soft administrative job, where he remained until the end of the war. Before he left the Squadron, Mannock ordered a member of his Flight to tear off his wings and to sew a yellow piece of cloth on instead. There is no doubt that this pilot suddenly realised that in air fighting the individual was supreme and that his own skill was the deciding factor in a fight. In a battalion or a battleship the individual is *moral*ly reinforced by the immediate presence of comrades, all sharing the same dangers and sustaining one another during action. The airman is isolated, lonely, and must fend for himself. Should he be wounded, or his machine disabled, he knows that it is only his own determination and ability which can possibly save his life. Some lacking in self-confidence fear to come to grips with such realities, and allow Matter to overcome the Will.

In place of this spineless individual there arrived from the C.F.S. a pilot whose spirit was the antithesis of the other, Lieutenant Sydney Carlin, M.C., D.C.M. Before the war, like Hunt, his occupation was that of a farmer; a Yorkshireman from Hull, he joined the local Company of the Royal Engineers. Proceeding to the war in 1914, he was soon wounded and had to have a leg amputated above the knee. For his bravery in action he was awarded the Military Cross and the Distinguished Conduct Medal as a ranker. Owing to his severe wounds he had been compulsorily demobilised, but, not content to perform duties of a non-combatant nature, he decided to learn to fly at his own expense. Having successfully completed a course, he presented himself at the Air Ministry, and was provisionally accepted as a pilot. His confirmation depended upon a report from Colonel Jack Scott, so he was sent to the C.F.S. for training. As far as landing was concerned, he turned out to be a poor pilot, but his remarkably cheerful spirit added to his pertinacity. This decided Scott to recommend his acceptance. As always, Scott was correct in his judgment. This one-legged airman soon developed into an air fighter of outstanding ability and tenacity, and he attacked enemy aeroplanes and balloons with equal sang-froid. Mannock took special interest in him—christened him "Timbertoes"—and his subsequent success made him proud of his protégé.

Carlin was concerned with Caldwell in one of the miracles of the War in the Air. While simultaneously attacking a Fokker, they collided and both went spinning into the depths below. This happened at 16,000 feet. At 8000 feet, Carlin succeeded in gaining a measure of control and managed by skilful flying to steer his machine back to our lines. Caldwell's machine, which was more damaged than Carlin's, would not respond to his attempts to regain control, but kept on spinning. Ultimately he decided that his only chance to get his machine out of the spin was to stand half-in and half-out of his cockpit, with the foot inside the cockpit pressing hard on the rudder on the side nearest him. He hoped that by standing in this manner he would counteract the spinning, and eventually gain sufficient control to get the machine back to our lines. He crossed the lines at about ten feet and then throttled back. Immediately, his machine nose-dived into the ground, and at the same moment Caldwell jumped! Turning a few somersaults on the ground, he eventually came to a halt near a dug-out, where some of our infantry were watching, speechless. When Caldwell gave himself a shake, got up and walked towards them with a broad smile on his face, they looked as if they were watching a ghost.

This almost incredible story does not end here. The accident happened about 6 a.m., and as no news of him had reached the Squadron by nightfall, everyone presumed that he had fallen in the enemy lines, and there was a dark depression hovering over the Squadron, Carlin in particular being in a state of great agitation. True to the Squadron tradition, however, the pilots, aided by the hope that he was safe, and the company of many visitors who had arrived to sympathise, "livened-up "the party after dinner almost into a "wake"; while it was in progress news was received from Lieutenant Spiers, the Recording Officer, that Caldwell was on his way back to the Squadron. His appearance was the signal for the liveliest night in the history of the Squadron, and Carlin, who was almost insane with depression, quickly recovered his normal composure only to "pass out" in complete happiness later in the evening!

The next day Caldwell led a Squadron patrol with greater determination than ever. When higher authority heard of this, he was ordered not to fly over the lines again without permission. He was allowed to fly on our side of the lines, however, and in this way he was able to have as much fighting as before, because he used to wander far over the enemy's lines and shoot down Huns which he never reported! He was indeed a great leader of men. Such men as he are rare.

On September 21st, at 16,000 feet over Armentières, Carlin fought his last fight in the war. With Caldwell leading, Hunt, Roxburgh-Smith, and Carlin dived on about twenty Fokkers. Carlin had a sudden feeling as if someone had knocked him on the head, and he remembered no more until he regained consciousness at 5,000 feet, when he saw the smoke and flame of tracer bullets all around him. Soon he realised his elevator control had been rendered ineffective by the two Fokkers who were sitting tight on his tail. He flew towards our lines as fast as he could go, and had the hardest of luck in crashing on the wrong side of the German barb-wire entanglements in No Man's Land. He managed to get clear of his machine and made a great effort to find an opening to get through the wire while our troops in the opposite trenches put up a magnificent machine-gun barrage to prevent any German soldier getting at him. While he was hobbling about from shell-hole to shell-hole, he was suddenly knocked flat by the butt of a rifle and jumped on by a couple of Huns. He was taken to a General in the line to be interviewed, and thence to a temporary prison at Lille, and later to Karlsruhe. In each place he was punished because of his refusal to acknowledge the rank of any German officer by addressing him as "sir." A few days after he was shot down, an enemy airman was made prisoner, and he informed us that "an airman with lots of decorations and only one leg had been caught trying to crawl through the barbed wire." This news was a great relief to the Squadron. Nowadays, our wooden-legged hero is happily engaged as a land agent in Kenya, working for a German firm!

Other pilots from the C.F.S. who lived up to Colonel Scott's high opinion of them as potential Hun-straffers included George Gauld, of Mimico, Ontario; Freddie Gordon, of Auckland, New Zealand; W. C. Goudie, of Vancouver; and Jules Ferrand, an American from Boston, Mass., who won a D.F.C. as the result of his first air fight, when he fought seven Fokkers on his own and shot down three of them, all of which were confirmed by pilots of other squadrons and "Archie," as the engagement took place about half a mile on the enemy side of the line. Ferrand's machine was so badly shot about that it collapsed on landing. He, however, was none the worse physically or mentally as a result of his adventure.

With the good weather which June produced, the number of Huns in the air on our front increased, and fighting became more interesting. However, the enemy still regarded the imaginary front line of the air to be over his own aerodromes, and the patience of Flight-Commanders was severely tested whilst they manoeuvred for a position which would compel the Hun to fight at a reasonable distance from our lines, particularly when a strong west wind was blowing, which was frequent. The enemy airmen invariably tried to make use of this strong west wind by attempting to draw our patrols well over their lines before an engagement commenced, in the hope that the wind would carry us over so far that we would run out of petrol before we could recross our lines. This ruse of theirs proved successful on more than one occasion. For example, Leefe Robinson, V.C., the destroyer of the first, Zeppelin over England, was enticed into such a trap whilst leading his Flight over Douai Aerodrome, with the result that Richthofen and his gentlemen were able to claim five easy victories; other British machines which were missing were more frequently victims of circumstances than of bullets fired by an enemy pilot, although they were often claimed as victories.

A letter dated June 7th informs Mannock's friends of the award of a bar to his Distinguished Service Order:

"74 SQUADRON,
R.A.F.
7.6.18.

DEAR COMRADES,

Thanks for the parcel. I am obliged to Mrs. Eyles for taking all this trouble. Will you please thank the lady for me.

They have given me the bar to the D.S.O., I enclose correspondence in connection therewith. D.S.O. and bar inside 11 days is not so bad for an old man. Total now 51. Officially only 47. No news of poor old Dolan. I have no hope personally. We have lost several people lately, but up to the present I have only been shot about the machine a bit. I have only to beat Mac and old Richthofen now. I hope I shall do it. The other day the C.O. and I engaged 9 Huns. We chased them miles over their own side. They would not wait. I got one.

Another occasion 5 of us engaged 12. I got 3. One in flames, one in pieces, and one nose-dived to the ground. Great times. Derek's mascot has lost an ear. In combat, I think! I am having a white one put on in its place.

Cheerio,

Regards to all at home.

Remember me to Mr. Smith and the others,

Yours,
PAT."

The citation in the *London Gazette* announcing the award of a bar to the D.S.O. ended: "A fine example of marksmanship and determination to get to close quarters. As patrol leader he is unequalled."

This letter gives a fair indication of the extent of our mastery of the air during the summer of 1918. It is doubtful if ever an enemy's scout formation was seen over our lines during this particular period, so complete was our domination. On the other hand, our pilots, who were drawn from all walks of civilian life, roamed the air at their own sweet will with hardly ever an attempt on the enemy's part to stop them. Our offensive tactics had succeeded in the one branch of warfare where sheer personal gallantry decided the issue as of old. Prodigious acts of valour on the part of our pilots would make Coeur de Lion's cheeks pale with envy. British airmen now proved themselves superior in personal gallantry—which, when every other computation is made, is the test of a nation's manhood supreme. Our pilots, man for man, had out-fought the Germans. The fighting spirit of the

German airman was enveloped with the despondent air of failure now shared by his comrades on the ground. The tactics of the enemy fighters took them nearer Berlin every day, and our pilots did indeed begin to wonder when the day would arrive when our machines would not have the range to engage them. As our pilots penetrated deeper and deeper into enemy territory after his fighters, we sensed the collapse of the enemy *moral*—it was slow and agonising; and from our point of view—sad. The unfailing spirit of sympathetic chivalry which we unconsciously felt for a defeated foe who had fought well, although not always courageously, surmounted the joy of ultimate Victory, which was now obviously only a matter of time. The British airman could indeed feel justly proud of his part in the Great Triumph.

His Majesty the King, after a visit of inspection of our Air Force in the field, at this time wrote to the Commander-in-Chief:

"I have inspected detachments of Royal Air Force. Its prowess and established superiority over the enemy make me proud to be General-in-Chief of this last creation in the Fighting Forces of the World."

Mannock from now on periodically visited squadrons for the purpose of teaching his tactics to fighting pilots, and as a result other patrol leaders were inspired to follow his guiding principles with varying success. Mannock not only imparted his tactics to other pilots, but he imbued them with the glorious offensive spirit of Nelson. The tactics of the sea and of the air are not unlike. Mannock considered that the principal duty of a fighting formation, as a battle squadron at sea, is to seek out the main hostile force and destroy it, by placing itself as speedily as possible alongside the enemy in a position of tactical advantage.

Almost daily members of his Flight and patrol were securing victories, which pleased Mannock as much as if he were adding to his own score. Only one of his Flight up to this time had not succeeded in downing an enemy, and he was the "baby" of the Squadron—"Swazi" Howe, the 17-year-old South African, born in Bremensdorp, Swaziland, a fair-haired, blue-eyed, slim little lad who looked no more than 15 years. He had enlisted a year earlier, and had only been accepted by giving a false age. He maintained the high standard of bravery which Beauchamp-Proctor, H. W. L. Saunders, and Hector Daniel had set their Afrikander compatriots, for he always fought with determination and disregarded danger. His shooting, however, was so poor that he could never bag a Hun. Mannock at last decided that at all costs he was to down an enemy and get blooded; and with this end in view he took Howe out day after day until he eventually succeeded in destroying a couple of scouts. It was during one of these flights that Mannock's machine was badly shot about as a result of a misunderstanding between himself and a flight of Camels. VanIra records the incident thus:

"Mick came back in a furious temper from a patrol this morning. He had taken 'Swazi' out on a private war to see if he could help him to get a Hun. At 11.20 a.m. he spotted half a dozen Albatrosses flying in formation near Armentières, and at the same time he noticed a flight of Camels patrolling near by, so he flew up to the leader and waggled his wings to attract his attention and to ask him to follow him, this being a recognised procedure. The Camels followed Mick while he manœuvred for position before attacking. Eventually he gave the signal to attack, and down he swooped on the completely surprised enemy. A dog-fight immediately commenced, and when Mick had time to look around to sum up the situation he discovered that he and 'Swazi' were alone and that some distance away was the Camel flight, flying away! Both Mick and 'Swazi' eventually made a safe get-away after expending all their ammunition, but each of their machines much shot about, both the tyres of Mick's machine were punctured, and as a result he turned a somersault on landing. He was so angered about the whole affair that he asked the C.O. to report the matter at once to Wing Headquarters. What apparently happened was, when the leader of the Camels commenced to dive with Mick, he saw another enemy formation approaching towards the fight from some distance away, so he thought he'd better go and intercept them. The result was that they sheered off and Mannock's fight was over before the Camels could return and join in the fray. They were, however, able to confirm that one of the Huns went down in flames. Mannock credited this victory to Howe."

A letter to his sister gives an indication of the state of his nerves:

"74 SQUADRON
(NOT 742 SQUADRON),
R.A.F.
16.6.18.

DEAR JESS,
Your letter dated 15th May to hand a few days ago. How careless of you to have wrongly addressed it. Your fault. Well, I am out here and have been out here since March. It is a pity you did not write sooner. You knew my address

quite well, and you also knew I was out here. Perhaps you did not feel like writing after a heavy day at the factory. Well, we will let the matter drop.

I am sorry to hear that Ted is crocked up. Still I think he is lucky to get out of it all. It will give you both a chance now of settling down, and he will probably get a cushy job on some War Work Committee or other. There are bags of opportunities for a broken-down old sweat!

Poor old Pat is going through the mill now. The Tank Corps is having a rough time of it. I hope he gets through all right. I suppose you are all still on the munitions job. It must be pretty hard work, but not quite so hard as the war out here. Things are getting a bit intense just lately and I don't quite know how long my nerves will last out. I am rather old now, as airmen go, for fighting. Still, one hopes for the best. I hope mother and Nora are getting along O.K. These times are so horrible that occasionally I feel that life is not worth hanging on to myself, but 'hope springs eternal in the human breast.' I had thoughts of getting married, but …?

I am supposed to be going on leave on the 19th of this month (if I live long enough), and I shall call at Birmingham to see you all.

Cheerio,
Yours,
EDWARD."

Pilots of the Squadron were now going home for a fortnight's rest leave, and Mannock's turn came on the 18th. This leave came none too soon—for his nerves were noticeably fraying. He was now continually talking about being shot down in flames. For weeks he had been engaged in air fights almost every day, some of which he had reported and others he had not troubled to. VanIra's diary for June 17th gives an idea of his activities during his last day in No. 74 Squadron:

"Bags of Huns again. Ideal for fighting, just a few billowy clouds about at 10,000 feet. Just at the right height for surprise attacks on Huns below.

After breakfast I went up with Mick's patrol. I felt I could do with a little inspiration from him, and I was quite frank with him why I was going up. He laughingly said, 'Van, old lad, I've often felt like you. Come up with me and I'll send one down, sizzle, sizzle, wonk! It will just put you right. You can fly on my left. You'll get a better view from there!'

At 9.30 I spotted our 'Archie' bursting over Berques, so I flew up to Mick's level and waggled my wings to attract his attention. I was only ten yards away. When he saw me he just laughed and pointed to the 'Archie.' Marvellous what eyesight he's got, despite his dud eye.

We commenced to climb eastwards at once, as the Hun was at 18,000 feet and we were only 15,000 feet.

I should hate to be a Hun, because he never knows from what angle he is going to be attacked over his own territory. For our part, when we are on our own side of the line we just dream of home and think of some sweet fairy—we never think of a Hun. To us the war does not commence until we are a few miles over the enemy's lines, and then it is usually only a case of dodging 'Archie,' and not our real objective, of killing Huns by fighting.

Well, to continue our patrol. At 9.45 we were getting close to the Hun. Mick decided on a head-on attack. About half a mile away, Clem, who was on Mick's right, was suddenly seen to drop out and dive for home. Mick and I saw him go simultaneously, and we immediately stared at one another and looked behind us. We both thought there may have been Huns diving at us and that Clem was giving us the tip. Later we found that his engine had konked. This little episode put Mick off his target slightly, but he continued on his deadly track. When the Hun—a lovely silver-coloured Halberstadt—was 200 yards away, he opened fire with a short burst. Immediately after he dived below the Hun and turning came up under his tail again. The formation did likewise. Our friend was not hit, but was diving steeply away—a foolish thing to do, as Mick had now only to dive at the same angle directly behind him and he was bound to be hit, as he was in a direct line of the flight of the bullets. It was a grand sight to watch. There was Mick just in front of me doing 180 miles per hour, with bullets pouring out of his two guns to the accompaniment of vicious barking. At 8,000 feet it was plain that the enemy had been hit, as he was going down at a steeper and steeper angle. I then pulled out and just watched the end. It soon happened in a cloud of dust followed by a roaring furnace!

My blood-lust had been reawakened and my confidence was returning. Good old Mick!

Later in the day 'A' and 'C' Flights did a combined stunt which ended in Roxburgh sending a Fokker biplane to his eternal home.

It was an extraordinary affair; it happened at 15,000 feet just east of Dickebusch Lake.

When first we saw it, it was at 19,000 feet. Mick and Roxburgh left the formation and flew underneath it, nearly at full throttle, the remainder of us flew on in front of it and acted as decoys trying to make it dive down on us. The Fokker was not having any. Mick eventually got sufficiently close to it to attract its attention and flew in front of it tempting it to come down to his own level. Eventually the enemy made a half-hearted attack, and it was laughable to watch Mick's machine swinging from side to side (he was kicking his rudder alternately), as he pulled the Hun's leg. Occasionally he would pump-handle his controls and the machine would wince about like a bucking bronco—very funny it was. I could imagine Mick roaring with laughter as he did it.

While the timid Hun was watching Mick's ridiculous antics, Roxburgh was getting closer and closer, and as I watched him, I was getting as excited as he must have been. I kept on saying to myself, 'Why doesn't he open fire? The Hun will see him in a second. For God's sake give him the gun, Rox.' At last I could see the tracer bullets leave his guns and a second later the Hun was tumbling down. I turned back immediately and made a dive for him in case he was bluffing. But when I saw him reeling over on his back, halting there for a few seconds, then suddenly flicking out of the position and making a steep vertical dive, then out of the dive after a drop of a few thousand feet and continue with a sweeping gigantic zoom which again ended by his being on his back, I knew that Rox had done his work well. The Hun pilot was dead or unconscious."

The next day Mannock went on leave, and from the R.F.C. Club he wrote to Eyles:

"R.F.C.,
BRUTON STREET,
*June 18.*

DEAR JIM,
Just heard that I've been promoted (Major) and am taking command of Bishop's squadron in France. I'm not

sure that I'm glad of the transfer, as I don't like the idea of leaving the old squadron, but it can't be helped now.

Well,

Cheerio,
PAT.

P.S.—Keep it out of the papers."

Eyles states that whilst on this leave, his friend became obsessed with the idea that he would be killed on his return to France. At times, as a result of nervous reaction, tears would come into his eyes and saliva would pour out of his mouth. A serious attack of influenza aggravated his depression, and there is no doubt that from a flying point of view he was a very sick man when he boarded the leave boat on July 3rd. But his high sense of duty made him too proud to give way to his feelings. He came direct from Boulogne to No. 74 Squadron instead of going to his new Squadron which was at St. Omer, and insisted on staying the night. He had no desire to leave his old Squadron, as he felt it was part of himself. During the evening when discussing his departure he was so overcome by the realisation of the impending severance of his connection with his, old comrades who had always shown implicit faith in his leadership and their high personal regard for him, that he broke down and wept. Promotion meant nothing to him; comradeship meant everything. Even the information on his arrival that he had been awarded the second bar to his D.S.O. did not console his harassed soul. The combination of parting with his dearest friends and the premonition of death were too much for him.

No. 85 Squadron were badly in need of a squadron commander who would lead them daily over the lines and get them into battles, as the pilots were full of the offensive spirit. Bishop, the Canadian V.C., and Mannock's predecessor, was renowned as a lone patroller, but not as a leader. Mannock soon modelled the Squadron into a first-class fighting unit, and the friendly rivalry which Caldwell and he set up between the two Squadrons made the Huns patrol nearer to Berlin than ever. Often, on the last patrol of the day, they would join forces and sweep the sky from Ypres to Lens. Later they would forgather at "George Robey's," and the night would be made merry. Mannock the Major was loved and worshipped by his whole Squadron. The pilots found in him a leader who could be trusted, whilst the mechanics discovered a strict but kindly master.

On the day he did not return, they wept. Strong men do not weep over trifles. During the short period in which he was in the Squadron, he developed squadron patrol fighting into a fine art. Lieutenant C. B. R. MacDonald, a Canadian, who served in No. 85 Squadron during the whole of the Squadron's sojourn in France, relates how Mannock used to organise his offensive patrols in order to trap the wily Hun. "Mick," he states, "would select one of the young pilots to fly with him in order to give him instruction, and together they would hunt about the sky at about 15,000 feet, whilst the rest of the Squadron would be about three-quarters of a mile away flying at a higher altitude, waiting their leader's signal, a red Very light, that he was about to attack. Then the war would commence in earnest, and Huns would be seen tumbling in flames or pieces or diving helter-skelter for the ground." On the 7th the Squadron had a successful fight with seven of the latest type of Fokker biplanes. The combat started at 16,000 feet and ended at 2,000 feet. Mannock gained two victories, "Nigger" Horn two, and Longton one, without loss to themselves.

On his return after a fight, Mannock collected his pilots as he always had done, and discussed the combat with them, explaining and helping each one individually. The inevitable result was that these men developed a perfect and almost childlike confidence in his leadership. Mannock, as always, made sure that by showing sympathy, helpfulness, and comradeship to his pilots, they would fight for him; the majority of men in face of danger will gladly surrender their wills to a successful and beloved leader, and Mannock knew this.

While with No. 74 he had several times experimented with the possibility of a whole Flight firing at the same time on the same target, but the results did not prove a success. He again tried it whilst with 85. One day he led a formation of four others who were instructed to fire simultaneously at a two-seater which he was going to single out for attack. The two-seater was manoœuvred into the desired position and Mannock gave the order to attack. But the pilots, being afraid of collision, opened fire too soon, and the Hun got away unscathed because Mannock was put off his aim by the sight of tracer bullets whistling past his ear. A few days later he tried the same form of attack, but this time with the formation more spread out. Again he achieved no success, for the same reasons.

He made one more attempt at this form of attack before definitely deciding to give it up. This time the experiment was different from the previous ones, because he attacked a formation of scouts, and the instruction had been given that each pilot was to attack his opposite number in the enemy formation, Mannock selecting the leader. Unfortunately during the dive the enemy saw them approaching and broke formation, with the result that our pilots became confused, and with the exception of the machine that Mannock shot down in flames there were no other successes. After this last failure Mannock ceased to experiment with this form of attack.

It would appear to the uninitiated that formation attacks would be a simpler way of disposing of an enemy in the air because of what appears to be a greater concentration of fire. In the same way as twelve shore guns have a better chance of hitting a battleship than a single gun, it seemed evident that twelve machines firing at an enemy would also stand a greater chance of shooting it down than one. The analogy, however, does not seem to apply, as the experience of Mannock and his flight proved. Pilots in an air fight in order to hit a target have to take definite aim at it and approach closely, before opening fire. It was discovered that the fear of collision prevented them from doing either. Of course at this time British pilots did not have parachutes, and it is possible that with the introduction of this last resource a war pilot's nervousness of collision may disappear.

On July 9th the R.A.F. suffered the most distressing calamity since the death of Ball. McCudden, while flying out from England to take over command of No. 60 Squadron, crashed at an intervening aerodrome as the result of stalling when taking off. Those who knew this great fighting pilot well were dumbfounded when they heard of the manner in which he was killed, for he was a brilliant pilot and the personification of carefulness in all that he undertook—hence his success. His gravestone could well be inscribed with the epitaph which "Leontius Scholasticus" struck for Ajax:

"The Telamoniam lies low in Troy, but he gave no foeman cause to boast of his death. For Time, finding no other man worthy of such a deed, entrusted it to his own slaying-hand."

He joined the R.F.C. before the war, became an observer and pilot, N.C.O. and officer in turn, winning medals for bravery in both ranks. He ended his career as a Major, having won the V.C., D.S.O., M.C., M.M., and French Croix de Guerre. His death was deeply felt by Mannock, because they had spent much of their time together during his last leave; also a delightful rivalry, entirely free of the green monster, had developed between them. Mannock felt the void left by McCudden's death as he meditated on his passing, and he gave the impression that he felt more than ever that the Shadow of Death was drawing nearer to himself. "I am going to avenge him," he told his friends. And the vigour of his attacks during the next couple of weeks testified to his determination to carry out his mission.

Occasionally they were tempered with an indiscretion, for in his eagerness to make sure of destroying his enemies he followed them down perilously close to the ground, often many miles over their lines. Consequently on the way back to our lines he was the target of all ground forces. These risks taken by others he deprecated, and any of his pilots who showed similar eagerness were severely censured. But these temporary indiscretions were the "writing on the wall"; his nerves were getting into such an unhealthy state that the excitement was intoxicating him. Every patrol and fight had become a narcotic; he was doping himself with the blood-lust; he could no longer resist the urge to follow the beaten enemy until he had seen his victim strike the ground; even then he had to fire a few shots into the wreckage to satisfy his soul. Mannock had reached an alarming stage of nerves which could have but one end in one imbued with his unquenchable spirit. Many have suffered in this manner, and those who have survived the war must have had to fight an even greater battle in the effort to return to normal. How many have failed! Peace has stripped these veterans of their last resources of emotional reserves. We meet them daily, men who faced death and untold horrors in the war, beaten and cowed by the remorseless struggle for existence, unable to harness their shattered emotions to the stresses and strains of civilian routine, and fleeing defenceless into the gutters of the world's highways. Much of our political unrest today is due to this callous misunderstanding of the war veteran's outlook which the war altered to an irretrievable degree. In a "get on at any price" world, these men had little chance to recoup their emotional reserves, and to our lasting shame we cannot yet adjust our social order to give the war veteran who has been unable to get to grips with life a chance to live the remainder of his days a little more easily than those who escaped the deluge. These men gave their all to save civilisation—but civilisation and peace have destroyed them.

Daily his Squadron swept the sky; daily enemy scouts went hurtling earthwards, some in flames, some in pieces, some out of control, and some only frightened by the fierceness of their attacker. Mannock now became savagely relentless, and it mattered little how they left the fray, for he would follow them down lower and lower until all his ammunition had been expended. On the 14th, he trapped a mixed formation of Fokkers, Pfalz, and Albatross in the vicinity of Merville, and his Squadron added five more victories without loss to themselves. Randall, Longton, and Rorison each crashed a machine, while their leader crashed a Fokker, and later, on his way back to the lines, sent a two-seater down out of control; again his unquenchable desire drove him to follow his victim down to the ground. This blood-lust had attacked other great air fighters, Hawker, Ball, Mayberry, Rhys-David, Harvey-Kelly, Guynemer, Dormie, Lowenhardt, Schafer, and Voss, and sent them to their glorious death. Mannock's turn was not far off.

Destroying enemies was not the primary aim of our Air Force, but the figures for the week ending July 17th give an indication of the intensive offensive activities of our fighting airmen. One hundred and seventy victories were claimed over enemy airmen, thirty-four balloons were destroyed in flames, whilst ninety of our machines were reported missing. Fierce battles of the skies were raging daily far over the enemy territory, thus enabling our cooperating aircraft to assist our artillery in their registration shoots, to make reconnaissances, and take photographs. These aerial activities were the prelude to the Infantry attacks, which were to result in the commencement of the Victory Advance. On the 18th, General Foch began his victorious offensive on the French Front by using a large number of small tanks which broke the German defences on a 27-mile front and advanced 2-5 miles towards Soissons-Château-Thierry. The next day on the British Front the enemy was pushed out of the Lys Salient, and Merville and Metteren and Merris were captured. These successful, although small, attacks on the two sectors of the Allied Front proved to be the turning-point in the last phases of the war. From now on, the determined, defeated, but not demoralised German soldiers retreated step by step to their Fatherland before the victorious Allies.

Mannock from the skies watched the British advance, and whilst his indefatigable spirit exulted, his weary flesh and overwrought nerves were already exhausted beyond ordinary endurance. Mannock now lived his days in a sustained frenzy of exhortation to his inner self. Outwardly more than usually calm, his keen, sensitive awareness of the underlying facts of the situation told him that the enemy was already defeated and that his stubbornness was merely being enforced by the Higher Command. The shattered remnants of the mighty hosts with which the Central Powers had hoped to subjugate Europe and enchain the world were at last "giving up the ghost." They were merely endeavouring by their desperate resistance to allay the harshness of the terms which they knew they had earned and which must surely be inflicted.

Mannock, divining the inevitable result, "flogged" his, breaking flesh with his indomitable will, and kept repeating his well-known phrase, "All tickets, please! Pass right down the lift, please! Now come on gentlemen, please, take your places for the grand finale," as if he were actor-producer and call-boy at some vast stage show, as indeed he was imagining himself to be. Actor-producer he was indeed in one of the greatest spectacles ever staged by history and he knew the Finale was at hand. Moreover, he knew his own end was near. He no longer wished to stage any special scenes of his own. The show was over. He sensed that the great cause for which he had striven had triumphed. All was now ready for the curtain to be rung down and for the actors to take their last stand. His own part was played. The footlights had lit his figure in an heroic blaze of glory and he knew he had played his part well. The applause at the finale meant nothing to his great spirit. His pilots could have that; the men he had schooled and nurtured were welcome to take the curtain—he was on his way to rejoin old comrades with whom he had played the early scenes. As he watched the enemy give up stronghold after stronghold which had cost so many lives, he counted the days of the approaching end with savage satisfaction and his heart was glad. In the last frenzied scramble for decorations and honours which were easier to obtain now with an enemy in defeat, the new pilots clustered moth-like round him in an excited circle to catch the reflection of his glory. Mannock did not mind. His tongue was no longer bitterly scathing and denunciatory of malingerers. He no longer scoffed at "society pets" and "base wallahs." He had mellowed in his own innermost nature, because he knew that the Spirit of Man had triumphed. Man—living man—was free once again, and the enslaving hosts of domination and serfdom were being smashed and hammered to pulp. The age-old everlasting struggle between reaction and progress was ending in overwhelming defeat for the former. "Sufficient unto the day is the evil thereof."

His mind rose above petty strife; what cared he now that poseurs and social climbers, upstarts and cowards, scrambled eagerly forward to share in the glory ? What cared he for the screaming patriots who howled their loyalty from safe retreats ? Edith Cavell had answered the *canaille*: 'Patriotism is not ENOUGH." What cared he for social climbers and lip-service toadies who vied with each other for favours of acquaintanceship with the be-ribboned war heroes? What cared he now for the million and one meannesses of the civilian order which had spent themselves in an orgy of the hastily militarised spirit of the Empire? Militarism—Kaiserism—Junkerism—were smashed utterly and completely, he fondly hoped for ever. The world of balances of power, secret treaties, paper alliances, and regional pacts was shattered beyond redemption, he imagined. Labour had obtained a new charter of freedom. Liberalism had vindicated itself. It had brought America in on our side and decided the final issue. The reactionary and bellicose spirit of Germany, despite the heroic endeavours of her young manhood pitched to a high degree of efficiency and schooled with a ferocious intensity tor success which no other armies had ever possessed, not excepting the Grande Armée of Napoleon, had failed to overcome the unorganised vague *fin-de-siècle* Liberalism of the Western Powers. What a lesson for history! What, then, could not an organised, disciplined Liberalism achieve if such a victory could be won by a nebulous Liberal idealism swathed in industrialism?

As these reflections washed in great waves of thought through his mind, he was becalmed. His offensive spirit began to ebb and his fuller nature manifested itself in many pleasant little mannerisms which made him so beloved of all. The veteran's visits to the Sisters' Messes grew more frequent. One noticed he took more care with his clothes and personal appearance. He even allowed his batman to sew a new row of ribbons on a uniform he had just ordered. His movements became less cyclonic and his greetings more composed. Mannock had lived his life. He felt the crisis over, not only for the cause of our arms, but he had conquered himself in the process. He had survived both only to find disillusionment in his own forebodings and fears. In his last letter to his sister Jess, he feels that he is nearing the end. "Occasionally I feel that life is not worth hanging on to.... I had hopes of getting married, but...?" The great warrior had shot his way through his own obsessions only to find that "life was not worth hanging on to any longer"! The flame of his wild lovable nature had burned itself through to a philosophy in a raging furnace, only to discover why Plato "wondered" at it all, and why Einstein innocently scoured the stars in the never-ending quest for knowledge. Man can only top his own physical and mental exertions by a personal example of living according to the best that is in him. From such are the leaders of the race recruited.

Where can the Messianic impulse for the creation of a Plato-cum-Mannock-cum-Einstein spring from? Each little flame spurts its fitful candle-light in the overwhelming darkness of the mysterious universe. Mannock's flame lit up the new comradeship and heroic ideals of the coining race of man with a hitherto hidden energy. The flaming cross of Christ was already under the searchlight beam of Marx and Mannock presaged the coming age in the fusion of his ardent spirit with the hot furnace of his inner thoughts. His incredible achievements drew their energy and will from this source, and when he felt that the victory had been won, his inspiration dwindled as the white heat of his energy waned.

On the afternoon of the 25th, Clements and I went over by car to St. Omer Aerodrome to spend the afternoon and evening with our idol and friend. As ever, he was the personification of liveliness in the Mess. His pilots also were in high spirits; their successes over the enemy and their happiness as a family made them so. Whomever we spoke to, we heard little else but talk of their offensive patrols and of Mannock's wonderful leadership. The *moral* of the Squadron had reached its peak. The enemy was spoken of as so much dirt. Mannock was delighted. Whilst we were having tea on the grass outside the Mess a couple of very pretty V.A.D. nurses from the Duchess of Sutherland's hospital, located near by, arrived to have tea with Mannock. This pleasant feminine touch added considerably to the enjoyment of the meal. The conversation naturally veered round to Hun-strafing, and as Mannock was explaining, amid roars of laughter, what it felt like to be shot down in flames, he suddenly said to a little New Zealander who was a comparatively new arrival, "Have you got a Hun yet, Inglis?" "No, sir," was the shy and almost ashamed reply. "Well, come on out and we will get one." Rising and asking to be excused for "a few minutes," off he and his happy comrade went towards the aerodrome. With their machines ready to take-off the leader gave the signal to taxi out, and in a few seconds he was in the air. His young companion, however, suddenly discovered to his dismay that the elevator wheel of his machine was jammed tight, and on examination it was found that the machine would not be able to fly after all.

Mannock circled once, then realised that Inglis was not going to join him, and set off alone for the lines. While he was away, the young pilot cursed, swore, worried, and walked up and down in front of the hangars impatiently waiting for the Master's return, secretly fearing he might not. Nearly two hours later an S.E. with a red streamer glided gently into the aerodrome, and young Inglis was happy once again. When he told Mannock what had happened, the mechanic was severely reproved for his carelessness, but as he was "a good man," no disciplinary action was taken. The disappointed pilot was told not to worry, and that he would be taken out at dawn the following morning. Everybody had got rather anxious as to Mick's long absence, as he was away for a longer time than usual, and his reappearance was the signal for much rejoicing, his health being drunk on more than one occasion. He told us that he had done his "damnedest" to secure his seventy-third victory, but he could not find a Hun which would satisfy his desire. He looked weary and drawn as he went to have his bath, so I accompanied him to his hut.

Once inside, I asked him how he felt; he then frankly told me that he thought that he would not last much longer. Suddenly he put his arms upon my shoulders, and looking me straight in the eyes with a suggestion of a tear in his, he said in a broken voice:

"Old lad, if I am killed I shall be in good company. I feel I have done my duty." Then, changing his expression and the tone of his voice into a more cheerful one, as if he was suddenly ashamed of having shown such emotion, he said, "Don't forget that when you see that tiny spark come out of my S.E. it will kindle a flame which will act as a torch to guide the future air defenders of the Empire along the path of duty." Then, linking his arm in mine, he led me into the Mess, singing "Rule, Britannia" at the top of his voice. Little did I think that within twenty-four hours these words spoken more in jest than in seriousness would live so vividly in my memory for ever. At the same hour the next day the greatest air tactician and air fighter of the war was dead. He had fulfilled his mission; the end which he had feared and predicted so often had come. But not from the bullet of an enemy air fighter!

In the darkness before dawn the following morning, the candle-lighted Mess produced a soothingly eerie sensation. The Decca played softly the sweet Irish melody—"The Londonderry Air." Mannock was quietly telling Inglis that he hoped to come across an early-flying two-seater, and that he would endeavour to get the Hun into an easy position before attacking. He instructed the tyro to make sure of taking careful aim and to get very close to his enemy before firing. The rest of the pilots and most of the mechanics of the Squadron were deep in their slumbers as their leader walked across the dewy grass to his machine for the last time. The first streak of dawn was lighting the horizon. The birds wakening with the dawn were singing their chorus with crisp vigour. Mannock drew his companion's attention to a particular blackbird which appeared to be leading the others. "Do you hear that bird?" he said to Inglis. "He is like me. He is full of the joy of life. He is wishing us luck." His mechanics, as he gave each a cheery "Good morning," little thought that this was going to be the last "Good morning," and that they would never again see their beloved commander. Perhaps it was just as well.

Away through the dimness of dawn two War Birds sped towards the Front, until they disappeared like wasps in the distance. It was not an unusual sight—it had happened dozens of times before. The Master at the crack of dawn taking the eager novice along to be blooded.

Almost at the same moment an enemy pilot and observer were soaring into the western sky with instructions to reconnoitre our trenches. These three machines were going to make war, and the God of War had decided that none should return to their aerodromes. At about 5,30 a.m. Mannock spotted this two-seater in the vicinity of Merville, and five minutes later both he and his enemies were lying dead, a short distance from each other within the enemy reserve trenches—their machines a twisted crumpled mass of smouldering wreckage, of charred wood and twisted steel. Death had at last issued his inexorable summons to the brave and beloved Micky Mannock. By the irony of Fate he had fallen a victim to the enemy at the moment of triumph.

His desire to make certain that the tyro was properly blooded, reinforced by the narcotic urge, blood-lust—call it what you will—to follow the defeated foe until he had seen the flaming mass dash itself to the ground, had caused him to fly too low, and the bullet of an infantryman had killed him. But he had died as he had so often expressed a wish that he might—at the height of his fame; at the moment of victory; and while teaching a beginner his art. That he fell in flames only confirmed his fears; but the fact that he did not fall a victim to the bullet of an enemy airman only vindicated his comrades' conviction that as an air fighter he was invincible and supreme.

Donald Inglis describing the tragic flight writes:

"My instructions were to sit on Mick's tail, and that he would waggle his wings if he wanted me closer. I soon found that I didn't have much chance of looking round, as Mick would waggle, and the only thing I could do was to watch his tail and stick tight, as he was flying along the lines at about thirty to fifty feet up and not straight for more than a few seconds, first up on one wing tip, then the other. Suddenly he turned towards home full out and climbing. 'A Hun,' thought I, but I'm damned if I could find one; then a quick turn and a dive, and there was Mick shooting up a Hun two-seater. He must have got the observer, as when he pulled up and I came in underneath him I didn't see the Hun shooting. I flushed the Hun's petrol tank and just missed ramming his tail as it came up when the Hun's nose dropped. Falling in behind Mick again we did a couple of circles round the burning wreck and then made for home. I saw Mick start to kick his rudder and realised we were fairly low, then I saw a flame come out of the side of his machine; it grew bigger and bigger. Mick was no longer kicking his rudder, his nose dropped slightly and he went into a slow right-hand turn round, about twice, and hit the ground in a burst of flame. I circled at about twenty feet, but could not see him, and as things were getting pretty hot, made for home and managed to reach our outposts with a punctured petrol tank.

'Poor old Mick,' all I could say when I got into the trench was that the b—b—s had shot my Major down in flames."

The normal time for pilots to be wakened was about 8 o'clock. But on this memorable morning, all the pilots were up and standing around in groups outside the officers' Mess, dressed only in pyjamas and overcoats, scanning the eastern sky half an hour earlier. The news had spread that the Major and Inglis had left at dawn and that they had not returned. "Oh," said an optimistic pilot, "it's all right. Mick has probably landed at No. 74 for breakfast. He is celebrating his seventy-third victory." Another cheerful soul supported the suggestion with, "There is no need to worry, chaps, old Mick is all right. There's no Hun good enough to get him." The more serious-minded said nothing, but thought a lot.

At 8 a.m. most of the pilots were sitting at the breakfast table enjoying the Decca, and the tragedy which had befallen the Squadron was still unsuspected.

Suddenly the telephone bell rang, Captain Horn answered it.

"Hello! Is that No. 85 Squadron?"

"Yes. This is Nigger Horn speaking."

"Oh! This is the Archie Battery near Hazebrouck speaking. Has Mannock returned?"

"No. Why?"

"Well, a couple of S.E.s, one of which had a red streamer on its tail and was flown just as Mannock usually flies, attacked a Hun about 5.30 a.m. and shot it down in flames; they then followed it down to the ground, and we have not seen them return; it looked as if they may have got shot down themselves. We are sure it was Mannock, because we know his tactics."

This information frightened most of the members, but some who were determined not to believe that any ill could befall their hero said, "What rot! How do they know his flying? His machine is like all others, and many other leaders fly a red streamer."

Yes, how did they know his machine, and in particular, his flying? They knew it because through their telescopes they had often watched him destroy enemy after enemy before. They recognised his preliminary cunning manœuvres, and the swiftness and relentlessness of his attack once he was satisfied with his tactical position. They recognised in that sudden short burst of fire, and an enemy falling in flames, the master hand of Mannock. He stood alone as the one air fighter they recognised in the vastness of the sky, without being in a position to recognise his features. This faith of the "Archie" gunners in their ability to recognise him in the air is the highest compliment which has ever been paid to an air fighter.

Half an hour later the telephone operator of the Squadron was becoming paler and paler, and his hand trembled more and more, as he wrote word by word this unbelievable message from the 24th Welch Regiment, who were holding the trenches opposite Lestrem:

"Major Mannock down by machine gun from ground between Calonne and Lestrem after bringing E.A. two-seater down in flames at Lestrem. Lieutenant Inglis shot through petrol tank landed on front line at St. Floris. Machine O.K., Pilot O.K. Machine likely to be shelled, salvage to-night if possible, more later. Machine at Sheet 36a S.E. or 36 N.W., K.31, D.14."

When the news became known, pilots who had not known fear turned deathly pale, and became momentarily speechless. A void within them seemed to eat away their very souls. For minutes they stared at one another as if they were in a trance. Then, as the weight of the blow lessened, they staggered to their huts and wept. The mechanics were similarly affected, and carried on their work with tears in their eyes and with a heavy heart. They had not only lost a just Commander whom they trusted and respected, but a friend to whom they could go with their private sorrows with absolute confidence of sympathy.

When the news spread among the Squadrons, a representative from all of those in the vicinity called on the Squadron in the evening to try to cheer up the pilots. No. 74, who had fought with Mick for months, were even more affected than No. 85, so Caldwell, Young, Jones, VanIra, and Roxburgh-Smith went over to assist in livening up the party. VanIra records the evening thus:

"Last night lots of fellows turned up at No. 85 to cheer up the lads. Among the star fighters were 'Mary' Coningham and Collishaw, both of whom assisted considerably in making the evening cheerful. It was a difficult business. The thought of Mick's charred body not many miles away haunted us and damped our spirits. There was more drinking than usual on these occasions; the Decca worked overtime; we tried to sing, but it was painfully obvious that it was forced, as there was a noticeable discord. We tried to prove that we could take a licking without squealing. It was damned hard. Caldwell said in his little speech after dinner that Mick would not wish us to mope. We never do it in No. 74, so let's liven up. And liven up we did—up to a point. The C. O. is really very cut-up."

When Inglis returned to the Squadron the next day and told his story, everyone realised that there was no hope. Several pilots flew low—at great risk to themselves—over the spot where the wreckage lay to satisfy their disconsolate souls, and their inflamed passion caused them to risk their lives unnecessarily as they proceeded to shoot up any German infantryman they saw in the vicinity.

Inglis in his combat report describes the fight thus:

### "COMBATS IN THE AIR

| | |
|---|---|
| Squadron No. 85. | Dated 26th July, 1918 |
| Type & No. of Aeroplane: | Time: 5.30 a.m. |
| S.E.5a E. 1294. | Locality: Lestrem-Calonne. |
| Armament: I Vickers, | Duty: Special Mission |
| I Lewis. | Result: Destroyed—One. |
| Pilot: Lieut. D. C. Inglis. | |

Remarks on Hostile Aircraft—Type, armament, speed, etc. Two-seater; Type unknown.

### Narrative

While following Major Mannock in search of two-seater E.A.s, we observed an E.A. two-seater coming towards the line and turned away to gain height, and dived to get east of E.A. E.A. saw us just too soon and turned east, Major Mannock turned and got in a good burst when he pulled away. I got in a good burst at very close range, after which E.A. went into a slow left-hand spiral with flames coming out of his right side. I watched him go straight into the ground and go up in a large cloud of black smoke and flame.

I then turned and followed Major Mannock back about 200 feet. About half-way back I saw a flame come out of the right-hand side of his machine, after which he apparently went down out of control. I went into a spiral down to 50 feet and saw machine go straight into the ground and burn. I saw no one leave the machine and then started for the line, climbing slightly; at about 150 feet there was a bang, and I was smothered with petrol; my engine cut out so I switched off and made a landing 5 yards behind our front line.

(Sd.) DONALD C. INGLIS, Lieut.

(Sd.) A. C. RANDALL, Captain, Commanding No. 85 Squadron."

It was quite obvious to everyone that there was not the slightest hope that Mannock could be alive. His Squadron, therefore, did not keep up the pathetic vigil which the famous French Stork Squadron performed when they lost their incomparable comrade and idol Guynemer.

There is a great similarity in the passing of these two warriors. Both fought their last fight with a two-seater; both were reported to have been buried in a certain place; either may be resting as the representative of a nation's sacrifice in the tomb of the Unknown Soldier, for neither grave has ever been traced, nor have the remains of their machines been found.

There was also a great similarity in their general conception of their duty. Reading Guynemer's talk with his father, who was advising him to take a rest, as quoted in Henry Bordeaux's fascinating book, *Guynemer, Knight of the Air*, one can imagine the son's replies as issuing from the mouth of Mannock.

"You need strengthening; you have done too much. If you should go on, you would be in great danger of falling below yourself, of being not really yourself."

The father continues to persuade, but the conversation is ended when the son remarks:

"We have given nothing as long as we have not given everything."

They both gave their all. Every pilot felt it was indeed something to have lived and fought with such men as Mannock and Guynemer. Their life and death were at once an inspiration and a proud inheritance.

The pilots of No. 85 knew the wish of their lost leader so they did not allow his loss to react adversely on their imagination or on their offensive fighting tactics, as the loss of Richthofen had affected his "circus." In fact, they fought with greater fury than ever.

The mystery of his grave is like that of thousands of others who found their last Rest in the shelled area. An Air Ministry letter from the Secretary of State for Air dated July 24th, 1919, to Eyles, states:

"The information which we have has been received through the Central Prisoners of War Committee, who apparently obtained their information from German sources. Major Mannock, according to this report, died on July 26th, 1918. It is regretted that no information is available as regards his place of burial."

A letter from the Imperial War Graves Commission dated June 2nd, 1921, to the Rev. E. Rogers, O.B.E., M.A., of the Church Lads' Brigade, is more informative. It reads:

"I am directed to inform you that Major E. Mannock, V.C., D.S.O., M.C., is reported to have been buried at a point 300 metres north-west of La Pierre au Beure in the vicinity of Pacaut, east of Lillers. I regret, however, to say that the officers of the Graves Registration Units have not yet been able to find the grave."

A final letter on the subject to Eyles from the Imperial War Graves Commission was not any more helpful:

"With reference to previous correspondence, I am directed to inform you that the inquiries which were being made regarding the burial-place of Major Edward Mannock, V.C., D.S.O., M.C., have now been completed. I regret to say, however, that it has not been possible to identify his grave.

As you are aware, Major Mannock was reported to have been buried at a spot 300 metres north-west of La Pierre-au-Beure on the road to Pacaut. Although all this neighbourhood has been searched, and the remains of all those soldiers buried in isolated and scattered graves reverently reburied in cemeteries in order that the graves might be permanently and suitably maintained, the grave of this officer has not been identified.

A special search has since been made for the grave, and the Representative of this Commission in France reports that the locality is now reconstructed and all the fields cultivated, and there is no surface evidence of graves any where in the vicinity. It is added that the remnants of an aeroplane were found, but unfortunately the condition of this aeroplane is so bad that no markings could be traced, all woodwork being burnt away and the metal rusted. The statements of local inhabitants differ as to whether this aeroplane is British or German.

A further inquiry was sent to the representative of this Commission in Berlin, to obtain more definite information as to the position of Major Mannock's grave. The reply, however, states that only the original report is available, and no sketch showing the position of the grave can be obtained; further that the report emanated from a German Intelligence Officer whose records were entirely lost during the retreat.

The records of the exhumation work in this area have been carefully searched, but there is no trace of a report of the finding of any grave which can be thought likely to be Major Mannock's. There was the grave of an unknown British airman found in this neighbourhood and identified by wreckage of an aeroplane. The date of this unknown British airman's death, however, cannot be ascertained. Although this grave was found some distance from where Major Mannock was reported to have been buried, endeavours have been made to identify the grave as that Major Mannock, but without success.

As the records held by the Air Ministry contain no references as to the locality of the crashes in a large number of cases, it is not possible to compile a complete list of casualties for the area in the vicinity of La Pierre-au-Beure and Pacaut. It has not, therefore, been possible to identify this unknown British officer, and I fear that it is not possible to say that the grave is Major Mannock's.

I need hardly add that any definite information which may be obtained will be communicated to you without delay, but I fear that there is now very little hope of this.

It is the intention of the Commission to erect memorials to those officers and men whose graves cannot be found. You may rest assured that the dead who have no known resting-place will be honoured equally with the others, and that each case will be dealt with upon full consideration of its merits as regards the site and the place of the memorial."

And so the King of Air Fighters passed into the Valhalla of heroes in the same unobtrusive manner that characterised his modesty in life; unheralded and unsung; just as he would have wished, his duty well done. A great man had passed. The bugles blared a dim shrill through the dawn at Roncesvalles. Roland was no more! East of Lillers the sky brightens today. The broken earth of France embraces in its blood-soaked, churned-up soil the charred remains of one of the most heroic spirits of our age. The blooded warriors stand mutely at the salute. Reverently they listen to the booming guns splashing the mud over his mutilated form. Mick Mannock is being buried with all the honours of the war—by the ages—and the heroes of all times, all races, are at once his grave-diggers and his mourners.

# V

## *King of Air Fighters*

Mannock's comrades, who knew and admired his achievements and personality, were not prepared to let them pass unnoticed or unrecognised. If any airman deserved the highest of all awards for bravery, they knew that he did, and they were determined that justice must be done to his great work.

They, therefore, agreed to combine and to agitate for the posthumous award of the Victoria Cross. Months of weary warfare rolled by, and then came the sudden Armistice. The war over, his comrades who were leaving the Air Force to return to civil employment decided that they could now press Mannock's claims with greater effect. Eventually an avenue was found which led to the ear of the Air Minister of the time, the Right Honourable Winston Churchill. The Air Minister caused the claims of Mannock's comrades to be immediately investigated, and as a result, on the eve of Peace Day, there appeared in the *London Gazette* the announcement that His Majesty had posthumously awarded the Victoria Cross to Major Edward Mannock "in recognition of bravery of the first order in aerial combat."

The Citation, having recorded many of Mannock's aerial victories, ended with praise which did justice to his great achievements and memory:

Note.—Any italics in this chapter are the author's.

"This highly distinguished officer, during the whole of his career in the Royal Air Force, was an outstanding example of fearless courage, remarkable skill, devotion to duty and self-sacrifice, which has never been surpassed."

The title of King of Air Fighters has at various times been applied to Ball and McCudden, the British heroes; to Guynemer and Foncke, the French aces; to Boelcke and Richthofen, the German idols; but never before to Mannock—the greatest of them all.

Ball and Guynemer were of the same mettle. They fought as much for the love of fighting as for their desire to kill their country's enemies. Often they "saw red," and many a time they returned with badly scarred machines as a consequence. They attacked the enemy regardless of tactical position, and fought until the last bullet was spent. To them air fighting was a gladiatorial combat to be fought among Knights of the Air. They set a standard of valour to their comrades which was accepted as the measure to emulate.

McCudden, Foncke, and Boelcke were tacticians. They fought on "Safety First" lines, and many were their victories as a result. Rarely did their machines return scarred from the combat. Theirs was duty well done.

Mannock and Richthofen, now the recognised aces of their respective sides during the war, were both expert individualists, as well as clever leaders of large formations. That they both displayed courage and aggressiveness is indisputable, although the quality of the one was better than that of the other. The question then arises: which of them overshadows the other, which of them was the King of Air Fighters? Let us compare their characters and records, and we will be able to realise why one is obviously greater than the other. At the same time it will be easy for the reader to understand why the British airman was the superior of the German, for the fighting tactics of Mannock and Richthofen typify the spirit of the race to which each belonged.

Mannock's character and achievements have already been set down, as far as it is possible to record them: the reader has no doubt by this time realised the impossibility of accurately estimating the number of victories which he had gained (or any British pilot as far as that goes) because of the locality of his fighting. There is little doubt, however, that purely in respect of numbers the two great aces are more or less on an equal footing.

In order to appreciate Richthofen's record it is necessary to describe Boelcke's tactics, for it was he who was Richthofen's master and instructor in air fighting. They are clearly exposed in Boelcke's letters.

The principles of the science of air fighting, which were specifically evolved by Boelcke, were the foundations on which others built. And it is of the highest importance to note how these tactics differed from those of Ball and Mannock, not only in principle, but in their actual effect on the traditions evolved by the respective belligerents. The German airmen, following the inspiration and lead given them by Boelcke, perfected the science of air fighting DEFENCE. The British, inspired by Ball and trained by Mannock, perfected the science of OFFENCE. The importance of this difference in method shaped the future course of the War in the Air to such a degree that, eventually, the supremacy of the air was unquestionably won for the British.

Boelcke, who must be accepted as the most admirable type of German fighting pilot, flew the very first Fokker Scout, which at the time was the only aeroplane in the war able to fire through the propeller (Garros having no imitators on our side as yet). This invention gave his machine an overwhelming advantage over any other type, irrespective of its superior performance. He makes the following naïvely contradictory observation in his own diary which shows up the German airman's mentality more eloquently and conclusively than any of the records written during and since the war by sympathisers with either side. His diary proves once and for all that the German airman looked on his own side of the lines as the place to fight in the air and, in fact, was trained so to do. He only ventured our side when the odds were definitely on his side. He did not dispute the *mastery* of the air at all. He merely defended the air above his own aerodrome as far as his own front-line trenches. The German airmen regarded the enemy side of the line as "Verboten" air. Our men, on the other hand, did not consider themselves in the war at all until they were well over the enemy's lines. An entry from his diary reads:

"Douai, 16.7.15.—In addition to its technical points my little single-seater possesses the advantage of giving me complete independence; I can fly when, where, how long and how I will. I have not yet caught anyone else over our lines— the event of 4.7 has given the French a mighty scare, and they treat my single-seater with holy respect. As soon as I appear on the scene, they bolt as quickly as they can. As I cannot catch any of them here, I go to look for them on their side of the lines where they think they can spot for their artillery in safety. I have to prowl about stealthily and invisibly, using every trick and wile I can manage. In this fashion I have succeeded in shooting at four of them, but as they always make a dive for home at once, I could not get any of them *because I cannot chase them too far behind the enemy's lines without exposing myself to their artillery.*

Most of the other gentlemen flying Fokker fighters—there are only eleven all told so far on the Western Front—think differently, and *do not intend to attack anywhere but behind our lines, because they can fight to a finish there only. That is certainly true, but the consequence is that they do nothing but go for joy-rides round our lines and never get a shot at the enemy,* whereas I have the pleasure of getting a good smack at the fellows over yonder. One must not wait till they come across, but seek them out and hunt them down."

How definitely the German airman had the inferiority complex about flying over enemy territory is verified by the "incomparable Boelcke" himself. That he preferred to fight on his own side of the lines, in spite of the superior performance of his machine, is made plain by the following quotations from a letter:

"As my first opponent went down deeper and deeper and his companions closed in on me, I had to finally assume that *I was over the enemy's lines. For that reason I broke off the fight*; as I had the superior speed and the Frenchmen promptly sheered off from me, I was soon alone once more.... I got my Fokker from Metz several days ago and flew it daily—to the great sorrow of Teubern, who consequently has nothing to do. Yesterday morning I patrolled a stretch of the front from Rheims towards the Champagne. Just as I was over Pontfaverger I saw a machine rumbling about behind the enemy's lines. *I kept my eye on him, and was highly delighted when I noticed the fellow coming across—apparently he had failed to spot me. For a fight behind our lines is something different from one on the other side, because the enemy cannot make a bolt for the ground.*

The Frenchman circled round our territory and then wanted to go home. But I barred his way: he came slanting across to me, and was cheeky enough to shoot at me. I calmly let him fire away, for the combined speed of two opponents meeting one another reduces the chance of a hit to practically nil—as I have already to get behind my man as quickly as possible.

As I was a few hundred metres above him, it worked very well. At the moment that I was directly over him I took my machine round and dived on him. Now things began to get a bit uncomfortable for him, so he tried hard to get away and flew round in circles.

But as the fellow shot up at me in a slanting direction, I quickly dropped down a bit deeper and came at him from behind. In air fights it is absolutely essential to fly in such a way that your adversary cannot shoot at you, if you can manage it. *Owing to my superior speed* I soon came up quite close—within twenty to thirty-nine metres of him—from which distance I put about two hundred shots into him. That was too much for him, and he preferred to dive headlong..."

So daring were the British airmen in their slow and cumbersome two-seaters that Boelcke records how Immelmann achieved his first victory by the fortunate coincidence of attacking an unarmed aeroplane which was actually carrying out a reconnaissance over their own aerodrome at Douai:

"Early on the morning of 1.8.15—it was Sunday—the clouds hung so low that the officer on duty telephoned it was no use going out to the aerodrome. So I was lying quite happily in bed when Fischer suddenly woke me and said there was an Englishman about. I jumped out and ran to the window. But as the Englishman was making for the Front and so I had no chance of catching him, I crawled back under my bedclothes, cursing. I had hardly got warm once more before Fischer rushed in a second time; the Englishman was coming back again. Well, if the fellow is so impudent, I thought, I'll get up quick and have a go at him. So all unwashed, with my nightshirt still on, but no puttees, I shoved along to the aerodrome on my motor-bike and came just in time to see those chaps—there was not one, but four of them—amusing themselves by dropping bombs on our aerodrome. I jumped into my machine and took off. But as the Englishmen flew home as soon as they had dropped their bombs and had very fast machines, I did not manage to get within range of them. I turned back sadly.

When I got over the aerodrome again—I could scarcely believe my eyes—there were another five machines that had come to pay us a visit with their bombs. So I went for the nearest, a monoplane. I got to grips with him nicely and peppered him well, but when I was close enough up to think that the next shot must send him crashing—Lord, my gun jammed! Oh! I was wild. I tried to remove the jam up there, and used so much force in my rage that the obstructing cartridge broke in half. So there was nothing for it but to land and get a fresh supply of ammunition.

As I went down I saw our other monoplane coming up and felt pleased that those English machines would at least get their tails twisted by it. While I was loading with new cartridges down below, I saw Lieutenant Immelmann attack an Englishman in grand style, and send him bolting. I climbed up again quickly to help Immelmann against the others. But they cleared off again as soon as they saw me arrive on the scene the second time, and I only had disappointment for my trouble. Meanwhile Immelmann had forced his Englishman to land; he put a bullet through his elbow, so that he had to come down as quickly as he could.

Immelmann was extraordinarily lucky over the whole business, I only gave him his first lesson on a Fokker three days before, i.e. I went up with him in his machine and let him help handle the controls. The day before he did his first solo and had great difficulty in pulling off his landing. He had never flown against the enemy in a Fokker and had never fired his machine gun before—*and then he had the luck to catch a defenceless biplane over our aerodrome, because the Englishman had left his observer at home to save weight for his bombs.* All the same, Immelmann did his job beautifully, and I congratulate him sincerely on his success. But I really am annoyed at my own bad luck; it was the first time for four weeks that I got an opponent bang in front of my gun, and then it must go and jam!"

In describing his "hardest fight," Boelcke actually boasts of the advantage of fighting over his own territory as his main inspirational idea in combat. The fact that the Englishman would have to fly straight some time in order to get back to his lines was like balm to his valiant spirit; he favoured this advantage to possessing the dash and offensive spirit which his opponents had.

Boelcke's letters and Richthofen's diary entries are a series of recapitulations of events where the Britisher is over on their side and they are constantly leaving their aerodromes to defend themselves! When they achieve the feat of downing an enemy the entire credit that they take to themselves is that of making one less go home. They leave entirely out of account the fact that the Britisher had to fight his way to them, often with obvious engine or gun trouble.

To the German, engine trouble during a fight meant nothing more serious than landing on or near his own aerodrome; for an Englishman it often meant capture. The spirit of our airmen made them try to glide back to our lines while being attacked all the time, although their effort was challenging almost certain death, which they preferred to being taken prisoner, as hundreds of combats over the enemy's lines are testified by the Germans themselves:

"And now comes the best part of the joke. On the 14th, *i.e.* yesterday, there was good weather in the morning. So I took off about 9 a.m., all fresh and lively again, to see after *my customers*. As the sky above Lille was clouding over, I shifted my hunting-ground to the south of Arras. I had hardly been flying for an hour before I saw shell-bursts round Bapaume way. While I was flying there, the Englishman seemed to catch sight of me, for the flew back. But I soon overhauled him. When he noticed that I was going for him, *he went into a sudden turn and attacked me.*

Now began the hardest fight I have had up to now. The Englishman tried all the time to get on to my back, and I tried the same to him. So we whirled merrily round each other, but as I had taken to heart my experience of Dec. 29th (when I shot away all my ammunition) I only fired when I had him well in my sights. Thus it came about that we went round each other for several minutes without my firing a single shot. The merry-go-round did not worry me, *because we were over our territory; I said to myself, 'some time or other he'll have to fly straight to go home.'* Then while we were circling he continually tried to work his way nearer to the front lines, which were not too far distant. On one of these occasions I succeeded in getting on to him and shooting his engine to pieces—I noticed that because after I attacked him he tried to reach the English lines (which were now quite near) in a long glide, with a column of oil vapour trailing behind him. I had to stop that.

His glide had brought him fairly low down, and so I had to attack him again. I caught him up just by our trenches at a height of one to two hundred metres and pounded him from close quarters with both my machine guns—I did not need to save ammunition now. We were both just above our trenches at the moment when I caught him. I then turned away; I could not find out where the other machine was, because I had to clear off myself, as I had not much petrol left.

I therefore landed at Flers village, where I received very kindly attentions from the divisional staff, and, much to my delight, learnt at once what had happened to the Englishman. After I turned away, the enemy machine landed at once close to the English trenches—at this spot the trenches are only one hundred metres away from one another. One of the inmates—the pilot—apparently climbed out of the half-wrecked machine and escaped into the English trenches in spite of the fire directed on to him by our infantry. Our field artillery then shelled the machine. One of the first shots was a direct hit, so that the machine took fire at once; the other inmate, probably the observer, who was already dead or badly wounded, was burnt with it. Only the skeleton of the machine remained."

In the copy of this letter which Boelcke sent to his brother, Wilhelm, there is a footnote drawing his attention to an important addition at the end which was a piece of private information for him:

"For you alone! The real reason of my retreat was that the Englishman shot my tank to pieces; I had only some petrol from the emergency tank; moreover the machine had been hit several times; one bullet went through the bonnet on to my chronometer, while another penetrated the sleeves of my overcoat and jacket. I must have got it from close range when we were about eight hundred metres up—it felt like a blow on the arm. When I saw that arm and engine were both in working order, I set about the fellow with both guns as a punishment. As I also came into the propeller wind at the moment when he hit me, and the machine side-slipped a bit, that chap must have certainly thought I was done for. But after-wards he was able to convince himself to the contrary. You don't need to be afraid I'll be too rash; I'm looking after myself all right."

The incomprehensible mentality of the German, a mentality which has puzzled politicians as well as soldiers, is well illustrated by the following. Boelcke professes he sees in the French airmen's attitude something to be despised—something contemptible, not consonant with real valour—but all the time he is telling us how he himself is practising the very precepts and tactics he affects to despise:

"*11.4.16—Business gets worse every day. The French never come across to us now; they only take the air a long way behind their own lines. Nevertheless, our service is not*

*light—this continual lying in wait without results is greater
strain than a jolly scrap."*

How well this attitude on the part of the German colours the
ever-recurrent theme in Mannock's letters home about the
German airmen's refusal to accept combat! Even as a tyro
Mannock sensed this defect in the German mentality and
this idea grew and grew in his consciousness until it later
dominated his whole offensive concept of action in a fight.
This knowledge filled all our airmen with a sense of
superiority which they never once yielded up to the enemy
right throughout the war.

German reports as to crashes, and their records of actual
destruction even on their own side of the lines, are not
always completely accurate, as has been shown. Thus, if it
was so difficult for a German airman to establish his claims
behind his own lines, how much more difficult was it for a
Britisher to prove his claim when he was constantly battling
over the enemy's side of the lines! If we appreciate this
difficulty, we can admire the high veracity and integrity of
Mannock, who never made a claim without witnesses, and
then only for those he downed without any possible doubt
whatsoever. His comrades constantly speak of this high
quality of their leader, and tell how impressed they were by
his unwillingness to accept credit for a victory until all
possible avenues for establishing its truth had been explored,
and the result had been verified by actual eye-witnesses or
participators in the combat.

Summing up, we cannot more eloquently prove our case
than by quoting the principles and rules of aerial warfare as
set down by the German master himself. He was asked one
day to state these principles for the guidance of his pupils

and famous *Staffel*, and here is what he wrote about flying over the enemy's side of the lines:

*"When over the enemy's lines never forget your own line of retreat!"*

From this it is clear that the German fighting pilot never conceived it his duty to look on the other side of the lines as his legitimate fighting ground.

When Boelcke was at his fighting zenith, the following episode illustrates that the master never broke his own rules, and apart from the fact that the combat was an uneven contest from the start, it must be remembered that the respective "aeroplanes" flown by the opposing contestants were not even comparably matched either in speed, manœuvrability, or armament. Yet the "great Boelcke" has usually to "lure" an enemy over to his own territory, even when the odds are already in his favour at the start of the combat! Even when he has the enemy completely at his mercy and shoots him down, he naïvely admits the vast superiority of his own craft:

"May 17th was a strenuous day. One of our artillery machines wanted to photograph the Côte Marre (to the west of Verdun), and asked me to come along as escort. On the homeward flight I saw shell-bursts near Douaumont, and went to have a closer look. I found four or five German biplanes there, along with several French scouts. I kept in the background for a while, and watched the enemy. Then I saw a Nieuport get cheeky and attack one of our biplanes. I dived on him, and thought my victory was certain, as I managed to get within close range unobserved. But there was too much way on my machine, so that I shot over him. He speedily bolted, and I followed close behind. I got several good shots at him, but I was up against an able opponent, who flew brilliantly. *I followed him for a while, but retreated behind our lines when several of his companions came to help him*, and watched out for the enemy that were still about. One that was flying much higher than I was came along and attacked me—we went into several joyous turns, and then he cleared off.

This little joke brought me down from my fine height of four thousand metres to two thousand. Then suddenly—I could hardly believe my eyes—eight double-engined Caudrons made their appearance over the lines between Douaumont and the Meuse, flying in pairs at four thousand four hundred. Such a low trick—I now had to climb right up to this height to get at them! But as those fellows flew so uncannily high, and took not the least trouble to come down to me, I did not come to grips with them. I tried to give one of them a dose from below, but they punished me with cold contempt, and flew homeward without troubling themselves about me.

All this took fifteen to twenty minutes, and once more I reached a considerable height. Then—I was over Douaumont —I saw two more Caudrons coming over Côte de Talou, and noted with great joy that they were at a lower height than I was. So I flew after them, but meanwhile they had recrossed the Meuse. Then, just in time, I saw another Caudron and a Nieuport diving down on to me. I engaged the most dangerous opponent first and flew straight at the Nieuport."

"*Douai*, 31.12.15.—The day before yesterday we had another merry day after the long spell of bad weather. In the morning I chased away the fellows who came across from

Arras, and when flying home, I saw shell-bursts to the west of Cambrai. So off I quickly went to look. I came just in time to see another Fokker—it was Immelmann—start a scrap with two Englishmen. I dived on the one nearest to me, but then saw that Immelmann had already taken him on, and given him enough, so that he was bound to go down soon. So I promptly went for the other, who was ready for a tussle. That was a fine fight. I had to deal with a tough fellow, who defended himself stoutly. But I forced him on to the defensive at once. Then he tried to escape me by turns, etc., and made an effort to get at me on my weak side. He did not succeed, but the only success I scored was forcing his machine ever farther down—we began at two thousand metres, and in a short time I fought him down to less than one thousand. Finally he could defend himself no longer, because *I had mortally wounded his observer*. It was now a comparatively easy job to shoot the fellow down, but when we got to eight hundred metres I ran out of ammunition, because I had previously used some of it on two others. That was his salvation. We now circled round each other, but neither could do the other any harm.

Finally, Immelmann came to my aid, and the fight began all over again. I kept on attacking merrily, so as to confuse the Englishman. We managed to force him down to one hundred metres, and waited for him to land, but he went on flying about like mad, all over the place, with the pair of us behind him. I tried to cut off his further progress by flying at him, etc.; then my engine gave out, and I had to land. I could just see my opponent disappearing behind the next row of trees, and thought he would land there; I was delighted, and arming myself with a Very pistol—I had no other weapon at hand—I rode across on horseback to take the fellow prisoner. But he had flown on. I made inquiries everywhere and rang up—no definite news obtainable. *Then in the evening there came a report that the Englishman actually flew over the trenches at a height of one hundred metres and got home.* Smart of the fellow; he won't have many imitators! Immelmann could not go on shooting at him because his gun jammed."[6]

The German air fighter took his lead from the example of Boelcke, whose spirit and tactics have now been revealed by his own admission. Boelcke's spirit was commendable enough, but was strictly limited in its aggressiveness, while his tactics were conspicuous by their strong defensive flavour. With the exception of a few German air fighters of the quality of Voss, all enemy pilots, including Richthofen, were imbued with their master's defensive spirit.

A study of Richthofen's character and tactics, as deduced from his own writings, makes it clear that his attitude towards air fighting was in some respects the opposite of Mannock's. A few quotations will suffice to make this point clear. According to his biography (*The Red Air Fighter*), Richthofen makes the following admissions:

*"During the whole of my life I have not found a happier hunting-ground than in the course of the Somme Battle. In the morning, as soon as I had got up, the first Englishman arrived, and the last disappeared only after sunset."*

"Sometimes the English come down to a very low altitude, and visit Boelcke in his own quarters, upon which they

---

[6] The quotations on the preceding pages are taken by kind permission from *Boelcke—Knight of Germany*, by Professor Werner, published by John Hamilton Ltd.

throw their bombs. *They absolutely challenge us to battle, and never refuse fighting.*"

"*It is better for one's customers to come to one's shop than to have to look for one's customers.*"

This latter assertion, beyond any doubt, definitely defines Richthofen's limited offensive spirit. In this blatant statement, written in cold blood, and published to the world, the German ace of aces condemns himself as a defensive fighter without any shadow of doubt. His record substantiates this assertion—he rarely fought on our side of the lines, and then—only just over, and against opponents with inferior equipment. A study of his victories confirms this: out of eighty which he claimed, at least fifty were two-seaters, so inferior in performance to his fast Albatross, with its two Spandau guns firing through the propeller, that they can be justly compared only with the victory of a kestrel hawk over a foraging fledgling sparrow, wandering far from its own nest. Of the remaining twenty-nine (for now we know definitely that at least one victim which he claimed he did not shoot down) many were single-seaters whose performance were decidedly inferior to that of Richthofen's aeroplane—the Vickers Fighter, the F.E. IS the D.H.2S, the Spad, the Nieuport, and the "Pup." As Richthofen was usually attacked over his own aerodrome, and often compelled to get out of bed, the victories are nothing to boast about. There were types of British machines whose performances compared favourably with the Albatross, and it is interesting to note how few of them he actually shot down; they were—the S.E.5, the Sopwith Triplane, the Sopwith "Camel."

The S.E.5 first appeared in France in 1917, flown by pilots of No. 56 Squadron, who threw down the gauntlet to the German air fighters; the famous pilots of the Squadron fought many battles with the Red Circus, but Richthofen himself appears to have been conspicuous by his absence in the dog-fights, for it was not until December 1917 that he was able to claim a victory over an S.E.5, although there were already 335 of them in France. His victim then was a pilot who had only been six weeks in France. His only other S.E.5 victim was a raw pilot. It is further interesting to note that Richthofen only shot down one famous British fighting pilot—Major Hawker V.C., who was, at the time, flying a much inferior machine—a D.H.2. Hawker challenged the German ace to a duel far over his own territory. Richthofen has made much ballyhoo and song of this fight in his book, and elsewhere, but when it is carefully analysed, it is only another "hawk versus sparrow" fight, with the sparrow fighting with the indomitable courage of a Britisher, courage which the Germans envied and secretly admired. Writing of the difference between the English and French fighting pilots, Richthofen says:

"Sometimes, however, the Gallic blood asserts itself. Then Frenchmen will attack. But the French attacking spirit is like bottled lemonade. It lacks tenacity.... But the English see in flying nothing but a sport... *They absolutely challenge us to battle, and never refuse fighting...* Therefore the blood of English pilots will have to flow in streams."

The British pilot fought with the spirit of abandon which Richthofen and his comrades could never understand. The tactics of OFFENCE were a mystery to them.

The Sopwith Triplane was a match for Richthofen's Albatross, and it is a significant fact that he did not shoot a single one of this type down, although it is on record that many engagements took place between our Triplanes and the "Circus."

The Sopwith "Camel," when it arrived in France in October 1917, was a match for any German aeroplane, but again Richthofen does not claim a victory over one of this type until March 1918, when it was then inferior in performance to his Triplane. In all he claims seven "Camel" victims; the respective pilots' service in France was—9 weeks, 5 weeks, 6 weeks, 3 weeks, 2 years, 7 months, 3 weeks. It is clear from a study of his record that the Baron picked out his victims with great discrimination. If he could arrange it he only fought "easy meat." It is widely declared, and there is little doubt, that he hovered above the dog-fights, and waited for an easy opponent, many of which were undoubtedly already "lame ducks," victims of one of his gentlemen, who had to do the spade-work before the master completed the task; or, as in some cases, he just followed the victims to the ground, eventually to claim them as his own victories.

That Richthofen was not always accurate in his statements is made clear in more than one recorded instance. That he claimed a Nieuport as crashed, which actually was not the case, has already been pointed out. That he wrote contradictory stories and occasionally exaggerated the intensity of combats can also be proved; for instance, on April 2nd, 1917, he describes a fight thus (the italics are mine):

"The second of April, 1917, was a very warm day for my *jagdstaffel*. From my quarters I could hear the drum fire, which was again particularly violent. I was still in bed when my orderly rushed into the room, and exclaimed: 'Sir, the English are here!'

Sleepy as I was, I looked out of the window, and really, *there were my dear friends circling over the flying-ground.* I jumped out of bed and into my clothes in a jiffy. My red bird had been pulled out of the hangars, and was ready for starting. My mechanics knew that I would probably not allow such a favourable moment to go by unused. Everything was ready. I snatched up my furs, and went up.

I was last to start. My comrades had started earlier and were much nearer to the enemy. I feared that my prey would escape, and that I should have to look on from a distance while the others were fighting.

Suddenly, one of the impertinent Englishmen tried to drop down on me. I allowed him to approach quite near, and then we started a merry quadrille. *Sometimes my opponent flew on his back, and sometimes did other tricks. He was flying a two-seater fighter.* I realised very soon that I was his master, and that he could not escape me.

During an interval in the fighting, I assured myself that we were alone. It followed that the victory would belong to him who was the calmest, who shot best, and who had the clearest brain in the moment of danger.

Soon I had got him beneath me without having seriously hurt him with my gun. We were at least two kilometres from the front. I thought he intended to land, but there I had made a mistake. Suddenly, when he was only a few yards above the ground, I noticed how he once more went off on a straight course. He tried to escape me. That was too bad.

I attacked him again, and to do so I had to go so low that I was afraid of touching the roofs of the houses in the village beneath me. The Englishman defended himself up to the last moment. At the very end, I felt that my engine had been hit. Still I did not let go. He had to fall. He flew at full speed right into a block of houses.

There is little left to be said. *This was once more a case of splendid daring. The man had defended himself to the last. However, in my opinion, he showed, after all, more stupid foolhardiness than courage. It was, again, one of the cases where one must differentiate between energy and idiocy.* He had to come down in any case, but he paid for his stupidity with his life.

I was delighted with the performance of my red machine and returned to the aerodrome. My comrades were still in the air, and they were surprised when we met later at breakfast, and I told them that I had scored my thirty-second machine."

When it is revealed in Richthofen's combat report that *the "two-seater fighter" was a cumbersome old B.E.*, a type which had been in France since early 1915, and a machine which could not fly on its back, it is quite unnecessary to make further comments regarding this tendency to exaggerate at times.

On the same day he forced down a Sopwith two-seater, a type which neither he, nor his comrades, favoured fighting. Captain Norman MacMillan, who served with No. 45 Squadron during this period, writes:

"No. 45 Squadron, flying 1½-strutters on the Ypres front from April to August 1917 (when the 1½-strutters were replaced by Camels) referred to their own aeroplane as 'Flapping Geese,' owing to their inferior performance compared with the Albatross D.3. During this period while I served with the Squadron, I cannot recall any No. 45 Squadron formation ever being attacked when over the lines except when the German scouts had an overwhelming majority—proportions of 18 to 8 or thereabouts—and such attacks were seldom if ever made to prevent us going to our reconnaissance destination, but took place usually when we were at the maximum distance from our lines and were on the point of turning back."

This fight on April 2nd was against a Sopwith two-seater of No. 43 Squadron. I now propose to quote Richthofen's own story of the fight—his combat report; and, finally, his victim's version of the fight will be compared with his own. The reader can judge for himself. Here is the story from Richthofen's book:

"Suddenly, we saw an English air patrol approaching from the other side. Immediately the thought occurred to me, 'Now comes number thirty-three.' Although there were nine Englishmen, and although they were on their own territory, they preferred to avoid battle. I began to think that it might be better for me to repaint my machine. Nevertheless, we caught up with them. The important thing in aeroplanes is that they shall be speedy.

*I was nearest to the enemy, and attacked the man at the rear of the formation.* To my delight, I noticed that he accepted battle, and my pleasure increased when I discovered that his comrades deserted him, so I had once more a single fight.

It was a fight similar to the one I had had several hours earlier. My opponent did not make matters easy for me. He knew the fight business, and it was particularly awkward for me that he was a good shot. To my great regret, that was quite clear to me.

A favourable wind came to my aid, and it drove both of us over the German lines. My opponent discovered that the matter was not as simple as he had imagined. So he plunged, and disappeared in a cloud. He had nearly saved himself.

I plunged after him, and dropped out of the cloud, and as luck would have it, found myself quite close behind him. I fired and he fired, without any tangible result. At last I hit him. I noticed a ribbon of white vapour. He would have to land, for his engine had stopped.

But he was a stubborn fellow. He would not recognise that he was bound to lose the game. If he continued shooting, I could kill him, for meanwhile we had dropped to an altitude of about nine hundred feet.

However, the Englishman continued to defend himself by shooting at me exactly as his countryman had done in the morning. He fought on until he landed.

When he had come to the ground, I flew over him at an altitude of about thirty feet in order to ascertain whether I had killed him or not, and what did the rascal do? He levelled his machine gun and shot holes into my machine.

Afterwards Voss told me that, if that had happened to him, he would have shot the aviator on the ground. As a matter of fact, I ought to have done so, for he had not surrendered. He was one of the few fortunate fellows who escaped with their lives. I felt very merry as I flew home to celebrate the downing of my thirty-third plane."

Here is his combat report: [7]

"Requesting my acknowledgment of my 33rd Victory:
Date: April 2nd, 1917.
Time: 11.15 a.m.
Place: Givenchy.
Plane: English Sopwith two-seater. Clerget Blin motor, type 2 without number.
Occupants: Sergeant Dunn and Lieutenant Warren.

Together with Lieutenants Voss and Lothar von Richthofen, I attacked an enemy squadron of eight Sopwiths above a closed cover of clouds on the enemy's side of the lines.

The plane I had singled out was driven away from its formation, and tried to escape me by hiding in the clouds after I had put holes in its petrol tanks.

Below the clouds, I immediately attacked him again, thereby forcing him to land 300 yards east of Givenchy. But as my adversary would not surrender, and even as his machine was on the ground, kept shooting at me, thereby hitting my machine very severely, when I was only five yards off the ground.

Consequently, I once more attacked him already on the ground, and killed one of the occupants.

(Signed) BARON VON RICHTHOFEN."

And, lastly, here is Lieutenant Warren's version:

"*I am afraid Richthofen in his report on his fight with Dunn and me must have mixed us up with somebody else.* I certainly wish Dunn and I had been able to put up as much

[7] The Red Knight of Germany, by Floyd Gibbons (Cassell), pp. 176 and 178-81).

resistance as the Baron credits us with, but actually it was rather a one-sided affair, almost entirely in Richthofen's favour. Poor Dunn was hit early in the fight, and was unconscious through most of it.

It was the first time I had ever taken Dunn up, although he was a veteran observer with, I believe, three Hun machines to his credit. My regular observer, an infantry officer who had been in the air about three months, had fallen off a horse the day before and broken his knee. Dunn was assigned as a substitute. The fact that we had never flown together before would be a disadvantage if we were attacked.

We left the aerodrome at ten-thirty in the morning. The weather was bad—rain and hail, with almost a gale blowing in the direction of the German lines. Our faces were covered with whale oil to prevent frost-bite. So many flyers had been laid up with frost-bitten faces that the use of the grease was compulsory, and a case of frost-bite became an offence calling for court martial.

Our Flight consisted of six machines from the Forty-third Squadron, with Major Dore as patrol leader. Our planes were Sopwith two-seaters armed with Lewis and Vickers machine guns, firing fore and aft. Our job was to photograph a section of the Second Hindenburg Line, east of Vimy Ridge, which, as you remember, was attacked just a week later. My plane and one other carried the cameras. The other four were escort.

We were flying in a V at about twelve thousand feet, and our direction was northerly. I was flying at the end of the V, in the last position, which made me the highest.

Richthofen dived down out of the sun, and took Dunn by surprise. The first notice I had of the attack was when I heard Dunn from his seat behind me shout something at me, and at the same time a spray of bullets went over my shoulder from behind and splintered the dashboard almost in front of my face.

I kicked over the rudder and dived instantly, and just got a glance at the red machine passing under me to the rear. I did not know it was Richthofen's. I looked back over my shoulder, and Dunn was not in sight. I did not know whether he had been thrown out of the plane in my quick dive or was lying dead at the bottom of his cockpit. I realised that he was out of action, however, and that I was quite defenceless from the rear. I endeavoured to get my forward machine gun on the red plane, but Richthofen was too wise a pilot, and his machine was too speedy for mine. He zoomed up again, and was on my tail in less than half a minute. Another burst of lead came over my shoulder, and the glass faces of the instruments on the dashboard popped up in my face. I dived again, but he followed my every move.

I had lost several thousand feet, but still below me at about nine thousand feet was a layer of clouds. I dived for it, hoping to pull up in it, and shake him off in the vapour. Bad luck again. The clouds were only a thin layer, you know, and instead of remaining in them I went completely through them, came out below, and found that the red Albatross, with those two sputtering machine guns, had come through with me.

Another burst of lead from behind, and the bullets spattered on the breech of my own machine gun, cutting the cartridge belt. At the same time, my engine stopped, and I knew that the fuel tanks had been hit.

There were more clouds below me at about six thousand feet. I dived for them, and tried to pull up in them as soon as I reached them. No luck! My elevators didn't answer the stick. The control wires had been shot away. There was nothing to do but go down, and hope to keep out of a spin as best I could. I side-slipped, and then went into a dive which fast became a spiral. I don't know how I got out of it. I was busy with the useless controls all the time, and going down at a frightful speed, but the red machine seemed to be able to keep itself poised just above and behind me all the time, and its machine guns were working every minute. I found later that bullets had gone through both my sleeves and both my boot-legs, but in all of the firing, not one of them touched me, although they came uncomfortably close.

I managed to flatten out somehow in the landing and piled up with an awful crash. As I hit the ground, the red machine swooped over me, but I don't remember him firing on me when I was on the ground.

I looked into what was left of the observer's cockpit, and saw poor old Dunn crumpled up on the bottom. He was quite heavy, and I had some difficulty in lifting him out. He was unconscious. I laid him down on the ground, and tore open his coat. He had been plugged through the stomach, apparently from the back. I lifted him and spoke to him.

'I think I'm done,' he mumbled, and then became unconscious. German infantrymen rushed out from dugouts near by; some of them brought a stretcher. We carried Dunn to a dressing-station in a stone hut. I was kept outside under guard. The doctor came out and told me that Dunn was alive, but would not last much longer. I never saw him again. Later, they told me that he died six hours afterwards. He was a stout fellow."

The inconsistencies in these three statements are great. The reader should not have much difficulty in deciding which is nearest the truth.

Lieutenant W. B. Giles, who was one of the observers in

the Sopwith formation, says: "Richthofen is talking nonsense when he states that the other Sopwiths deserted Lieutenant Warren and Sergeant Dunn."

"The facts of the case are these," writes Giles:

"The Sopwiths were attacked by a formation of Huns, two or three times our strength, and each machine naturally being overwhelmed, had to fight for its life. I doubt very much if Warren was only attacked by Richthofen, because each machine appeared to me to be fired at by different enemies at short intervals. Richthofen, in following Warren down, must have left the dog-fight early, because it continued for a long time, and the Huns only left us once we had crossed our lines."

From this obviously truthful statement of Giles it is again apparent that not only were Richthofen's reports exaggerated and incorrect, but that, also, he left his formation to get on with the stern business of fighting while he followed down the "lame duck" to claim it as his victory.

Mannock's character and record appear to be almost the complete antithesis of Richthofen's. Mannock never made exaggerated claims: Richthofen often did. Mannock often gave credit of a personal victory to a comrade, to encourage him: Richthofen never did; he did the opposite. Mannock had no thirsting desire for decorations or self-glorification: Richthofen lived for both. Mannock was not jealous of other airmen's achievements: Richthofen at one time was jealous even of his brother. Mannock had no desire to kill just for the sake of killing: Richthofen's destructive and vainglorious nature made men's, birds', or animals' lives equally cheap.

Mannock was the personification of modesty: Richthofen was boastful and conceited. Mannock was loved and admired by all men: Richthofen was not loved. Mannock was the spear-head of every attack, and fought where the battle raged hottest: Richthofen moved to his place of security on the fringe of the battle as soon as it had commenced. Mannock was a leader with the "Nelson touch": was Richthofen?

Mannock's high qualities of leadership were enhanced by the knowledge his comrades had that, where the fight was raging at its very hottest, there the leader was. where ever the red streamer flew, the great Britisher was at war with the enemy hosts, and thus was formed that enduring phalanx of offence which translated several separate machines into a single attacking unit of which the thrusting tip was the leader himself.

Richthofen rested his fame in the first instance on Wolff's agency. In the second instance, the German Air Service had received a very good thrashing during the first battle of the Somme, 1916, and as a result, it was re-equipped with good fighting machines, which, when flown by good pilots, played havoc with the slower British machines which continued to appear daily over the German aerodromes. Because of this offensive policy of the British, Richthofen was enabled to build up his reputation chiefly by attacking isolated, slow, and cumbersome two-seaters, whose pilots were too venturesome. It was the Baron's practice to sit aloft (as he often boasted), and by cunningly using his formation as decoys, to swoop down out of the blue on to a straggler who had lost height or position in a clash with the Baron's gentlemen.

A remarkable and striking vindication of the superior

attacking spirit of the Britisher Mannock is the fact that he hardly ever sought battle with enemy two-seaters. Mannock stressed the importance of striking at the enemy fighters each and every time, in his lectures and instructions. "Don't forget," he used to say, "we are fighting scouts, and that our job is to clear them out of the sky before we attack any old fat two-seater." Richthofen's preference for attacking two-seaters is indicated by the fact that he eventually shot down nearly twice as many two-seaters as single-seaters. With Mannock the reverse was the case. Mannock sought combat with his equals. Richthofen hid himself from his adversaries in the clouds as he hid himself behind trees in his home forests whilst stalking game. He pounced on the "lame duck" who had lost position in the fray by segregation from his companions as the result of a chance shot or engine failure. Such a quarry was an easy prey for two fresh Spandaus in the hands of a novice, let alone for the steel sights of Germany's ace of aces. "Everything below me is lost," he boasted. Everything below him, including his own comrades, had usually fought themselves to a standstill before the redoubtable German plunged into the mêlée. Thus was patent the inner sense of craft and cunning developed by the hunter instinct. This instinct shadowed all Von Richthofen's work on the Front, and eventually forged the tradition of the German Air Forces.

Mannock deliberately placed himself and his formations between the enemy and their own aerodromes. He forced them to fight their way home. By these means he established a superiority complex in the formations he led, by proving to his colleagues the enemy's patent disinclination to give battle unless he was well within his own lines. These definite offensive tactics were so inculcated into Mannock's pilots, that it became an accepted tradition of his Squadron to make the enemy fight if he ever wanted to get home again.

Is it therefore unreasonable to claim that, pilot for pilot, the Britisher eventually proved himself superior to the German as an air fighter? Is it ungracious to assume that any impartial judge of these momentous years will unreservedly award the palm of honour to the greatest of the Allied air fighters, Mannock? Is it therefore not a just and honourable discrimination to make, that the glorious title of King of Air Fighters of the War 1914-1918 belongs by right of conquest to Major "Mick" Mannock?

# VI

## *L'Envoi*

"Clean, simple, valiant, well beloved, Flawless
in faith and fame."

—Kipling

The lies told about the last Great War were bigger, more outrageously ingenious and distorted than in any previous wars, simply because the last war was a Great War. It was, in fact, the greatest war in history, as even school-children and the American film showman attempt to show in bathos and absurd emotionalism. The lies were the biggest and the most aggravatingly distorted that ever came from man's imagination. The eddy of half-truth which flowed through the rivers of propagandic lies on both sides can only be compared with the gold content in quartz. Unquestionably, and abundantly proved already, a very rich pure vein of the heroic spirit was discovered to present more deep-seated than ever before in the spirit of man. But it has taken years to extract the gold from the earth the war has blown up. The sifting process has proved, as we have shown, that the hero himself (caught up by the emotional waves the heat of his time engendered) was as likely to lapse into error and misstatement as the weakest spirit was liable to whine and resort to cowardly retreat. Thus it is perhaps excusable for men such as Richthofen and Boelcke, not to mention the lesser spirits who stood out so prominently amongst the enemy airmen, to colour their outlook with the temper of their times.

Further analysis has been carried out with the aim of discovering the quality of the offensive spirit of our particular hero, Mannock. We discovered during our labours that his unique character was utterly unlike the conventional hero types usually symbolised by the enemy and the Allies. The nearest approach to the type of our hero amongst the French was that immaculate cavalier of the air, Guynemer. Amongst the enemy, the one character who came closest to our concept of the ideal stimulated by our researches into Mannock's history was the chivalrous, brave, and resourceful Voss. Voss it was who, in a Triplane, fought the most daring air battle of all time. Fighting against six of our airmen, all of them aces, including the famous McCudden, the wonderful Etonian, Rhys-David, the redoubtable Bowman—he was wounded unto death. He recalls the end of Lancelot; his life-blood was streaming from him, but this brave daring spirit refused to yield. Neither seeking nor taking advantage of any surprise tactics, he attacked this formation of famous aces until he was himself shot to pieces and his plane a flaming relic. All who witnessed the fight unreservedly admit it to have been the most courageous and most deserving of praise of any ever put up by the enemy in France.

It was, of course, a fight against impossible odds, but it was proof of the fact that if the German airman as a whole had been possessed of the Voss spirit, the story of the war in the air might have been differently written.

The phenomenon we call human nature appears to us, therefore, to work in sudden spasmodic outbursts of savagery, barbarism, and chivalry. Man attempts to erect civilisation on this flimsy foundation, even to prosper, to what ends we have not yet divined.

By the discovery of fire, man was enabled to withdraw from the protection of the jungle and use the new weapons which fire enabled him to mould. Man, from being the most hunted of animals, became the most feared hunter. Fire enabled him to mould iron and make weapons, and his mastery grew until it overshadowed the earth.

The invention of the flying machine marks a stage in the evolution of man comparable only with the invention of fire.

As before, man is faced with extinction or survival on a plane infinitely higher in the scale than he has ever achieved. As before, he is mercilessly hunted and persecuted by the creations of his own imaginative genius in the sciences of chemistry and physics.

As before, man is hemmed in by the confines of the jungles of nationalism, colour, race, and by economic barriers of greed. As before, the new inventions threaten his own destruction unless man conquers the ether.

The open spaces of the atmosphere beckon to man to overthrow the boundaries of countries. Flying is the means by which man will unite the world. The aeroplane has given to man a third eye. No longer does man share the instincts of the hunter with its cunning and deceit brought about by the feeling of the unknown. As airman he sees an expanse covering so vast an area that his perspective and delineation of thought are carried into a new sphere of vision. Ask any pilot of a fast single-seater about his feelings on a crisp June morning at, say, 10,000 feet. The exhilaration is something which can only be pathologically explained as seeing things whole instead of by bits and pieces, as the earth-bound man does. Seeing things in "wholes," therefore, is seeing things afresh, stripped of their false and illusory trimmings of relative perspective.

Who knows that by his conquest of the air, man has not destroyed all races, all colonies, all creeds, and all boundaries? The whole world is now united by atmosphere. The airmen during the war sensed this new power instinctively, and for them there was a new experience which was cemented into a reality because an entirely new concept of the hero had grown.

The fact is that the days of the perfect war are past. The perfect war is one in which the contestants are as unevenly matched as possible. From such conditions the classical hero was born and raised to mastery. The significance of the popular historical hero is to be found precisely in those conditions which he represents and symbolises.

Mannock symbolises for us a new "hero type." His great unselfish warm nature produced, under the stress of high-speed scout-flying and persecution of the enemy, a new technique of the spirit of man. He did not seek medals and blood for glory. He sought the destruction of a spirit which, to his keen mind, was a dangerous obstacle to the future progress of humanity. His was a nature rich enough to hold in contempt the petty jealousies, vanities, and obsessions which surrounded him. Mannock possessed intelligence to such a high degree that he could assume indifference to the sentiments of the common herd. When he led his Squadron he was like the King Eagle feathering his flock. His mind was free from the poisonous obsessions of glory which stimulate weaker spirits to acts of valour. With him the performance of the valorous act was the natural and obvious performance of his duty as he conceived it to be, and that duty was to defeat and demoralise the German military spirit. That was why, when he died, his Squadron and all those in France who knew him, wept.

They wept as strong men do when they know that something unutterably precious has departed from them.

They wept because they knew in their hearts there was no other to take his place. They prayed that they might be like him; and in the wonderful revival of the fighting spirit which set in immediately after his death, Mannock lived on. He taught us something fresh by his life and work. He taught us that the *moral* value of a belief is an unconquerable force, and faith is invincible and can engender still higher degrees of courage and endurance than have ever been thought possible in man.

He taught us that the vain aspiration by which the militaristic hunter spirit seeks to enslave humanity can be shattered by a higher spirit, and in that he proved the touchstone of valorous effort in overcoming fear. His spirit did not know defeat. His life was a message for all the higher civilised spirits who strive for peace today, not out of fear, but because of necessity. By the way he did his job, he gave us the clue to living the valorous dangerous life in order to achieve the higher destiny of man. He eclipses the fictitious hero of the classics and substitutes a new concept in our estimation of the invincible spirit of man. He proved that Carlyle was a writer of nonsense, that there is reserved for the human race a higher instinct for life than selfishness, which must ultimately be the key to unlock the supreme riddle of life. The love his comrades bore him was not a mere admiration of his superiority, for all men around him were valiant. He sublimated courage to the service of spirit, and he employed ruthless measures to defeat ruthless aims by a keener and more sensitive intelligence and understanding of the task in hand.

He lives on today in the memory of those who survived the war; and with the passage of time and the bursting of the balloons of lies told about it, his glorious memory grows ever brighter, until today it forms one of the highest inspirations of our Air Force.

Of him it can be said that if courage, selflessness, integrity, and modesty are man's highest nature,

"THEN MANNOCK WAS A WHOLE MAN!"

# *Author's Acknowledgments*

I have great pleasure in acknowledging the very kind assistance given by the following in providing material for the book, et cetera:

My Wife.

The Air Ministry, for granting permission to quote a number of Major Mannock's combat reports which are Crown copyright.

Flight-Lieut. Bernard John Brady, D.S.M. (retired).

Squadron-Leader Seton Broughall, M.C., D.F.C.

Flight-Lieut. Guy Carter, A.F.C.

Flight-Lieut. C. B. Dick-Cleland (retired).

Flying Officer E. S. D. Drury.

Mr. G. de B. Epstein, Johannesburg.

Mr. A. E. Eyles, Wellingborough.

Flight-Lieut. Thomas H. French, D.F.C.

Mr. Glyn Jones, Llanelly.

Group Captain the Rev. Archibald McHardy, M.C., M.A.

Major Francis Moller, M.C., D.F.C.

Captain J. Morris, M.A. (late Air Historical Section).

Captain A. Frazer-Nash.

Squadron-Leader H. D. O'Neill, A.F.C.

Wing-Commander J. M. Robb, D.S.O., D.F.C.

Mr. Ronald Spiers, Glasgow.
Captain E. Grattan-Thompson.
Mr. James VanIra, Pretoria.
Flight-Lieut. Neville Vintcent, D.F.C.

In addition, the author is indebted to the writers and publishers of the following books, from which extracts have been quoted:

*An Airman's Wife*. (Herbert Jenkins.)
*A Short History of the Royal Air Force.*
*Boelcke—Knight of Germany*, by Prof. Werner. (John Hamilton.)
*Flying Fury*, by Major McCudden, V.C. (John Hamilton)
*Guynemer, Knight of the Air*, by Henry Bordeaux. (Chatto & Windus.)
*Red Air Fighter*, by Von Richthofen. (The Aeroplane and General Publishing Co., Ltd.)
*Scarlet and Khaki*, by Wing-Commander T. B. Marson. (Jonathan Cape.)
*The Flying Dutchman*, by Anthony Fokker. (George Routledge & Sons, Ltd.)
*The Red Knight of Germany*, by Floyd Gibbons. (Cassell)
*The War in the Air*, by H. A. Jones. (Oxford Press.)
*War Memoirs of David Lloyd George*. (Ivor Nicholson & Watson, Ltd.)